SMUGGLERS, BROTHELS, AND TWINE

Smugglers, Brothels, and Twine

*Historical Perspectives on
Contraband and Vice in
North America's Borderlands*

Edited by
Elaine Carey and Andrae M. Marak

The University of Arizona Press   Tucson

The University of Arizona Press
© 2011 The Arizona Board of Regents
All rights reserved

www.uapress.arizona.edu

Library of Congress Cataloging-in-Publication Data
Smugglers, brothels, and twine : historical perspectives on contraband and vice
in North America's borderlands / edited by Elaine Carey and Andrae M. Marak.
    p. cm.
  Includes bibliographical references and index.
  ISBN 978-0-8165-2876-9 (hbk. : alk. paper)
    1. Transnational crime—North America—History.   2. Smuggling—North
America—History.   3. Prostitution—North America—History.   4. Border
security—North America—History.   5. Borderlands—North America—
History.   I. Carey, Elaine, 1967–   II Marak, Andrae M. (Andrae Micheal)
    HV6252.N7S68 2011
    364.1097—dc23   2011027210

16 15 14 13 12 11   6 5 4 3 2 1

For
Robert Himmerich y Valencia, friend and mentor

1

Contents

Acknowledgments

This collection evolved from ongoing conversations at conferences with a diverse group of colleagues. As scholars of Mexico and the US-Mexico borderlands, we wanted to expand the questions to include the northern and the southern border to provide a broader picture of North American contraband and vice flows. Moreover, we hoped to offer greater comparisons of all three countries at different points in time. We have been privileged to work with a great group of scholars over the past couple of years. We would like to thank our fellow authors in this collection. Some we have known for years, others we have met and worked with closely only since 2007. Others, we have yet to meet in person but have developed a professional relationship with through the flows of communication that new technologies permit, a central aspect of the late twentieth century and an important facet of current transnational flows.

An edited volume demands the cooperation of all the contributors. We have been very fortunate in finding a group of incredible scholars who offered their expertise, responded to suggestions, and assisted us in crafting the manuscript. Moreover, their work and feedback greatly improved the manuscript. We also would like to thank the four anonymous reviewers who offered profound encouragement and feedback from the beginning. In both of our careers, we had never received such constructive and glowing reviews. Those comments not only improved our own analysis of transnational flows but also offered suggestions for future areas of consideration. Patti Hartman, who has since retired from the University of Arizona Press, worked closely with us on the development of the manuscript.

Throughout the process, we have enjoyed the help, discussions, and work of many colleagues, especially Peter Andreas, H. Richard Friman, Samuel Truett, Scott Morgenstern, Kathy Chamberlain, Mark Edberg, Froylán Enciso, Mark Findlay, Paul Gootenberg, Herman Herlinghaus, Regnar Kristenssen, Marlene Medrano, Gabriella Sanchez, and Elijah Wald. Our institutions, St. John's University and California University of Pennsylvania, have also offered tremendous support, financial and otherwise. Elaine thanks Dorothy Beck of Interlibrary loan at St. John's University Library; Larry Sullivan, Ellen Sexton, and Ellen Boegel of the Lloyd Sealy library at John Jay College of Criminal Justice; and Barbara Traub, Astrid Emel, and Bill Manz at Rittenberg Law Library. She also thanks Javier and Lucas. Andrae Marak thanks Laura Tuennerman, Cindy Speer, Bill Meloy, Reuben Naranjo Jr., Bernard Fontana, Thomas Sheridan, Alan Ferg, Bernard Siquieros, and, most important, Angie, Flannery, Delaney and Rowman Marak.

This book is dedicated to Dr. Robert Himmerich y Valencia who introduced us to the study of the Borderlands and its people, the farming of blue corn, and the wonders of tractors.

SMUGGLERS, BROTHELS, AND TWINE

Introduction

Elaine Carey and Andrae Marak

The United States and Canada share a 3,145 mile border, while with Mexico the United States shares a 1,969 mile border; both borders have clearly occupied different places in the historical imagination. Nonetheless, these boundaries have always been permeable, allowing for the flow of goods, services, and cultural practices, legal and illegal, licit and illicit. Cattle rustling, drug running, tax evasion, sex tourism, and human trafficking are only a few examples of transnational contraband and vice practiced in North America. In this volume, the borders of North America serve as the central locations to examine the consequences of globalization as it intersects with hegemonic spaces and ideas, national territorialism, and mobility (or lack of mobility). We recognize that contraband and vice in the Americas and elsewhere are not new. In a corrective to the often present-focused, knee-jerk analyses of transnational issues, the authors in this volume "bring history back in."[1] Focusing on historical case studies of contraband and vice provides an interesting and often overlooked way to make sense of international relations and the nation-building process. The purposeful inclusion of obscure and forgotten cases also broadens our understanding of the diversity and complexity of these issues.

Concerns over contraband and vice have always been of central importance to nation-states (and empires). Prior to Europeans' arrival in the Americas, Mesoamericans created counterfeit cacao beans, which competed with genuine cacao beans as the main currency in the region.[2] Contraband remained a central fact in colonial New Spain as in independent Mexico, where up to half of all silver left the region bound for the Philip-

1

pines without passing through the customs house.[3] Smuggling was equally an issue in colonial Massachusetts and New York, where the English were unable to enforce taxes on molasses and other goods.[4] Contraband continues in the modern era. Economic crises, the collapse of governing institutions, changes in elite and/or public perceptions of propriety/vice or shifts in laws create new demands for particular products that fuel profit-making from contraband.[5] While studies of eighteenth- and nineteenth-century contraband examine specifically the illegal trade of certain commodities that were legal but highly desired, more recently questions of contraband have expanded to include the transnational flows of people, crime, narcotics, alcohol, vice, and even ideas.[6]

The chapters in this volume use bottom up, nonstate, and denationalized perspectives to create a pioneering comparative border study in North America. By embracing Paul Gootenberg's approach in *Andean Cocaine*, we seek to show how transnational flows across North America have worldly connections within the hemisphere and beyond.[7] In addition, by avoiding the "framework of national history" in exploring transnational flows, we hope to elucidate borders, border crossings, failed border crossings, borderland regions, and the people who inhabit these spaces (i.e., borderlanders).[8] Borders not only serve as contested spaces that divide people, leading to the social construction of seemingly distinct races, nationalities, genders, and cultural practices, but they act as barriers across which social, political, cultural, and economic networks function. In other words, they bring people together.[9] Furthermore, the inequalities manifested at borders provide opportunities for those with the necessary political, cultural, social, and economic capital to take advantage of these nebulous spaces.[10]

Candelilla — a waxlike substance extracted from native plants and useful in a range of products from cosmetics to chewing gum — offers an obscure but illuminating example of illicit flows. The smuggling of candelilla boomed in the 1950s because the Mexican government limited production, held down prices, and required that producers send their candelilla to a government-run refinery in Saltillo, Coahuila. American manufacturers who wanted candelilla had to purchase it from an agent in New Jersey. Into this void stepped Jim Casner, a Texas businessman, and a plethora of *candeleros* (candelilla makers) who created a clandestine "system of drop points and independent truckers" to move the candelilla across the border in much the same way that drug and human traffickers work today. Interestingly, increased border surveillance and policing did not end the trade in the 1980s; this business only died out when candeleros began to make more money by selling their labor in the United States.[11]

Economic inequalities and other forms of marginalities created by borders provide opportunities for transnational entrepreneurs, in turn reinforcing the "need" for strengthening borders with fences, customs workers, policing agencies, and laws that legitimize gross disparities across the region.[12] These inequalities, and the failure of states to prevent people, vices, pollution, and cultural practices (among other things) from permeating, penetrating, and crossing borders, extend the possibilities of converting every location across the entire continent into a potential borderland, with different effects on different classes of people.[13] Government policies, actions, and inactions serve to create these interior "borderlands" regions.[14] Border crossings are rarely unidirectional as portrayed in the press, in spite of the predominant focus on peoples, products, and practices penetrating hegemonic spaces from the outside.[15]

In an attempt to better capture — and avoid demonizing — the nature of transnational flows, we embrace Itty Abraham and Willem van Schendel's model for understanding transnational flows. They warn against falling victim to the myth of nation-states engaging in a valiant struggle against the transnational flows of crime and vice. In its place, they adopt a non–state-centric approach that makes a distinction between what nation-states deem to be legitimate (i.e., legal) and what different groups of people think is legitimate (i.e., licit).[16] By applying this analysis to the past, we shatter the assumption that only those things that are legal are licit and that all things that are illegal are illicit. Furthermore, we demonstrate the possibility that what is licit for some groups (at some points in history) may be illicit for other groups (or similar groups at different points in history), regardless of its legality or illegality.[17] This approach reflects the fact that the flows of goods, peoples, ideas, and other items do not easily fall into either one category or the other.[18] A good or commodity may be legal in two separate jurisdictions, but become illegal when crossing from the first to the second. Finally, moving away from state-centric views of the flows of goods and ideas helps us to avoid adopting the norms that hegemonic powers try, often with some success, to foist on others while ignoring the fact that they (and their citizens) engage in the same practices.[19]

Our avoidance of state-centric explanations must not be taken as a complete rejection of the importance of nation-states; they are vitally important. As Tyler Stovall has recently argued, "The essence of transnational and global history is not the absence of the nation, but rather a critical interrogation of its relationship to other levels of the human experience" and, we would add, of its relationship with state, regional, and local governmental and nongovernmental entities.[20] We embrace a bottom-up approach to understanding the nation-state. Some scholars argue that nation-states gained control over borderlands by defining the physical space with laws and controls and over the people who populated the zone by ethnicity, nationality, and gender (as well as other social categories). In some respects, this is true. For example, the US-Mexico border has historically provided the US and Canadian agricultural sector (and increasingly other sectors as well) with a large pool of cheap, flexible, and exploitable labor (undocumented immigrants). Nonetheless, the top-down model of nation-states with control over the border and its people ignores that borderlanders have historically engaged in cross-border commerce, whether legal or illegal, which has created the uniqueness of the culture in the region.[21] The rise in the policing of borders historically has been and continues to be often inefficient if not downright useless.[22] Increased policing does, however, provide nation-states with a tool to construct "an image of state authority" (i.e., sovereignty) and communicate "moral resolve." In essence, the idea of deterrence is and has been more important than its practice.[23]

The different degrees of cooperation that Canada and Mexico offered the United States in preventing the passage of alcohol into US territory during Prohibition present interesting examples of debates over sovereignty and morality. Mexico agreed in 1925 to work closely with the US Treasury Department to prevent the illegal exportation of alcoholic products into the United States even as the Mexican government allowed former US distilleries and brewers to reincorporate in Mexico. The Canadian government, on the other hand, refused to provide assurances to the US government that they would prevent ships laden with legally produced goods that were illegal in the United States to leave Canadian ports.[24] More recently, the focus on ever-hardening borders ignores the impact that globalization has had on political borders. Treaties such as the North American Free Trade Agreement (NAFTA) have actually undermined nation-states' control over borders (even as their policing of them has expanded). Some scholars and pundits decry this loss of control as a phenomenon that imperils the future existence of those states.[25]

By studying the historical flows of contraband and vice across North American borders, these chapters seeks to instill greater understanding of borderlanders, the actual agents of historical change, who often remain on the periphery of most historical analyses that focus on the state or on policy.[26] As noted, the three countries' shared borders remain porous despite attempts to regulate certain behaviors and certain classes of people for many years. The contributors in this collection demonstrate the participants' perspectives along the border that relied on vast transnational networks and territorial movement.[27] In recent scholarship, illicit trade has garnered greater attention as a hindrance to capitalism and democracy and as contributing to the rise of transnational and international crime.[28] Historically, the three nations under consideration defined criminal activities with shifting definitions and power relations.[29] Contrabandistas, smugglers, and border dwellers creatively construct their networks and demonstrate a fluidity in territorial responses. Conversely, bureaucracies are slow and rigid, while governments are unable to reach a general agreement.[30] In turn, government officials disagree on policies and constructs of the illicit. As Abraham and van Schendel elaborated, "The political and geographical limits of sovereignty imply the presence of competing authorities, whether other states or nonstate ideological affiliations, and thereby constitute foundational crises of authority."[31] In turn, "individuals and social groups that systematically contest or bypass state controls do not simply flout the letter of the law; with repeated transgressions over time, they bring into question the legitimacy of the state itself by questioning the state's ability to control its own territory."[32]

To examine the political, economic, and social shifts that developed from the transnational movement of goods, people, and ideas, we consider the analytical categories of race, class, modernity, and gender that explore the historical evolution of transnational contraband and vice across North America. These chapters explore official discourses about vice, "deviance," and illegal trade in comparison to their quotidian reality. Chapters focus on the ways in which relations of power created opportunities to engage in "deviance" for different actors, but also question the constructs of economic reality versus concepts of criminal behavior. Looking through the lens of transnational flows of contraband and vice, the authors develop a new understanding of nation, immigration, modernization, globalization, consumer society, and border culture.

Despite the many ways in which we could have brought the volume together in an attempt to provide a useful framework for the individual chapters, we decided to divide the chapters into two major sections: "Establishing Borders" and "Consolidating National Space." "Establishing Borders" examines cases where specific tangible goods or peoples crossed national boundaries. We begin the section with Robert Chao Romero's "Chinese Immigrant Smuggling to the United States via Mexico and Cuba, 1882–1916," which explores the first "illegal aliens" to be smuggled into the United States from Mexico. Romero points out that, mirroring the conditions surrounding the continued entrance of undocumented immigrants into the United States today, trafficking was not only viewed as legitimate by those who engaged in it (most especially those being trafficked), but also that it was inseparable from many licit businesses. In turn, Romero explores the sophisticated transnational smuggling ring that circumnavigated US laws and policies. Brenden Rensink's "Cree Contraband or Contraband Crees? Early Montanan Experiences with Transnational Natives and the Formation of Lasting Prejudice, 1880–1885" also provides us with a historical case study that has many current-day applications. Rensink argues that early prejudice beleaguered Cree efforts to secure permanent settlement in Montana and shaped the narrative of white-Cree interactions throughout the region for decades. In fact, the US federal government played on Montanans' fears of the Cree to engage in state-driven rhetoric aimed at reinforcing internal and international boundaries. In effect, the federal government used the Cree to (re)establish its sovereignty even if it had little or no control over the Cree's border crossings. Sterling Evans's "Contraband Twine: Harvests, Smuggling, and Tariffs in the US-Canada Borderlands in the Early Twentieth Century" brings front and center the social construction of illicitness by nation-states (in this case, of a seemingly harmless product, twine). His chapter supports Adelman and Aron's argument in favor of the hardening of borders in the late nineteenth and early twentieth centuries that "turned borderlands into *bordered* lands."[33] Finally, George Díaz's "Twilight of the Tequileros: Prohibition-Era Smuggling in the South Texas Borderlands, 1919–1933," illuminates how US efforts to enforce Prohibition not only failed but helped give rise to more sophisticated and violent international gangs of smugglers.[34] He demonstrates how the shift from borderlands into bordered lands undermined nation-states outright control of their borders.[35]

The second section, "Consolidating National Space," explores border crossings that do not necessarily involve anything tangible crossing a border. The promotion of ideas and ideologies across international borders by transnational moral entrepreneurs often causes the mere threat of border crossings (of drugs, certain social practices, or particular kinds of peoples) to create a moral panic. Holly Karibo's "Detroit's Border Brothel: Sex Tourism in Windsor, Ontario, 1945–1960," demonstrates that the dynamics along the US-Canada border parallel those along the US-Mexico border in important aspects, even if the two borders hold very different places in our historical imagination. Karibo also engages Abraham and van Schendel's concept of licit and illicit, arguing that the binary is too simplistic. She notes that the police and other law enforcement officials selectively enforced antivice laws;[36] this resulted in the rise of "unofficial forms of cross-border tourism." Finally, her work shows that we need to explore not only border crossings but also the failure to cross borders. In the case of Windsor, it was the white, not black, working class that crossed the border to engage in the sex industry, engaging in a form of "white flight." In "Official Government Discourses about Vice and Deviance: The Early-Twentieth-Century Tohono O'odham," Andrae Marak and Laura Tuennerman argue that scholars must expand the definition of vice to include the everyday and the mundane. They also note that the power to define vice and determine the processes by which these vices should be eliminated "are inextricably linked to patterns of inequality."[37] That this is the result of two sets of borders, one legal — the US-Mexico border — and the other metaphorical (but equally powerful) — indigenous/nonindigenous — is no mistake.[38] Dan Malleck's "Crossing the Line: Transnational Drinking and the Biopolitics of Liquor Regulation in Ontario, 1927–1944," explores the ways in which ideals and vices penetrate porous borders. Malleck argues that, from the perceptions of many residents and officials in Ontario border communities, the American represented a dangerous "other," corrosive to the idealized social order. This "othering" of American drinkers had its roots in perceptions of cultural difference and interpretations of the dangers of affluence on a sober body politic. Elaine Carey's "Selling Is More of a Habit than Using: Narcotraficante Lola la Chata and Her Threat to Civilization, 1930–1960" documents the thirty-year career of Lola la Chata, a female Mexican heroin peddler and trafficker, and the efforts of police, government officials, and diplomats on both sides of the border to undermine her criminal empire. An examination of the evidence reveals la Chata's transnational threat and her fluidity and flexibility in responding to policy shifts in Mexico, the United States, and Canada. Finally, Marcel Martel's "Preventing the Invasion: LSD Use in Canada during the Sixties," explores the role that the US-Canada border played in the debate over the regulation of LSD use in Canada, as well as how references to the United States played a role in the debate. It is also a case study of one province in particular: Ontario. Although nonmedical use of LSD was a North American phenomenon, Ontario exercised its political authority within the limits set by the Canadian federal structure. Despite these limits, and unlike other provinces, the Ontario government promoted solutions based on a mixture of education, health resources, and prevention. Canadian proponents and opponents of drug use had specific views on the border and the role of the state. Ideally, the border could shield Canada from this invasion, but in practical terms this was very difficult since the border was seamless.

The book concludes with an Afterword by Josiah McC. Heyman and Howard Campbell, who contextualize the reflections of this historical study of borders and flows on the contemporary debates that both scholars study.[39] They note that studying the ways in which nation-states have historically criminalized activities that some subsegments of society found to be licit (and that often revolved around differing concepts of the market; i.e., a focus on reciprocity) should inform our investigations into the ways in which borderlanders (and others) understand transnational contraband and vice today. In fact, the historical case studies in this volume often demonstrate how we arrived where we are today and how such changes, forcibly imposed but still negotiated, may occur in the future. Perhaps most important, these negotiations (or at least responses and counterresponses) have served to strengthen both the state and criminal organizations, usually at the cost of everyday people. Heyman and Campbell focus on the rise of Mexican drug cartels that resulted from increased US and Mexican antidrug enforcement (coupled with the militarization of the border).

We might use the US-Mexico border case to draw some interesting parallels for the future of the US-Canada border should we adopt similar policies there. Canada is the United States' number-one export market, and the North American Free Trade Agreement (NAFTA) has served to further integrate the two countries. Increased trade has also increased opportunities for smuggling. Perhaps no place is a better example of border integration than the Mohawk Nation of Akwesasne. The Mohawk Nation straddles the US-Canada border across the Saint Lawrence River — taking in parts of upstate New York, Ontario, and Quebec — but the indigenous residents consider themselves part of one community. It is a location of multiple jurisdictions (the Akwesasne Reserve in Canada and the St. Regis Mohawk Tribal Reservation in the United States as well as New York, Ontario, Quebec, the United States, and Canada), claimed sovereignties (US and Canadian police are forbidden on the reservation), and difficult geography; in other words, it is great for smuggling (an issue not prioritized by the Akwesasne Mohawk Police). Cigarettes, liquor, weapons, and — as recently dramatized in the independent movie *Frozen River* — people are commonly smuggled across this subsection of the US-Canada border. The engagement of Mohawks in smuggling has divided tribal members, led to continued fights over tribal sovereignty, and resulted in continued "regulatory anarchy."[40] Of course, smuggling and its effects are not just isolated to the Mohawk Nation. It forced Quebec to lower its cigarette taxes in hopes that doing so would undermine the incentives for smugglers (and purchasers).[41] Although the US-Canada border holds a much different place in the historical imagination, we can imagine a possible future where the response to smuggling there mimics that currently being deployed along the US-Mexico border, one that focuses on increased regulation, interdiction, militarization, and technological sophistication. We can also imagine a response from smugglers, one where small-time players are pushed aside to make way for the more savvy and professional criminal organizations that want to take advantage of the increased profits offered by greater levels of state involvement.[42]

It is our hope that the following chapters provide much-needed context for the contemporary debate about issues surrounding transnational flows, including transnational migration, commerce, the sex trade, and drug and human trafficking. A deeper historical understanding is especially important in today's increasingly globalized world, one in which the agents of nation-states often use the fear of the penetration of hegemonic spaces by "others" as grounds to expand their reach and power in spite of the fact that their doing so in the past has seldom solved any of these problems. In fact, in spite of increased globalization, many of the historical case studies in this collection follow the same patterns as our current borderlands problems. Many of the solutions offered by nation-states today are the same as in the past and will likely lead to the same negative consequences. In the end, it is our desire that present-day students, academics, politicians, and policymakers can gain a deeper understanding of the lessons that history has for us about transnational flows.

PART ONE

Establishing Borders

CHAPTER ONE

Chinese Immigrant Smuggling to the United States via Mexico and Cuba, 1882–1916

Robert Chao Romero

On July 1 or 2, 1911, Chinese immigrants Hom Hing, Ah Fong, Lee Lock, Sam Seu, and Leu Lin, accompanied by their Chinese-Mexican compatriot Joaquín Mon, drove by wagon from Ensenada to Carise, Lower California.[1] Hom, Ah, Lee, Sam, and Leu were received at the vicinity of the border by two Mexicans, Francisco Rios and Antonio Solis who were contracted to take them safely across into the United States.[2] Hing promised to pay the Mexican guides $120 for their services, Lock agreed to pay $405 in gold for safe transport to the United States, and Seu contracted to pay $300 for his delivery to the "land of the flowery flag." On the third of July, the five Chinese immigrants, together with Rios and Solis, entered the United States through San Ysidro, Lower California. Following their illegal crossing at San Ysidro, the group proceeded to the city of El Cajon in San Diego where they were hidden by their Mexican guides in a straw-stack on a hill located close to Riverview Station. Five days later, while en route to Anaheim, California, Hom, Ah, Lee, Sam, Leu, Rios, and Solis were spotted by Immigration Service Inspector in Charge Harry H. Weddle near San Marcos, California at about three o'clock in the morning on the railroad tracks of the Santa Fe railroad. Following an escape attempt, the group was arrested and subsequently interrogated by Weddle and his partner, Chinese Inspector Ralph L. Conklin. On their inspection and interrogation of Rios and Solis, Weddle and Conklin learned that the five captured contraband immigrants were consigned to Chinese individuals residing in Anaheim, California. Moreover, according to the smuggling arrangement, Rios was contracted to receive $150 for each contraband Chinese after safe delivery to Anaheim and on the presentation of a special letter of identification given to him by Joaquín Mon of Ensenada written in the Chinese language.

Following the successful apprehension of Hom, Ah, Lee, Sam, Leu, Rios, and Solis, inspectors Weddle and Conklin proceeded north to Anaheim, California, in pursuit of the Chinese agents to whom the five smuggled immigrants had been consigned. As part of their plan, Weddle and Conklin stopped first in Santa Ana, California, where they recruited sheriff employee George Placencia to pose as Francisco Rios. On July 15, 1911, Weddle, Conklin, and Placencia traveled to Anaheim seeking to locate the intended recipient of the smuggling letter. Posing as Rios, Placencia learned from an elderly man, Ngan Fook, that the correspondence was addressed to the "big boss man," Chin Tung Yin, who resided in Los Angeles. Fook further explained to Placencia that Chin would meet with him the next evening in Anaheim to discuss the arrangement. On the evening of July 16, 1911, Placencia met with Fook and the "big boss man" in the Anaheim Chinatown, and they worked out a plan for the delivery of the contraband Chinese described in the secret letter. Following an initial miscommunication as to the settled-on place of meeting, Placencia, together with inspectors Weddle and Conklin, drove to meet Chin and Fook at a small Chinese garden located approximately one mile east of the city of Anaheim. On arrival at the garden, Weddle and Conklin parked their car on a side road and hid themselves behind a blackberry bush. Placencia proceeded to meet the "big boss man" who was waiting for him in a house located in the Chinese garden. At the meeting, Chin paid Placencia $10 for expense costs and promised to pay him the balance of the amount owed after the delivery of the Chinese immigrants. Moreover, Placencia was instructed to meet Chin at the railroad station the following morning and travel to Los Angeles Chinatown where he would receive remuneration for services rendered. After their discussion, Placencia led Chin and Fook outside to the blackberry hedge where they were arrested by inspectors Conklin and Neddle. The US attorney subsequently dismissed charges against Ngan Fook for conspiracy to violate immigration laws related to Chinese exclusion; Francisco Rios and the "big boss man" Chin Tung Yin were acquitted of their charges by a jury.[3]

As suggested by this vignette, the smuggling of Chinese immigrants into the United States during these years was a sophisticated business, involving an elaborate transnational network of Chinese agents and non-Chinese collaborators.[4] In fact, Chinese immigrant smuggling was part of a broader Chinese transnational "commercial orbit," involving China,

Mexico, Cuba, and the United States. This commercial orbit was developed by entrepreneurial Chinese businessmen who made fortunes through the transnational flow of undocumented immigrants, laborers, and commercial products into the United States and Mexico.[5] This economic orbit, moreover, functioned contemporaneously with the Canadian and Mexican smuggling networks discussed by Sterling Evans and George Díaz later in this collection.

The organized smuggling of Chinese into the United States through Mexico began in the late nineteenth century as a response to the Chinese Exclusion Act of 1882 and thrived as a lucrative business until 1916 when the trade came to a screeching halt as a consequence of the interruption of transpacific steamship passenger service during World War I.[6]

The Chinese Six Companies, a transnational Chinese immigrant fraternal organization headquartered in San Francisco, directed the illicit smuggling traffic from Havana, Cuba.[7] The Six Companies was first organized in San Francisco during the mid-nineteenth century as an immigrant fraternal organization comprised of representatives of the seven major Cantonese families residing in San Francisco and was charged with the defense and representation of the collective socioeconomic and political interests of the Chinese immigrant community. Formed initially to provide a unified collective voice for the Chinese of San Francisco, the organization eventually developed an international commercial network, and some members of the Six Companies were transnational merchants invested in various types of import-export ventures, including, in addition to the illegal smuggling of immigrants via Mexico, the reported importation of opium and the white slave trade.[8] According to US Treasury Department special agent reports from the late nineteenth century, Havana was both the headquarters and distribution point of the Chinese immigrant smuggling business organized by the Six Companies of San Francisco.[9]

Moreover, the Six Companies possessed a strategic insider connection in Havana, which allowed for the flowering of the illegal immigrant trade during the late nineteenth century. In 1896, Chin Pinoy, chief representative of the Six Companies, directed and managed the Chinese smuggling business from his office in Havana.[10] In addition to being eastern chief of the Six Companies, Chin concurrently held the position of Chinese agent for the Southern Pacific Railroad Company, the Morgan steamship line, and a line of the Ward Steamship Company sailing from Tampico, Mexico, to New York.[11] Treasury department agents estimated that these three transportation companies for which Chin served as Chinese agent carried approximately four-fifths of the Chinese immigrants who eventually illicitly entered the United States during the 1890s. Leveraging and building on this key insider connection, the Six Companies developed not only a flourishing immigrant smuggling business but also an impressive transnational smuggling network involving representatives in China, Mexico, Cuba, Canada, and various cities of the United States, including El Paso, Tucson, San Diego, New York, Boston, and New Orleans. The existence of this vast transnational smuggling ring challenges the existing literature, which asserts that the nebulous areas of the US-Mexico borderlands had become, by the early nineteenth century, political borders that defined individuals by categories of race, ethnicity, gender, and national origin. As evidenced by this vast transnational smuggling network established by the Six Companies, during the late nineteenth and early twentieth centuries such socially constructed categories remained slippery and fluid despite the best efforts of the US government to define the Chinese by race and nationality and to exclude them from its territory.[12]

The Six Companies devised a multiplicity of schemes, procedures, and techniques to maximize smuggling efficiency through these various US ports of entry. The smuggling procedure described in the example of the "big boss man" Chin Tung Yin and his partner in crime, Ngan Fook, for example, closely resembles a popular scheme devised by the Six Companies to illegally transport Chinese immigrants into the United States via Sonora and Baja California during the early twentieth century.[13] According to this scheme, Chinese residents of the United States would make smuggling arrangements for friends or relatives desirous of immigrating to the United States through the Six Companies representative of their local town. As part of this procedure, the local US agent would proceed to contact a Chinese agent in a port city such as Shanghai, and the immigrant friend or relative would be instructed to travel to that city. On arrival at the port city, the immigrant would receive basic training in both the English language and in American cultural etiquette and then would be transported to Mazatlán, Manzanillo, or Guaymas, Mexico via Chinese steamer. Chinese immigrants were met at Mexican ports by Six Company representatives who distributed them temporarily into various jobs related to their future employment in the United States. Following further inculcation in American culture and preliminary job training, immigrants traveled by train to Nogales, Sonora, and then from Nogales they were transported to border cities such as Mexicali, Naco, or Agua Prieta, where they would be delivered across the US line by a Mexican guide to a Six Companies agent waiting for them in a local city. On arrival in the United States, illegal Chinese immigrants were assigned new identities — according to this common scheme, the identity of citizens born in the United States. Chinese immigrants appropriated entire falsified biographies that established their legal claims to be in the country, and in the event that they were taken to court by immigration officials on suspicion of entrance into the United States in violation of the Chinese exclusion laws, Six Company representatives hired false witnesses to corroborate their fabricated identities. The absence of official municipal birth records as a consequence of the 1906 San Francisco earthquake and fire, furthermore, made it more difficult for immigration authorities to disprove the false identities of Chinese immigrants who claimed to be born in San Francisco and contributed to the popularity of this smuggling procedure. Immigration Service official Clifford Alan Perkins claimed that this strategy of assigning false identities became so effective and common that, over time, government officials ceased to challenge suspected illegal aliens on these grounds and "that if all of those who claimed to have been born in San Francisco had actually been born there, each Chinese woman then in the United States would have had to produce something like 150 children."[14]

In addition to this popular scheme of smuggling Chinese immigrants into the United States through the use of Mexican guides and the assignment of fictitious identities, the Six Companies also devised various illicit "substitution" procedures based on the abuse of the "in transit" privilege. Many Chinese immigrants not legally entitled to reside in the United States under the Chinese exclusion laws were allowed to land at American seaports and travel "in transit" through the United States en route to Mexico and other destinations according to legal loopholes in US immigration policy. In addition, according to the "in transit" privilege, Chinese laborers were also allowed to travel through US territory "in transit" from Mexico or Cuba en route to China via American seaports such as New York City. The Six Companies developed a multiplicity of "substitution" methods to circumvent US immigration law through the creative manipulation of the "in transit" policy loophole.

The Joseph Lamb case provides an example of one such successful "substitution" method devised to beat the Chinese exclusion laws.[15] In mid-May 1891, forty Chinese immigrants arrived in New Orleans aboard the Southern Pacific Railroad traveling "in transit" to Havana, Cuba. The forty passengers landed originally at the port of San Francisco, and following a stay of about one week in New Orleans, were scheduled to depart to Havana from nearby Algiers, Louisiana, on board the SS *Arkansas*, a Morgan steamship owned by the Southern Pacific Company. During their week-long layover in New Orleans, the forty Chinese immigrants vacationed and visited freely with their compatriots residing in New Orleans while under the supervision of Joseph Lam, Southern Pacific Chinese agent at this Cajun port. Sometime during their one-week stay in New Orleans, passengers Fong H. and Leong Y., along with three other of their immigrant countrymen, made deals with five residents of the New Orleans Chinese community to be "substituted" in their stead. According to this arrangement, the five New Orleans residents switched places with their five countrymen traveling "in transit" to Havana for a fee somewhere in the range of $100 to $125. As legal residents of New Orleans, the hired substitutes, in addition to the handsome fees, received a free trip to Havana and, because of their legal entitlement to be in the United States, could return to New Orleans whenever they desired. Two of the contracted substitutes were, in fact, citizens of the United States and "professional" substitutes. Following the swapping of identities, the five Chinese laborers originally destined for Havana slipped away illegally into the United States, presumably blending themselves into the local Chinese community of New Orleans to avoid detection by immigration authorities. The Six Companies also utilized a similar strategy to "substitute" Chinese merchants for Chinese immigrant laborers traveling "in transit" through US territory by train to Chihuahua, Mexico, from the seaport of San Francisco.[16]

In addition to this practice of "substitution" en route to Cuba and Mexico, the Six Companies also developed a creative scheme of circumventing the Chinese exclusion laws by substituting Chinese laborers from Mexico and Cuba traveling "in transit" through the United States to China via the port of New York City.[17] According to further legal loopholes in US immigration policy, Chinese immigrants from Mexico and Cuba, although not entitled to immigrate to the United States, were allowed to travel through US territory via railroad to seaports such as New York, and from these ports to depart to China by steamship. On arrival at the seaport, lists of "in transit" passengers were created by immigration officials, which included descriptions of age, physical appearance, and last place of residence of each immigrant. Following the construction of descriptive lists and the posting of bonds for each passenger, Chinese immigrants en route to China, like their compatriots traveling "in transit" through the United States to Latin America and the Caribbean, were allowed to visit freely in the port city under supervision of other Chinese agents while they awaited departure. According to Treasury Department agents, some Chinese laborers abused the "in transit" privilege by swapping places with Chinese merchants during their port city layover. As part of this substitution scheme, Chinese laborers gained illegal residence in the United States and their compatriot merchants received, ostensibly, a free trip back to China as well as likely remuneration for their services. Moreover, in addition to earning a free visit to their homeland, because of their legal exemption from the Exclusion laws, merchants were allowed to return to the United States whenever they desired. An incident involving the detention and investigation of seven Chinese immigrants at the New York port of Malone on February 24, 1896, clearly illustrates this "in transit" to China "substitution" scheme. In February 1896, Land Ah Hop, Chong Ah You, Chong C. Tuck, Chong Kung Foon, Lie Ah Long, Lam Ah Lin, Loy Kong Tin, and four other Chinese immigrants from Mérida, Mexico, and Havana, Cuba, arrived at the port of New York aboard the Canadian Pacific Railway traveling "in transit" through the United States to China. Prior to their scheduled departure to China, and following a layover in New York City, nine of the original eleven "in transit" passengers appeared before Deputy Collector N. W. Porter and Chinese Inspector H. E. Tippett in Malone, New York, on February 24, 1896. Discrepancies between the descriptive lists and the physical appearances of passengers appearing that day, as well as faulty responses to governmental queries made by Chinese passengers, convinced Porter and Tippett that seven illegal substitutions had taken place during the layover stay in New York City. In addition, substitution suspicions were also raised by Tippett's observation that most of the Chinese interrogated spoke English, although they purportedly arrived in the United States from Spanish-speaking host countries. Porter and Tippett based their assessment largely on the following specific descriptive list of inconsistencies:

Land Ah Hop: According to the descriptive list created on the initial arrival of the "in transit" passengers in New York City, Land was 5 feet 6 inches tall, possessed a distinctive scar on his forehead, and had his left ear pierced. On inspection on February 24, the person purporting to be Land was only 5 feet 3½ inches tall, had no scar on his forehead, and no piercing in his left ear.

Chong Ah You: Although listed as 5 feet 6 inches tall with last place of residence being Havana, Cuba, on February 24 appeared to be only 5 feet tall and cited his last place of residence as Mérida, Mexico.

Chong C. Tuck: According to the descriptive list, Chong was a teenager of fifteen years of age, 5 feet 1½ inches tall, and last lived in Havana. On inspection prior to departure, the person claiming to be Chong appeared to be twenty-five to thirty years old, was 5 feet 3½ inches tall, and stated Mérida was his last place of residence.

Chong Kung Foon: During interrogation Chong stated he was thirty-five years old instead of twenty-five years old as recorded in the descriptive list and was not the same height as listed in the government list.

Lie Ah Long: Like Chong Ah and Chong C., Lie cited an incorrect last place of residence and was of different height than that described in the list.

Lam Ah Lin: On governmental query, said last place of residence was Mexico instead of Cuba. Also, Lam was shorter than detailed in the description and lacked facial discoloration described in the list.

Loy Kong Tin: Stated he last lived in Mérida, instead of Havana as recorded in the descriptive list.

Based on these many conspicuous discrepancies, Porter and Tippett denied cancellation of the penal bonds posted by the Canadian Pacific Railway on behalf of Land, Chong Ah, Chong C., Chong Kung, Lie Ah, Lam, and Loy.

In addition to these "substitution" schemes involving the swapping of Chinese passengers en route to Cuba and China via the ports of New Orleans and New York City, convicted illegal Chinese immigrants of Los Angeles and San Diego devised an ingenious "deportation substitution" procedure involving the collusion of US immigration officials.[18] According to governmental deportation policy, Chinese immigrants convicted in Los Angeles and San Diego of entering the United States in violation of the exclusion laws were transported by train from these southern California locations to the Alameda County Jail in Oakland and then from Oakland were taken to steamers in the port of San Francisco and deported to China. According to the "deportation substitution" scheme, Chinese detainees paid bribes to immigration officials while en route to the Bay Area and were allowed to swap places with other Chinese immigrants desirous of returning to China. Vouching for the efficacy of this substitution technique, Treasury Department agent officials during the late nineteenth century reported the sightings of many convicted and purportedly deported Chinese immigrants in the city of San Francisco. Intrigued and stirred to action by rumors of this illegal immigration scheme, Datus E. Coon, Chinese inspector at the port of San Diego, conducted an interesting investigational experiment in August 1890, which proved conclusively the reality of the rumors. As part of his plan, Coons, in secret cooperation with the US commissioner and jailor, photographed seventeen Chinese immigrants convicted and scheduled to be transferred and deported from San Diego.

Two sets of prints were delivered to the collector of the San Francisco Port, one by Coons through registered mail, and another by the San Diego collector, and it was requested that the identification of deportees be verified prior to admission at the Alameda County Jail through comparison with the mailed photographs. If the prints matched, then this would indicate that Chinese deportees were substituted somewhere in the Bay Area; if the photos did not correspond correctly, then this would constitute strong circumstantial evidence that the substitutions took place sometime during the lengthy sally from southern California to Oakland. Coons's curious experiment proved the existence of the insider immigrant trading scheme, but not through the tests he had devised. Although the two sets of photographs arrived safely at the San Francisco collectors' office according to plan, thirty-three of the thirty-four prints were stolen from the collectors' desk before they could be used.

As a final abuse of the "in transit" privilege, many Chinese immigrants during the late nineteenth century landed at American seaports and traveled to Mexico and Cuba through US territory only to surreptitiously reenter into the United States after an ephemeral stay in their supposed Latin American countries of destination. According to one common procedure developed by the Six Companies, Chinese immigrants arriving by steamship in San Francisco traveled "in transit" by train to the city of Torreon in the northern Mexican state of Coahuila. In Coahuila, they were received by Six Companies agent Mar Chark, alias, "Bum," who distributed them to strategic smuggling points along the three-thousand-mile US-Mexico border.[19] For his services as distribution agent, Mar Chark, described as a "middle aged, good looking, shrewed [*sic*] Chinaman," received a monthly salary of one hundred dollars from the San Francisco Six Companies headquarters.[20] Laredo, Texas, served as one such strategic site for smuggling into the United States utilized by Mar and the Six Companies. Many Chinese immigrants passed "in transit" through Eagle Pass, Texas, into Mexico, and reentered the United States furtively in the vicinity of Laredo, Texas. From Laredo, they were transported to a location near San Antonio aboard freight trains of the International and Great Northern Railroad companies. In addition to Laredo, the border city of Juarez in Chihuahua, Mexico, also served as a popular surreptitious gateway of reentrance into the United States for Chinese "in transit" passengers.[21] By the late 1890s, this abuse of the "in transit" privilege by Chinese immigrants had become so egregious that, according to W. P. Hudgins, special agent of the US Treasury Department, at most 20 percent of all Chinese laborers entering Mexico between the years of 1894 (the date of the signing of the US-China treaty which legally established the "in transit" privilege) and 1897 still resided in Mexico in 1897. The remaining 80 percent "mysteriously disappeared," presumably smuggled into the United States in flagrant abuse of the treaty privilege. Immigration officials such as Hudgins, in response to these rampant "in transit" smuggling abuses, advocated for amendments to the 1894 treaty that would limit passage in bond to Chinese immigrants traveling through US territory en route to transatlantic port destinations.[22]

To facilitate the smuggling of illegal Chinese immigrants into the United States, both "in transit" passengers to Mexico and those arriving directly at Mexican and Cuban ports, the Six Companies developed an elaborate underground market for the illicit sale of forged and fraudulent merchant, laborer, naturalization, and habeas corpus certificates. Chinese laborers desirous of entering the United States purchased forged and fraudulent merchant and laborer certificates through agents in China, Mexico, Cuba, and the United States.[23] Moreover, Chinese immigrant smugglers devised an ingenious variety of methods to both procure and create bogus immigration documents. In the late nineteenth century, Havana served as a central market for the purchase of both naturalization and merchant certificates.[24] Chinese laborers in Havana purchased fraudulent merchant papers acquired through the collusion of Chinese agents in New York City and the Chinese consul of Havana, as well as old US certificates of citizenship naturalization originally procured in New Orleans and delivered to Cuban Chinese agents. According to one popular procedure, Chinese laborers in Cuba desirous of immigrating to New York City sent photographs fastened to large blank pieces of paper to Chinese agents in the Big Apple who transformed the photos and leaves of paper into fabricated merchant certificates complete with official seals, signatures, and notarization. In further circumvention of the Chinese exclusion laws, the Chinese Consular General of Havana also colluded with laborers desirous of immigrating to the United States through the issuance of merchant passports which falsely alleged merchant status.[25] In New Orleans, conniving entrepreneurs of the bogus immigration certificate racket even secured illegal copies of naturalization papers belonging to dead people and distributed them to willing buyers who attempted to use them to gain entrance through various US ports, such as Eagle Pass, Laredo, and Key West, Florida.[26] Not to be left out of the lucrative document forgery bonanza, West Coast labor certificate counterfeiters in San Francisco and East Coast passport brokers in Boston also abetted the illegal immigration of Chinese laborers through the illicit commercial provision of false documentation.[27] In sum, utilizing a variety of creative certificate procurement schemes such as these, Chinese smuggling agents in China, Mexico, Cuba, New York, New Orleans, and San Francisco developed a sophisticated and elaborate black market for the sale of bogus immigration papers, which facilitated the illegal entry of thousands of Chinese laborers into the United States during the late nineteenth and early twentieth centuries.

Conclusion

Unbeknown to most contemporary Americans, Chinese immigrants were the first "illegal aliens" to be smuggled into the United States from Mexico. Legally excluded from immigrating to and permanently residing in the United States as a consequence of the passage of the Chinese Exclusion Act in 1882, Chinese immigrant laborers circumvented American exclusionary policy through the use of Mexico as a surreptitious gateway into the United States. Thousands of Chinese immigrant laborers entered Mexico through Pacific seaports such as Manzanillo, Mazatlán, and Salina Cruz, or were "in transit" through US territory during the late nineteenth and early twentieth centuries, only to slip across the border into the "land of the flowery flag" after an ephemeral stay in "Big Lusong" (as Mexico was called). Organized by entrepreneurial Cantonese immigrants of the San Francisco Six Companies in cohoots with transnational agents in China, Mexico, Cuba, and throughout the United States, the illegal traffic of Chinese immigrant laborers flourished well into the early twentieth century until its demise following the interruption of transpacific steamship travel during World War I.

CHAPTER TWO

Cree Contraband or Contraband Crees?

Early Montanan Experiences with Transnational Natives and the Formation of Lasting Prejudice, 1880–1885

Brenden Rensink

Introducing their edited volume on transnational crime, Itty Abraham and Willem van Schendel mused that today's global media has made a cottage industry out of *talking* about illicit international trade.[1] As societies gravitate toward well-controlled, regulated, and ordered environments, careful policing of internal and international borders is integral. The state and its public citizenry are wary of unsettled, undocumented, and uncontrolled populations because they obfuscate the "legibility" of society, and hence the ability to order it.[2] When crime transcends supposedly controlled boundaries, these anxieties increase. To make order from chaos, societies and states often seek to define what constitutes illicit transnational behavior and identify who is committing such trespasses. Public verbalization and acceptance of these definitions aims at bringing a return to order. Foreign, transient, or otherwise peripheral elements of society are often targeted in these efforts. As modern globalization draws exponential links across borders and between nations, cultures, and economies, this process of anxiety, public rhetoric, and attempted enforcement will grow. An example of these phenomena can be drawn from the outcry and debate that raged across the Forty-ninth Parallel between Montana Territory and the Canadian provinces of Alberta and Saskatchewan in the early 1880s.

The Chippewa-Crees of the Rocky Boy Reservation

About one hundred miles northeast of Great Falls, Montana, and sixty-five miles south of the US-Canada border, lie the Bear Paw Mountains and the Rocky Boy Indian Reservation. Rocky Boy tribal members, a combination of Chippewas and Crees, are unique among the reservation tribes of the northern Great Plains. Unlike other tribes in Montana or the Dakotas, their history has firm roots north of the Forty-ninth Parallel in terms both geographic and legal. Prior to the 1916 creation of the reservation, the US government officially classified the Chippewa and Cree bands that would eventually settle on the Rocky Boy Reservation as "foreign" Indians. As such, they were subject to deportation and did not have the same legal relationship with the US federal government as other Indian tribes in the region. For more than thirty years, the experience of Chippewas and Crees was subject to the capricious winds of change as driven by local press, and by economic and political interests. Throughout the Crees' quest for legal settlement in the United States, individual Montanans and some groups occasionally and vigorously rallied behind their cause, but the predominant sentiment toward them was negative. Until the establishment of the Rocky Boy Reservation in 1916, various bands subsisted on the peripheries of Montanan cities and Indian reservations, making consistent and determined, though ultimately unsuccessful, overtures to the United States for federal recognition.

While an obscure story in the broad scope of North American geography and history, this narrative of transnational indigenous activities and response of local Montanans sheds light on late-nineteenth-century borderlands history as well as the modern crises of globalization and illicit transnational vice. The interactions of Crees from Canada and Montanans during this period poignantly reveal the process of defining illicit behavior itself as well as identifying individuals and groups perpetrating it across international boundaries.[3] This process evolved internally within the society "receiving" inbound traffic, in this case, Montana, without the involvement, voice, or input of the group being labeled as transnational criminals, in this case, Crees. Divorced from broader contexts of *why* Crees from Canada were circulating south of the Forty-ninth Parallel, for how long they had been doing so, or what traditional claims they may have had to lands and resources in the United States, Montanans formed hasty opinions concerning them and devised plans for terminating their transnational presence.

The territorial-federal context in which these narratives unfold is a familiar one in the history of the American West. A combination of agricultural, ranching, mining, merchant, and urban-booster interests were all vying to establish communities, promote growth, and move their communities from territorial status to statehood in 1889. Their project was to implant American civilization in Montana and reap the harvest of national incorporation therefrom. As was the case in other developing territories, the assimilation, subjugation, or elimination of Native peoples was an integral factor in achieving these goals. By 1880, when the Crees accelerated transnational movements, Blackfeet, Bloods, Piegans, Crows, Gros Ventres, Assiniboines, Sioux, Salish, and Pend d'Oreilles, among others, had all been under treaty for decades. This reveals why the foreign Cree presence was so troubling. Montanan politicians, elites, boosters, and other settlers assumed the phase of dealing with nontreaty, and thus uncontrolled, Native populations was long behind them. The continuation of Native issues and troubles was accepted, but a fully uncontrolled and transnational Native "threat" was not. Crees from Canada loomed as a threat to the Anglo Montanan project to incorporate fully their developing territory into the nation as a state.

These contexts, however, were not explicitly discussed in response to Cree activities. Rather, Montanans cast the transnational Cree presence south of the line in terms of inherent illegality. Transnational trade or immigration was not the issue, but rather *Native* transnationalism. As noted in this volume's introduction, what nations define as licit for one group may be illicit for another.[4] At other times, Montanans linked the illegality of Crees' physical border crossing with the contemporary fears concerning illicit transnational trade of contraband stolen livestock. Thus Montanan, and by extension, federal, interest built prejudice on two foundational perspectives: all transnational Cree movements were inherently illegal, and Cree activities across the line regularly involved the transportation of contraband. Conflating these two concepts, Montanans regularly described transnational Cree movements in terms of inherent illegality, regardless of whether contraband goods or illicit trade were actually crossing the border. When actual stolen property was involved, it was always intertwined with how Montanans viewed the very presence of "foreign" Indians south of the line. Cree bodies were illicit as much as the stolen property they were accused of transporting across the line. Hence this early history is one of *Cree contraband*, where the stolen goods transported were the focus of Montanan ire, and of *contraband Crees* where their very corporal presence caused offense.

Cree contexts for their transnational movements were either ignored or explicitly discounted as local, territorial, and federal policies were crafted. Unsatisfied with treaty arrangements in Canada, and unwilling to forfeit territories and resources to which they held longstanding traditional rights, transnational Crees followed previously established migratory patterns southward in search of bison, trade, and settlement. The intersection of traditional indigenous activities with new geopolitical structures and jurisdictions extends along the US-Canada and US-Mexico borders. Rarely, if ever, did Euro-American empires consult indigenous geopolitics in assigning or attempting to impose new border regimes. Crees in Montana were certainly not consulted as prejudices were formed; they and future inbound Cree immigrants and refugees would all endure their legacies. Important to the Cree narratives in Montana, and surely important to modern groups and individuals whose transnational movements draw the ire of anxious nations and societies, quickly formed prejudices exact long-term consequences. In this instance, enduring foundational relationships and prejudices formed among Montanans about Crees from 1880 to 1885 led to determined and lasting resistance to foreign Native settlement.

Establishing a Cree Presence on the US-Canada Border

The arrival of Crees to the border itself stands in the broader context of eighteenth- and nineteenth-century Native migrations out of the Canadian northeast that far predate the late-nineteenth-century tensions in north-central Montana.[5] Over the two and a half centuries leading up to 1880, Crees from the eastern woodland areas between the Great Lakes and Hudson Bay made a slow but steady push to the west and south. The Crees shifting territorial boundaries were documented during their prolonged contact and interaction with French, English, and later, Canadian and American traders, settlers, and government officials.[6] The tensions along the Montanan borderlands in the early 1880s thus stood as the most recent in a long succession of migratory developments that had brought them across the northern Plains and into the foothills of the Rocky Mountains both north and south of the Forty-ninth Parallel. Although an alarming development in the eyes of 1880s Montanans, it stood as the logical outcome for peoples who, for centuries, had migrated and adapted to new socio-economic and military realities in their ever-expanding and -contracting homeland landscapes.

However dynamic the nature of traditional indigenous territories, these proved utterly incongruous to Euro-Americans, who were guided by their conceptions of policed international boundaries. Whereas Anglo residents of the United States' northern borderlands viewed the border crossing of "Canadian," "British," or "foreign" Indians as a blatant desecration of the sanctity of international boundaries, Crees and Chippewas did not. This disparity is significant: from the earliest Cree-Anglo interactions in Montana, Montanans labeled the inbound Natives' presence as inherently and thoroughly illicit, whereas Crees viewed their actions as wholly natural and rooted in historical and geographic tradition. New national identities, as assigned by the international boundary, imposed severe consequences on Cree bodies without consultation, treaty, or debate. All associated Cree activities were translated through the lens of their physical crossing's illegality. Be it migration or transnational trade, all were read through the prejudice of contraband, illicit trade, or vice.

In reality, Crees would have given significant input if Montanans had solicited their voice when forming policy concerning them. Shared Cree and Chippewa traditions included lands south of the Forty-ninth Parallel as part of their homeland territories. One legend tells of two young men who traveled to lands clearly south of the Forty-ninth Parallel where they saw "Great Rocks" that had snow on them during the summer, a "Great Water" that lay west from those high peaks, a warm country to the south where "there [were] trees with sharp branches . . . sharp needles," and of herds of "buffalo as far as they could see" on the more immediate northern Plains.[7] Another tradition explained that Montana's Bear Paw Mountains were "marked for [their people]," as a tribal elder was shown them in a dream and told that they were going to be a homeland, a "rich place for his grandchildren someday."[8] Traditional Cree territories were redefined as transnational by Euro-Americans. The two views were incompatible. "We recognize no boundaries, and shall pass as we please,"[9] stated Chippewa chief Little Shell in 1882. This pronouncement is emblematic of broadly held Native conceptualizations.

Defining the Cree Presence in Montana

Though the Crees' early interactions with American traders were amicable, by the 1880s they confronted a different American populace when they crossed the international border.[10] By the late nineteenth century, trading posts had given way to aggressive settlement, and farmers and ranchers viewed the Cree as a threat.[11] Whereas many regions in the eastern United States had wrested control from Natives decades and even centuries earlier, these far-off hinterlands were contested ground. In this environment, previous acceptance of northern Indians was increasingly cast in the negative light of territorial violations, contraband transportation, and theft.[12] Thus began the process of defining Crees as an illicit presence. Transnational Cree legal and extralegal activities assumed new importance as they crossed jurisdictional lines. Their transborder movements, whether involving transportation of stolen goods or not, were viewed as illegal because Native crossing itself was illegal.

United States military correspondence of the late nineteenth century expressed broad fears about such unregulated Native crossings. An emerging policy was manifest in various campaigns to track, number, and eventually deport groups of "foreign Indians." Loath to return to an era of daily "bloodshed and pillage by the Indians," local Montanans consistently drove federal policy toward the forced removal of "foreign" Indians throughout the 1880s.[13] With continual fears of attacks from the North from actual resistance groups such as Sitting Bull's exiled Sioux or even some remnants of Chief Joseph's Nez Perces, government officials quickly began favoring the deportation option rather than simply tracking transborder movements as had been done in years previous. To execute effectively such plans, US officials sought to clearly classify Natives as domestic or foreign so that appropriate action could be taken: deportation for the foreign and stewardship over the domestic. By imposing such strict definitions over the region's Native peoples and stemming the illicit flow of human traffic, US officials hoped to make some sense of order out of the seeming chaos of these peripheral borderlands, thus ameliorating the anxiety of local borderlands residents in Montana Territory.

Commanders at Fort Assiniboine translated latent fears of uncontrolled Native movements or outright attacks from across the line into action later in the summer of 1881 by enacting direct military action against border-crossing Natives. The language by which Crees were described reveals important truths in how the US government was beginning to define and view "foreign" Indians. "Send out as strong a force as possible under a careful officer to notify *the foreign Indians* to return to their own country, and so prevent them from driving the game away from the hunting grounds of *our own Indians*," orders at Fort Assiniboine read.[14] The orders reveal a succinct division and definition of indigenous peoples as foreign and domestic. The United States saw transnational Natives inherently as "illegals," whereas Natives themselves often did not. Many understood the jurisdictional divide the border represented, and used it as a tool of active resistance, fleeing across the line when it was to their advantage. However, there is no evidence to suggest that Natives accepted the boundary's legal right to restrict their migratory patterns, assign new national identities, or deny them access to traditionally used lands and resources.

Public response to the so-defined illicit transnational Cree movements and government efforts to deport them are likewise revelatory. In late August 1881, the local *Benton Weekly Record* filed two reports of the looming threat of some three thousand Indians who had already crossed the line and were "coming this way." Placing hope in the Assiniboine garrison, the *Record* felt the two cavalry companies and one infantry company, each armed with artillery pieces, would easily intercept and "drive them back."[15] Had General Thomas H. Ruger not sent these forces, commented the *Record*, the local stockmen were ready to organize a posse of their own to halt the Indian advance.[16] Despite the fact that the Crees were likely travelling with their families and holding no disposition for conflict, a fact admitted by the *Record*, northern Montana locals were adamant that the government support their desire to eliminate any Native incursions from north of the line. They were as concerned about the illicit presence of foreign Crees as about suspected criminal trade, theft, or contraband. Hence, as Cree families traversed well-established routes, following bison into the Milk River country, Anglo Montanans pointed desperately to the international boundary, demanding it be respected and threatening to enforce it themselves.

The determination of Anglo borderland residents to shore up any porous sections of the border clearly stemmed from a looming uncertainty about unregulated Native mobility. Domestic Indian policy was in place to deal with "American" Natives south of the line in Montana Territory. Troops stationed at regional forts with well-established protocol offered a sense of security to newly arrived Euro-American settlers, merchants, and ranchers. In principle, the perceived threat presented by wandering nontreaty Indians, whether domestic or foreign, was the same. In practice, however, the presence of *foreign* Indians south of the line posed unique problems. With no negotiable terms of treaty or reservation status, US officials had no established policy of recourse for dealing with inbound Crees. Even if they pursued deportation, US officials had no jurisdiction for ensuring that Crees leave the borderland region entirely and alleviate anxieties in northern Montana. Instead, the continued looming presence of Crees encamped just a few miles north of the line would persistently undermine the perceived stability of the region. More important, their proximal and unregulated presence eroded the confidence of settlers, ranchers, and US Army officials alike to impose order over their surroundings. Border proximity and the jurisdictional bisection of Native groups into foreign and domestic left the Montanans impotent in assuring their own sense of security. It was not a singular concern of Native depredations or of illicit transnational trade, but rather, the combination of the two that proved so disconcerting.

Evolving Transnational Cree Activities and Montanan Prejudice

Despite concerted efforts in the summer of 1881 to establish border security, fall brought continued uncertainty. Just as Montanans had feared, previously deported Crees hovered just north of the boundary and soon resumed transnational movements by late September and mid-October.[17] First, word made its way to Fort Benton that Crees were driving off cattle and horses on the Price and Company ranch on the Marias.[18] Soon thereafter, one hundred lodges of Crees were reported in the big bed of the Milk River, though apparently causing no damage.[19] One week later, a military detachment stumbled on two hundred lodges of Crees camped on Woody Island Creek, north of the Milk River and just a few miles south of the border. Likely consisting of the familial bands anticipated earlier in August, the Crees offered no resistance and left the next day toward the line.[20] Reports of troublesome bands fighting with Piegans near the Sweet Grass hills further complicated Anglo concerns.[21]

For Cree bands near Woody Island Creek, movement within the strip of land between the South Saskatchewan and Milk Rivers, divided laterally by the border, was undertaken regularly and with little regard for the international line. The environs between the two waters provided a natural corridor for their hunting and foraging, and the bisection of this naturally bounded geography was entirely arbitrary in their perspective. Their appearance south of and apparent dispassionate return north of the line speaks to the regularity and unfettered, almost nonchalant, nature of their border traverses. Some 150 miles to the west, two rivers likewise bounded the Sweet Grass Hills — the Milk on the North and Marias on the south. Presented with another naturally bounded geographic corridor, Cree activities seemed unfettered by the arbitrary presence of the international border. Indigenous geographies were made of open prairies, bounded by waterways and arboreal belts — intersected by competing Native spheres of influence. Traditional Cree geographies did not feature proverbial "lines in the sand," bifurcating the natural world along unnatural lines, latitudes or longitudes. Hence, whether moving across the imposed Forty-ninth Parallel in large family groups near Woody Island Creek, or raiding south of the line in the Sweet Grass Hills, Cree movements followed environmentally established, rather than internationally negotiated, geographic corridors.

As the winter of 1881 set in, Crees followed the regular pattern for Natives on the northern Plains of Montana, Alberta, and Saskatchewan: reducing mobility and establishing more sedentary camps. The lull assuaged Montanan's nerves. By mid-February 1882, however, whatever respite the weary Montanan populace had enjoyed ended. A report coming from the Kipp Ranch, located between the Milk and Marias rivers near Cut Bank and Browning, cited Canadian Indians as stealing some twenty-five horses near the first of the month. On tracking the raiding party, trader Eli Guardipee reported that the thieves had butchered one horse for food and eventually returned the rest, though in a deplorable condition of abuse.[22] Compounding these losses was the fact that the raiders had targeted the best animals.[23] Two weeks later, a chilling report offered a more detailed picture of "feloniously inclined" Crees and their operations in the region:

> They come from across the line over the divide at the end of the Milk River range, strike across to West Butte, thence to the head of Wilson Creek and following it down come to the Marias Valley, the land of fat horses. Having gathered as many of these together as time and opportunity allow, they have before them a ride of only sixty miles or so to get across the line with their plunder. There have been no less than seven raids on the horse herds in this vicinity within the last year. The latest one is reported by Sol Abbott who came to town yesterday on Friday night.[24]

Specifically identified as Crees, their route into the Marias Valley indicates Cree utilization of natural geographies as well as an ability to adapt to the imposed geopolitical implications of the international border.[25] For Crees whose ancestors had recently migrated across various competing Native spheres of influence, the business of negotiating boundaries, exploiting weaknesses of competing groups, and adapting to new geographic and geopolitical developments was well established. If relations with Canadian officials were unsatisfactory or game became scarce, making use of Montanan resources was the clear choice. On discovery that Montanans would not pursue them back into Canada, astute Crees used this fact to their advantage. Though a unique and new development, it follows in long-established traditions of adaptation and survival.

This account illustrates specific Montanan fears of transnational Native border crossings as well as Crees' willingness to simultaneously ignore and co-opt the border's supposed impermeability. As depicted by the Montana press, Crees were almost taunting locals with their usage of the border — leaving Montanans powerless to pursue their stolen livestock across the line. In this light, Crees were no longer a simple nuisance that inappropriately crossed south of the line. Now they seemingly leveraged the line to their advantage, raiding "the land of fat horses" and escaping "across the line with their plunder." This new distinction is significant. The initial definition of illicit transnational human traffic was now compounded with actual contraband, or stolen goods, being transported north of the line and out of US jurisdiction. Montanan prejudice evolved accordingly.

In an attempt to stave off the plunder and flight of transnational contraband, Sheriff John J. Healy of Choteau County rode out with deputies in early February 1882 to apprehend some of these thieves, assumed to be Crees. After five weeks, Fort Assiniboine received word that some one hundred Indians and Métis had captured and detained Healy and his men.[26] Three companies under the direction of General Ruger rode to rescue Healy and his men from any possible "dangerously hostile intentions" that their captors held against them. Two days later, Colonel Guido Ilges, who had considerable experience in the region after confronting Sitting Bull there previously, followed Ruger's march.[27] Healy was freed without major incident. The Indians and Métis involved had no desire to engage in a large-scale confrontation. They were in Montana to utilize resources, not fight a war. Healy's subsequent report enforced this concept. While returning to Fort Assiniboine, he encountered a camp of Crees, "had them running for the Queen's possessions in an hour," and sent other "Northern trespassers" across the line as they burnt houses and "struck terror into the hearts" of the troublesome parties.[28] As Healy and other parties continued along the Milk River Valley in search of Cree leaders Big Bear and Lucky Man, they sought to impress on all "Northern trespassers" their strict intolerance for their violation of the international boundary. It was likely pragmatism, rather than terror, that convinced Crees and others to withdraw. Having left Canada for avenues of economic activity that would bring them the greatest benefit but also the path of least resistance, Crees likewise withdrew from the United States for the same reasons. For the moment, returning to Canada was the most prudent choice.

The reported presence of Big Bear south of the line was of particular concern to Montanans. Big Bear was a nontreaty Cree from Canada whose warriors were "considered the most desperate horse thieves in Montana." Army personnel echoed extreme displeasure in Big Bear's appearance. One soldier stationed at Fort Assiniboine wrote of Big Bear's band, "I never was tired of a Tribe as I am of this one."[29] Statements like this likely stemmed more from frustration over the army's inability to control Cree movements than personal interactions with Big Bear's Crees. Civilian voices similarly posited that Big Bear was no doubt "causing trouble on this side of the line."[30] The entrance of Big Bear into Montanan public discourse transformed Montanan prejudice. Well-known from Canadian reports as a charismatic, yet stubborn, Native leader, Big Bear's figure put a more tangible, and prosecutable, name and face to oft-reported instances of Cree horse thieving and supposed depredations.

The May 4, 1882, edition of the *Benton Weekly Record* featured no less than three articles on Big Bear and typified the tone of news coverage and underlying local anxiety concerning his presence in Montana. When fifty Crees under the direction of Chief Little Eagle interfered with a commercial wagon train, an event with which Big Bear had no involvement, his name was nevertheless pulled into discussion. Although these reports did not accuse Big Bear of impeding the wagon train, they pointed out that Big Bear was back at his previous camp on Beaver Creek along the Milk River and "had no intention of going across the line."[31] His very presence was of interest because of its inherent illegality as determined by white Montanans and the troublesome reputation that he brought with him from Canada. And, if he was not directly involved with the events surrounding the wagon train, his camp was certain to be involved in the "Annual Spring Opening of Aboriginal Cussedness — Horse-Stealing and Other Outrages." As the *Record* editorialized, "Big Bear, the Cree, is on Beaver Creek and his camp is sure to be a centre of horse stealing operations and a refuge for dangerous renegades and cut-throats from all tribes."[32]

Increasingly upset and frustrated with the continued appearance of Crees south of the line, and their inability to stem their trade of contraband livestock back into Canada, Montanan settlers debated possible solutions. The *Benton Record* highlighted various problems to address. First, some military successes, such as Captain Klein's burning and dispersal of a large Cree camp, were ultimately inconsequential. As quickly as Big Bear had fled on Klein's arrival, the camp immediately reformed and continued "smuggling and rebuilding their houses." The *Record* explained the problem in the following terms:

> [A]s hostile Indians are always mounted and are trained to the hardest kind of riding, it is strange that infantry should always be sent out against them — particularly here in Montana, where the Indians as a rule, rove about and commit their depredations in scattered bands. The post at Assiniboine is intended to guard and patrol a vast section of country, and in view of the immense distances to be traversed in all expeditions, and the fact that the Indians to be watched are well mounted as we have stated, why in the name of common sense are there not more companies of cavalry stationed there?[33]

As conditions were, some feared that Big Bear and others would continue to dodge units and "laugh at the soldiers" before quickly returning to "their old stomping ground as if nothing had happened."[34] As Patrick Burke, a US Army Signal Corps member stationed in Helena, wrote to his father, "The Indians north of here under Big Bear . . . always strike where least expected and then scatter off over the line before the troops can follow."[35] Big Bear's band understood these borderland dynamics, the peripheral weaknesses extant in growing Canadian and American empires, and was wise to exploit them. If, but for a time, his people could persist in nomadic traditions, they could live off the bounty of the northern Plains and the added resources unwillingly provided by Anglo settlers and ranchers. If border security was to be enforced, it would require significantly more force than had hitherto been available.

Along with increased numbers, Montanans argued that troops must be allowed to more actively engage Native bands. Perhaps, if the military was given sufficient latitude to *impel* the Natives to comply with their demands, they could succeed. As explained in the *Record*, the troops sent out from Fort Assiniboine were under strict command "not to fight Indians until they are first attacked."[36] As evidenced by the fact that Big Bear and his band had "simply dodged" Captain Klein's April expedition, this made for ineffective border enforcement. Big Bear understood that any force sent against them was rendered utterly impotent, given the Crees did not fire first. By evasion and withdrawal, Crees, Métis, and others had veritable free range over the borderlands. The *Record* concluded, "Until a large body of cavalry is stationed at Assiniboine, and greater discretion is allowed officers in command, expeditions from the post against Indians and half-breeds, must necessarily prove abortive and expensive."[37] Without such action, Anglo residents of northern Montana believed they were effectively at the mercy of the various Native groups that circulated north and south of the Forty-ninth Parallel.

The *Daily Independent* in Helena sarcastically echoed the perceived injustice of this inversed power differential. Commenting on Big Bear's repeated pattern of evading US forces by crossing the border and then returning, the *Independent* related "the hostiles from the Queen's dominions declare their intention of running the Milk river region to suit themselves." Then, they quipped: "Wonder what Uncle Sam is going to do about it? Perhaps the Secretary of the Interior will recommend the removal of the troops from Montana *for fear they may degrade the morals of the reds*. As he has recommended the removal of troops from the Indian agencies in Dakota, it would be no surprise if he next recommended the removal of the troops from all the Indian countries."[38] The bitter sentiment expressed is telling. Northern Montanans were already anxious concerning the state of their "domestic" Indian issues. The seemingly endless threat of foreign Indians, over which apparently they had no control, was vexing. Crees "from the Canadian side . . . [were] engaged in their usual spring sports," and Montanans, for the time being, were left without recourse or security.[39]

Much to the delight of worried Montanans, Big Bear and much of his band returned to Canada in the spring of 1882. For a short time, attention toward perceived Cree troublemaking reoriented itself northward — following Big Bear's return toward Fort Walsh in Canada. Fifty odd miles north of the international border in Saskatchewan, and situated on the southeast flank of the Cypress Hills, Fort Walsh was a place that Crees had frequented for quite some time. Hence the coverage of horse-thieving along the Marias and Milk rivers shifted to reports of similar activities in the regions surrounding the Cypress Hills.[40] These reports read much like those previously south of the line, telling of thieving, warfare between Crees and other tribes, and the struggles of British authorities to quell such violence. Throughout, Big Bear's persona loomed. He had caused trouble in the region before his self-imposed, two-year exile to Montana. In the view of the Montana press, his troublesome tendencies had continued in Montana and were again being furthered in Canada. The press painted Big Bear, his band, and all associated with him in menacing terms. This would prove a pivotal precedent for future relations among Crees, the local Montanan citizenry, and US Army officials stationed in regional forts.

As Big Bear attempted to secure treaty agreements more favorable for his people, the destitute condition of his and other bands of Cree would again drive some south of the border as summer waned. Word reached Fort Belknap in mid-July that small groups of Crees were revisiting their familiar hunting grounds along Woody Island Creek. These were summarily confronted, relieved of their guns and horses (all branded), and turned north to the border.[41] Detachments from Fort Assiniboine faced similar conditions. In July and August, large parties of Crees and Métis were captured, stripped of guns, ammunition, and stolen horses and directed to return north and not cross the line again.[42] Threatened to be "more severely dealt with" if found south of the boundary again, the groups quickly retreated north.[43] As Big Bear's negotiations waxed on with Canadian officials, however, Crees faced dire circumstances and possible starvation north of the line. One observer wrote, "They are literally in a starving condition . . . their clothing for the most part was miserable and scanty in the extreme . . . [little children] had scarcely rags to cover them . . . it would indeed be difficult to exaggerate their extreme wretchedness and need."[44] While some, like Big Bear, decided to remain north, others being "slowly and deliberately starved" took to the border.[45] Throughout the fall of 1882 and well into the winter of 1882–83, Crees continued to cross south in search of desperately needed resources.[46]

In December 1882, Montanans rejoiced at the news that Big Bear had surrendered to Canadian authorities and accepted newly negotiated treaty terms. The *Benton Weekly Record* explained the significance that this event had for residents of northern Montana:

> There is much importance attached to Big Bear's accepting the treaty, in as much as to him can be ascribed the major part of the depredations committed by North Cree Indians. He has disturbed the people of this Territory by his raids upon stock, and his war parties have more than once within the past few years alarmed the settlers north of Benton . . . and while it may be a somewhat embarrassing confession, it is none the less true that Montana settlers have only the Montana Indians to fear since Big Bear's yielding to the treaty.[47]

Some eight to nine months removed from Big Bear's return to Canada, Montanans still looked to his influence as pivotal — for better or for worse. They mistakenly supposed that Big Bear's signing would end Cree depredations south of the line. Two misconceptions were apparent. First, Montanans assumed that all Plains Crees were under the direct control of Big Bear or other chiefs associated with him. Second, they assumed that as members of such an all-inclusive hierarchical social structure, all Crees would follow Big Bear's surrender and settle somewhere beyond the immediate proximity of the border. Almost immediately, continued Cree activities laid bare the inherent fallacy in these beliefs.

Finalizing Cree Illegality

In fact, as the winter of 1883 transitioned into spring, Montana experienced a sharp escalation in Cree border crossings and horse-thieving, rivaling those of previous springs. In one alarming instance, a Cree party that numbered some two hundred warriors crossed south of the line. Following familiar lines, but also stressing the unique nature of the threat, the *Daily Independent* wrote that "the Crees, about 200 strong, are moving down the Marias killing cattle, stealing horses, and fears for the safety of the settlers are entertained. It is the biggest Indian raid for years."[48] In the days to follow, reports streamed in about surrounding ranchers and settlers whose cattle and horses Crees targeted as well as the efforts of the garrison from Fort Assiniboine to drive them back north.[49] The strength and extent of the Cree incursion was so surprising that national press syndicates reported on the matter and raised alarm:

> Runners and scouts bring information of the most daring raid of the Cree Indians, who belong properly beyond the Canadian line, that has been made in many years. The party, supposed to number 200 braves, are represented as moving along the Marias River, killing cattle and other stock as they go. At daybreak on the nineteenth instant, a small war party of Piegans, headed by Little Dog and two white men, had a sharp engagement with the Crees, killing two of them and securing their scalps. Two Piegans were wounded and one horse was killed. The bodies of ten oxen were found near Fort Conrad, which had been killed by a marauding band, and forty horses were driven off by the same party near the same place. The Indians seem to be heading toward the Dominion.[50]

The tone of national coverage presented Crees in the most recalcitrant terms: focused on wanton, gratuitous destruction of property. In their previous complaints of transnational Cree movements, and their illicit trafficking of contraband, Montanans had suggested that Crees were not "what may be properly called hostile Indians," but rather a troublesome nuisance.

Now, however, echoing the *Washington Post*, the local press wrote of reckless destruction of property and "the biggest and best executed raid that [had] occurred on the Marias for a long time."[51] A salient point was thus revealed. The continued development of transnational Cree movements was inextricably linked to conditions north of the line, but not always with the causal connections that Montanans anticipated. Failed treaty negotiations in the late 1870s had prompted Crees to cross in to Montana, and much to the consternation of Montanans, the inverse relationship was not necessarily true. With Big Bear's compliance, the majority of Canadian Crees were under treaty, but this did not terminate their transnational presence. Many persisted to negotiate traditional geographies.

Conflict between transnational Crees and Piegans in Montana during the spring of 1883 prompted Montanans to clamor for more lasting solutions.[52] Both nations were at the point of starvation, and this fueled their mutual "intention to kill cattle wherever they find them" and determination to make raids on one another.[53] Some favored the establishment of new military forts and posts nearer to the international border.[54] The need to curtail the slaughter or stealing of livestock was apparent, but the mounting intertribal antagonism and violence complicated concerns. To make matters worse, Montanan papers reported supposedly "well grounded fears" that Big Bear himself was gathering an immense force to storm across the line, avenge Cree deaths, and make general war on Piegans, Assiniboines, and Gros Ventres.[55] Although the report of Big Bear's intentions proved false, it revealed continued anxiety about his looming presence. Some Cree raiding did ensue, even led by his son Little Bear, or Imasees, but it stood in direct opposition to Big Bear's wishes.[56]

In the late spring and early summer of 1883, Cree-Montanan interaction followed much the same pattern. Transnational movements were repelled and charismatic leaders were targeted in hopes of controlling subservient bands. Louis Riel, who was living in Montana at the time, was thus arrested for suspicion of inciting Crees to cross the border and Missouri River to "murder the whites." The targeting of Riel was similar to that of Big Bear and underlined a belief that eliminating the threat of charismatic individuals may reduce broader problems.[57] Unabated, Crees continued to range the prairies north of Fort Benton and US Army officials from Fort Assiniboine vied to capture and deport them. In response to reported Cree depredations, soldiers would directly confront Crees and instruct them to return north.[58] Despite such actions, Montanans' perennial frustration remained: deportation was their only recourse. Lamenting, the *Benton Weekly Record* wrote, "It is to be regretted that something cannot be done with these Indians after all the time and trouble spent in capturing them. They will hardly be turned loose on the other side of the line before they will return again to commit more depredations."[59] This complaint was now becoming all too familiar.

During the summer of 1883, Lieutenant Colonel Guido Ilges moved against the Crees led by Little Pine with mixed success. Commander at Fort Assiniboine, Ilges had been sending mounted infantry units against the Crees for months, but eventually set out himself. After rumors of his defeat, Ilges returned with "nothing of great importance [being] accomplished." He captured and deported some Crees, but as was becoming abundantly clear, this meant little in terms of long-term solutions to the problem.[60] Canadian officials were announcing plans to move Crees farther north, but the immediate situation continued unabated. Exacerbating concerns was the announced transfer of an infantry company stationed on the Marias. This, complained northern Montanans, left "the country wholly unprotected from the Cree raids."[61] A few months later, Patrick Burke, then stationed at Fort Maginnis, lamented that the trouble was likely to continue: "I think there is going to be some serious trouble with the Indians this summer in this country. They come from north of the line and murder settlers and steal their horses and get away before the soldiers can follow them. One thing is certain; if the boys get a chance they will show them no mercy."[62] During the remainder of 1883 and into 1884, Burke's contingency and others saw a significant decline in Cree cattle and horse thefts from settlers. Altercations between Crees and other Indians in Montana, however, continued.[63]

Conclusion

In the spring of 1885, the Northwest Rebellion broke out in Saskatchewan and Manitoba as Métis under the leadership of Louis Riel and others revolted against Canadian authorities. When word reached Montanan papers of Cree involvement in the uprising, the reported actions dovetailed neatly with the prejudices locals had built against Crees during the preceding years. Included in the instigative parties, Crees were perceived as "starting on the warpath" in Canada.[64] Further reports that Big Bear's band was involved galvanized the worst prejudices that had already formed against the Crees. The linking of Big Bear's negative reputation from Cree border crossings in the early 1880s to his involvement in the bloody Northwest Rebellion dominated the minds of Montanans as subsequent waves of inbound Crees arrived.

The developments of 1885 would have likely been enough to set US policymakers and Montanan interests against the prospect of offering federal recognition to future incoming Cree immigrants. Never in the business of assuming extra responsibilities for Indians, the United States and local Montanans were even more reticent to accept stewardship over so-called troublesome Crees. With layers of prejudice stacked against them from previous horse-thieving or cattle-rustling incidents, border violations, and the Northwest Rebellion, Crees found their efforts to settle in Montana ill-fated from the start. When Big Bear's son Little Bear fled into Montana after the failed 1885 Rebellion, Montanan policy defaulted to the entrenched bias of previous experiences.

For the preceding five years, the media frenzy concerning reported Cree depredations, thieving, and illegal border crossing had kept frontier settlers at high alert. The very "foreign" presence of Crees frustrated urbanites, ranchers, and farmers alike, and the local press made sure to consistently reinforce these prejudices. The impotence of US military units to enforce border security against the entry, exit, and reentry of Crees exacerbated such angers. Similar events of Native thievery committed elsewhere in the United States were dealt with summarily under established Indian policy. Uncontrolled Native transport of contraband across the United States' northern borders, however, was different. The perceived transnational Cree threat was uniquely problematic.

Throughout the early and short pre-1885 history of Cree-Anglo interactions in Montana, Crees were afforded little, if any, welcome south of the line. They were, in the eyes of many borderlands whites, purveyors of vice: specifically, the theft or slaughter of livestock. This, in and of itself, however, does not explain the underlying "moral panic," as termed by Josiah Heyman and Howard Campbell in this volume's afterward, surrounding transnational Crees in Montana Territory.[65] For Montanans, Cree activities were not simply an example Native depredation. They were an uncontrolled foreign presence, illicit in their very transnational corporal presence, and intent on illicit transnational behavior. As livestock thieves, Crees were not simple purveyors of vice, they were engaged in international smuggling. From the Crees' perspective, they were utilizing resources and lands to which they had traditional rights. Ancestors of Big Bear relate that he felt the Northwest belonged to him, valued its vast riches, and saw how

Anglos were then reaping the benefits of what was rightfully belonged to his people.[66] As incongruous as the arbitrary bisection of Native geographies by the Forty-ninth Parallel was with traditional Native understanding of territorial boundaries, the juxtaposition of these competing perspectives of Cree activities in Montana exacted lasting consequences on the histories of both Crees and whites.

Likewise, the proximity of the border itself was a transformational power in the lives of Crees and white Montanans. It recast and reconfigured the histories of all parties involved, adding layers of geopolitical and international complexity nonexistent elsewhere in the country. The transformation of the region from porous borderlands into policed borders, as fueled by increased white settlement, left indelible marks on Plains Crees.[67] While not resembling a strict Turnerian process where the region moved through discernable phases, the dynamics and histories of Native migration, white settlement, and border enforcement were tightly intertwined as they fitfully progressed. The evolution of the established, though porous, boundary into a geopolitical tool for controlling the movement of desirable or undesirable populations was concurrently influenced by increased white settlement and transnational Cree migrations. Without Cree border crossing, white settlement may not have demanded that their northern frontier be better policed. Likewise, without increased white settlement, transnational Cree activities may have continued without cause for alarm. It was the intersection and combination of the two historical narratives along the border in northern Montana that caused the nature of the region's borderlands to evolve.

Local Montanans, like most societies faced with possible chaos, hungered for order. Facing possible disruption to the ordered society they were in the midst of establishing, they quickly defined the licit and illicit, domestic and foreign. For the individual Crees and other foreign Natives thus defined and labeled, the traditional (though evolving) Native geopolitical landscape in which they were actors was not consulted. Their self-perception as rightful residents of lands arbitrarily bisected by Anglo borders was a view not simply overlooked, but forcefully ignored. How might the consideration of Native perspectives have augmented the Montanan definition of vice, contraband, and illicit transnational behavior? As transnational Cree migration and trade (whether licit or illicit) was defined and interpreted without the Crees' input or context, the history of all involved parties was predestined for conflict. Ironically, the dominant society's quest for order fated the region for chaos. Thus relegated to lives of destitute homeless wandering in Montana, generations of Crees suffered from this condemnation. Consultation with inbound groups would have ensured peaceful coexistence or successful segregation, but the opposite virtually guaranteed conflict. Sadly, Crees decades-removed from those initial years of Cree border crossings, hunting south of the line, and livestock-thieving would suffer the consequences of persistent prejudice. Defined collectively as illegals within their own lands, Crees, everything they carried, and all they did in their transnational world were contraband, illicit, and vice.

CHAPTER THREE

Contraband Twine

Harvests, Smuggling, and Tariffs in the US-Canada Borderlands in the Early Twentieth Century

Sterling Evans

American-made binder twine became a hot commodity for smuggling into Canada in the early decades of the twentieth century. Farmers relied on grain binders (before the advent of combine harvesters) and the twine they required for tying sheaves, or bundles, to harvest wheat and other grain crops. As a necessity without which farmers could not survive, binder twine was controlled by cordage manufacturers who set its price and distribution. But when some states in the upper Midwest started manufacturing twine using inmates at their state prisons to compete against the larger cordage companies, and started selling it for considerably less than corporate manufacturers, Canadian farmers sought ways to import and smuggle the less expensive twine across the Forty-ninth Parallel. At that point, Canadian cordage companies, centered primarily in Ontario, began an active campaign against the use of American twine, and especially prison-made twine from the United States, arguing against its supposed lower quality. Likewise the Canadian government worked to end the trade in contraband goods, not only by developing its own prison twine mill at the federal penitentiary in Kingston, Ontario, but also by beefing up customs and inspection policies, and by slapping expensive duties and tariffs on all US-made twine. The policy caused outrage among farmers and farmers' organizations in the Prairie Provinces (Manitoba, Saskatchewan, and Alberta). The history of this borderlands scenario represents a little-known but compelling chapter in North American agricultural, commercial, and contraband activity between Canada and the United States.

The story of contraband twine, however, may seem to be far less notorious or poignant than the history of smuggling alcohol, controlled drugs, prostitutes, or immigrant workers into the United States from Canada. Certainly during the era of Prohibition in the United States, there was great borderlands contraband activity that conjures up stories of daring whiskey runners, smuggling rings, and organized crime, as well as the development of a kind of border tourism business for thirsty American "refugees from Volstead."[1] Or, in terms of contraband agricultural activity, while the illicit trade of twine represents a clash of the American market system, it has perhaps gone down in history as far less notorious than borderlands cattle raiding.

Nonetheless, as this chapter will show, illegal twine that flowed into Canada caused considerable outrage among the Canadian cordage industry and prompted substantial policy shifts and changes in inspection regulations. In fact, the smuggling of illegal articles like twine into Canada fell in the same legal category as "narcotics and intoxicating liquors" with "all shipments across the line" needing to "be covered by shippers' declarations."[2] This then fits the general theory of "illicit trade," which Moisés Naím has defined as "trade that breaks the rules — the laws, regulations, licenses, taxes, embargoes, and all the procedures that nations employ to organize commerce, protect their citizens, raise revenues, and enforce moral codes."[3] All of those conditions apply well to what the Canadian government sought to protect by enforcing regulations against contraband twine. Ottawa sought to protect farmers from what was perceived to be highly inferior twine, and sought to protect the Canadian cordage industry from what could be unfair competition from south of the US-Canada border. Smuggling of commodities, whether of the intoxicating and psycho-active kinds, or of the industrial materials kind, was all illegal and thus to be regulated and controlled. As John Lea has explained, because "crime has no ontological reality," the criminalization of even seemingly innocu-ous commodities like contraband binder twine is part of a greater "social reality."[4] It is also part of the "transnational flows," as Elaine Carey and Andrae Marak have described them in their introduction here, of goods made illicit by the "fear of penetration of hegemonic spaces by 'others' as grounds to expand their reach and power," as we shall see below.[5]

This story of smuggling in Canada is based on that nation's (and all wheat-growing countries') dependence on the mechanical reaper/binder, or more simply, binder — an implement used for harvesting grain crops. The development of the binder in the 1870s gave farmers a significant labor-, time-, and money-saving advantage over the older reaper that cut but did not bind sheaves of wheat to await threshing.[6] The key was in the knotting device that tied twine around bevels of grain stalks as they were being cut in the field, thus allowing field hands to gather the sheaves and pile them upright into stooks (shocks in the United States). The knotter went down in history as one of the greatest of all agricultural inventions.[7] Historian Merrill Dennison has argued that "next to the wheel, the cutter bar, and the reel, the invention that did the most agricultural mechanization was the automatic knotter," and that it "has exerted a more profound influence in the world's economy than any other of man's technological accomplishments, save possibly the locomotive." Binders on average reduced the manpower requirement during harvest by 25 percent, and one Canadian farmer-writer explained that a worker with a team of horses and a binder could do in a day what previously took six workers to do.[8] The farmer or hired worker who operated the binder was, as another historian put it, "the king of harvest." The hard work and long days of harvest also exuded a special and contagious excitement. "A field of thick shocks always brought a sense of well being — or well doing!"[9]

Wheat became the predominant crop in the northern Plains borderlands. The mechanization of harvests was particularly important with the soaring world demand for grain during World War I and the interwar years when the big wheat expansion in both countries occurred. In the United States, harvested bushels of wheat rose from 36.7 million in 1890 to 69.2 million by 1938. In Canada, the rate of expansion was even more dramatic, rising from 42.2 million bushels harvested in in 1891 to more than 540 million bushels by 1940. By then, 95 percent of the country's wheat was grown in the Prairie Provinces where the percentage of all Canadian farms located there jumped from 24.3 percent to 67.3 percent, and where wheat acreage expanded from almost zero to 27.7 million in the same years. Canada then went from supplying 5 percent of the world's total exported wheat in 1911 to 40 percent by 1930.[10] During the First World War, farmers in the Prairie Provinces engaged in a "Patriotism and Production" campaign to stimulate grain production as part of "a duty the farmers owed the Empire," as one farmer in Alberta put it.[11] In 1915 — a record-setting year with a perfect climate for crop production throughout the northern Plains (for example, farm production in Saskatchewan increased by a record-breaking amount) — farmers brought in 300 million Canadian dollars more than the previous greatest yearly earning. The farmers did it "through hard work, good management, determination, and patriotism," a newspaper article concluded, and with "no need [for] flag-waving processions along the highways [nor] martial music to stimulate their patriotism."[12]

Farmers in western Canada quickly adopted binders to harvest so much wheat.[13] Although the contraptions seemed bulky and complicated, with 3,800 parts and common breakdowns, as one Canadian recalled "they were accepted at once and for nearly fifty years nobody considered an alternative." The reduction in their cost from the original $350 in the 1890s to $155 by the 1910s further popularized the implement. By 1915 even imported US binders were selling for around $105.[14] The Canadian government, however, imposed stiff tariffs on American implements, starting at 17.5 percent in the 1850s and up to 37.5 percent by the 1880s to help protect Canadian manufacturers. The tax added about $19 to the sticker price of US-made binders, a policy that clearly annoyed many Prairie Province farmers and US implement manufacturers, especially International Harvester (hereafter IH). These added costs did not stop the American firms from competing for the Canadian market. In 1911 at the Winnipeg Port of Entry alone, the government collected nearly $4,000 in duties on imported binders.[15]

With so much wheat and hundreds of thousands of binders to harvest it, especially during World War I and its aftermath, the demand for twine that the binders required increased exponentially. Depending on yield and conditions, an average of two to six pounds of twine was needed for every acre of wheat, or as some farmers averaged it, two pounds of twine to harvest every thousand pounds of grain. By 1900, then, more than half of all the hard fiber imported into the United States was used for spinning binder twine. For the next three decades, Americans consumed around two hundred thousand tons of twine and Canadians another thirty-five thousand tons a year.[16] Cordage companies across North America quickly retooled to increase production and had to seek out the right kind of fiber to make the most reliable and affordable binder twine. They experimented with "pure manila," a fiber made from abacá rasped from the bark of Philippine manila plants (related to bananas), sisal and henequen-agaves from Mexico's Yucatán Peninsula, jute from India, and a variety of other fiber-producing plants from Java, New Zealand, and the Caribbean. Ultimately, the industry settled on manila, sisal, and henequen as the fibers that tied the tightest sheaves, were naturally repellant to insects, and worked the best in the binder's knotter. Sisal and henequen, shipped from relatively nearby Yucatán, became the clear fiber of choice for manufacturers and farmers alike across the United States and Canada.[17] By 1910 reports showed that 90 percent of the twine used in the United States was made from sisal (a generic term that the industry used to mean both sisal and henequen). Sisal imports to the United States jumped from 39,000 tons in 1910 to 117,000 tons by 1911.[18] This scenario of a Mexican commodity on which US and

Canadian crops depended, then, became as I have called it elsewhere, a "henequen-wheat complex" that casts this history in a proto-NAFTA framework for the greater North American West in the late nineteenth and early twentieth centuries.[19]

As one of the largest manufacturers of binders, IH also came to dominate the sisal importation and twine manufacturing trades. By 1914 IH was consuming nearly twice as much imported fiber as the other twine manufacturers combined.[20] It opened up three huge twine mills in the United States (in Chicago, New Orleans, and St. Paul) and one in Canada (in Hamilton, Ontario). The Hamilton operation set out to compete with Canadian firms, especially the Brantford Cordage Company that developed large mills in Brantford, Ontario, and Winnipeg, Manitoba, and advertised itself as the "the world's largest exclusive binder twine manufacturers" and the largest twine producer in the British Empire.[21] IH faced many other competitors, the biggest of which was Plymouth Cordage of Massachusetts that had been making rope since 1837. Although Plymouth waged a veritable battle of the twines by its claim of marketing a better-quality product, and by opening a Canadian mill in Welland, Ontario, it never came close to manufacturing the volume of twine made by IH. In fact, IH became the largest fiber trader in the world with a whopping 90 percent of the binder twine market by 1902 (although that figure would drop somewhat in later years).[22]

To eliminate the threat of cheaper imports flooding the market, both the United States and Canada imposed tariffs on imported twine (but not on the importation of raw fiber). In Canada, as early as the 1890s the government's tariffs on foreign-made farm implements extended to cordage products with a three-cents-a-pound duty on imported twines. But while only about 14 percent of all binder twine in Canada in the 1890s was American-made, it was an important source for Prairie farmers during harvest, with some farmers arguing that the US twine was superior in quality. Thus farmers and their organizations lobbied for an end to the "absurd duty," as the Regina Leader in wheat-rich Saskatchewan called it, on imported twine. The newspaper reported in 1892 that the tariff amounted to an "annual tax" that earned the government $144,000 paid by western farmers. The populist organization the Order of the Patrons of Industry worked hard to end the tariff and by the end of the century sent petitions with more than twenty-five thousand signatures to Ottawa requesting the duties be lifted. And members of the United Farmers of Alberta (UFA), angry about the high prices on imported twine, passed a resolution at their annual convention in 1927 saying how they "emphatically do protest against any duty . . . [on] twine" and sent it to Prime Minister William MacKenzie King.[23]

A government representative responded by arguing that Canada "derive[d] no revenue whatever from duties on binder twine," that the Americans had a similar tariff that prevented Canadian twine from entering the United States, that there was no true twine "monopoly," and that there were sufficient numbers of Canadian manufacturers supplying twine to preclude Canadian farmers needing US imports. Parliament never ended the tariff, but the situation did resolve itself a bit when by 1910 Canadian production of twine increased to such a level that supply made prices drop from eighteen to seven cents a pound.[24] Nonetheless, despite the tariffs, by 1925 the amount of twine imported from the United States and Europe jumped to more than half of the binder twine used in Canada. In the four years between 1919 and 1922 alone more than 120 million pounds of twine, worth nearly $22 million, were imported into the country.[25]

The stiff competition in the cordage trade significantly increased when, as a direct response to IH's "trust" in controlling the industry and prices, state-subsidized twine factories in penitentiaries began making binder twine in 1891. The idea of setting up convict-labor mills to provide state farmers with lower-priced twine for their harvests and to give inmates useful work originated with officials at the Stillwater State Prison in Minnesota. Soon thereafter, officials at the Ontario Central Prison in Toronto, the Kingston Federal Penitentiary in Ontario, and state penitentiaries in North and South Dakota, Kansas, Wisconsin, Michigan, Indiana, Missouri, and Oklahoma followed Minnesota's pattern by manufacturing twine that was usually a cent a pound cheaper than the brand-name products. Officials at Plymouth Cordage complained that the state-subsidized twine plants, with their remarkably lower wages paid to inmates, unfairly competed against private industry and argued that theirs was "the only industry in the country subject to prison competition."[26] And IH warned its customers on both sides of the border that "when you have a chance to buy at lower prices . . . you have no assurance that this saving will not be more than offset by short weight, short length, or lost time due to breaks in the binder." This scenario was unfortunately altogether too real for farmers in South Dakota in 1919 and 1920. Inmates in the state penitentiary there sabotaged the manufacture process, producing faulty twine and thus creating havoc with harvests those years.[27] Such occurrences, however, tended to be rare. According to a contemporary study, most prison-made goods did not compete that significantly with commercially manufactured ones, except for binder twine, which did represent a real threat to the commercial market.[28]

Despite the efforts of IH, other US and Canadian cordage companies, and penitentiaries to produce enough twine, there were periods in the late nineteenth and early twentieth centuries when dangerous shortages in western Canada threatened harvests, prompting farmers to search for contraband cordage from south of the border. There were different reasons for these shortages. In 1894 with production increasing at the twine plant in the Kingston Penitentiary, Canadian cordage companies decreased their shipments of twine to the Prairie Provinces. When the prison shipped far less than was expected, a shortage of twine resulted.[29] International factors that threatened fiber supplies also caused shortages or hoarding. For example, in 1899, when the American War in the Philippines was raging, blocked ports there slowed the flow of manila fiber to cordage companies (although some Filipino producers smuggled contraband manila into the United States).[30] At other times rail problems caused delays in twine shipments that would understandably alarm farmers. The bumper-crop years themselves created conditions in which harvests exceeded the amount of twine available, especially toward the end of the season when supplies ran short. Such was the case in Alberta in both 1912 and 1913 when farmers duly worried about the lack of twine holding up the harvests. With shortages came higher prices for the twine, as is the general rule of supply and demand, further outraging area farmers.[31]

This especially became the case during the 1930s when Depression-era farmers had no extra money to spare. It was common for farmers to take out bank loans for their harvesting expenses — including the purchase of binder twine — then pay the lien off when they sold their grain. During the Depression, however, many banks halted the practice, leaving farmers without credit to buy supplies and causing farmers and farmers' organizations to petition the federal government for help. The general secretary of the United Farmers of Alberta cabled Prime Minister R. B. Bennett saying that the UFA demanded that "credit for twine be . . . [provided] through banks. Many fields will not be cut if credit not obtained. Immediate action necessary." Another Albertan wrote Bennett explaining that in his district there were "200 farmers who cannot obtain any advance from the banks, merchants, or twine dealers and unless the government come to their assistance and does so at once they will be unable to get the twine to harvest the crop."[32] The same was true in Saskatchewan. In 1931 the council of the rural municipality (county) of Grass Lake passed a resolution citing how "a majority of the farmers of this municipality are not able to secure their twine requirements having no funds of their own and credits being refused" and sent it to the minister of agriculture in the Bennett government.[33]

The shortages and the rapidly expanding wheat industry in western

Canada stimulated calls for creating new binder twine plants in Winnipeg and Brandon, Manitoba ("positively the best distribution centre for the West today," according to officials there in 1910), and for experimenting with other fibers for twine production, especially flax that could be grown in the region.[34] Factories in Brandon, and Rosetown and Saskatoon, Saskatchewan, attempted to obtain federal support for spinning flax fiber that "would be a great boost to the farmers," and would "constitute a very real boon and blessing to our agricultural community." Likewise, some farmers in Saskatchewan renewed efforts to grow industrial hemp as a usable twine fiber and sold their harvest to a cordage company in Manitoba.[35] Twine from locally grown fiber became even more urgent after the Mexican Revolution (1910–1920) when a new socialist-leaning government in Yucatán demanded higher prices for raw fiber to improve wages of henequen workers and to fund improvements in education and social services. A state fiber-regulating agency raised its market price for raw henequen from 13.2 cents per kilogram in 1915 to 50.6 cents by 1918, which duly outraged cordage manufacturers, twine dealers, and farmers throughout the United States and Canada. The rate increases also caused sisal growers in East Africa, Haiti, Brazil, Java, and elsewhere to compete more aggressively in the international fiber market, eventually leading to the demise of Yucatán's predominance in the trade.[36]

None of the ventures to raise local fibers in Canada solved the urgent need for binder twine, especially when unanticipated shortages occurred. To avoid ruined harvests, farmers did what they needed to do to get the best priced twine possible, which included illegally obtaining penitentiary twine from the United States. There had always been a problem of keeping US twine out of Canada, especially since overproduction in the States caused American producers to attempt to sell their excess stock in Canada. For example, as early as 1894, reports in Canada showed that there was a fifty-thousand-ton overproduction south of the border, and that cordage companies were trying to dump four-year-old twine in the Canadian market.[37] Likewise, as an attorney representing the Canadian cordage industry pointed out to Prime Minister Wilfrid Laurier a few years later, because Canadian harvests were later than those south of the border, Canada became "a dumping ground for surplus twine at slaughter prices," or when shortages occurred, Canadian farmers had "to pay exorbitant prices for twine."[38] This was no exaggerated fear of industry. A business report entitled "The Binder Twine Situation in Canada" showed that there were "ten independent companies" (including the Kingston Penitentiary) making twine in the country, and that those firms had "sufficient machinery to manufacture more than twice the amount of binder twine consumed" in Canada. Yet, to prove why protective tariffs were needed, it showed that nearly 75 percent of the twine used there was still being imported from the United States. "The American harvest is earlier than the Canadian and the American manufacturers are only too glad to dispose of their surplus twine at any figure than carry it over for another season." But, the report continued, if that kind of dependency continued "when there is a large crop in the United States, Canada will have no twine."[39] And with the even cheaper US prison twine, the problem accelerated. In 1924, responding to farmer complaints of twine shorter than stated on labels, the Ministry of Commerce and Trade conducted an investigation and discovered that the twine had been illegally imported into Canada. Custom agents then seized a shipment of "unmarked balls" of what was determined to be from a US penitentiary (although the records do not indicate exactly how much was seized nor from which state it was sent).[40]

The Canadian cordage industry grew even more alarmed about the illegal shipments. In 1925 officials at Brantford Cordage begged for Ottawa's attention to the matter, decrying how "persistent efforts have been made to ship American prison-made twine into the Canadian Northwest." They asserted that penitentiary twine was of inferior quality ("irregular and unreliable") due to the "class of labour" in the penitentiaries ("free labour factories"). They also claimed that the twine bore "labels intended to mislead the public" of its origin, which would lead to "grave injustices to the farmers" of Canada, and lobbied strongly for increased border inspections to keep out the prison twines. Likewise, the United Farmers of Manitoba passed a resolution in 1928 requesting that the federal government increase its inspections to keep defective twine, like the organization accused prison twine of being, off the market.[41]

However, some Canadian farmers were disgusted with brand-name twines manufactured in their own country, arguing that often the twine was mislabeled, had irregular lengths, and was of poor quality. Such was the case with A. J. Cotton — known as the "Wheat King" of Manitoba, who angrily complained to officials at the Massey-Harris Company in Toronto about their bad twine. Claiming that the "Blue Ribbon" Manalla [*sic*] twine he purchased was of shorter length than stated on the label and of far "inferior quality," he wondered why Massey-Harris had "the cheek to ask me to pay for the privilege of binding my crop with your inferior cord," and why they thought he would be "ignorant and . . . not the know the difference" of the various standards. He went on to say it was a "barefaced piece of dishonesty" and "an imposition that cannot be overlooked" for which "the company should be brought to task for trying to obtain money under false pretences." Finally, he argued, "I have dealt with your company for a number of years in Ontario and here in Manitoba and I intend to stop right now unless we get some fairplay."[42]

Farmers throughout the Great Plains and Midwest were generally very satisfied with penitentiary twine and clamored for more than the state mills could produce. It was indeed a popular commodity, and wheat states like Kansas and North Dakota could in no way keep up with the demand for their prison-made twine. Despite laws against out-of-state sales in some states, requests streamed in from farmers from other states who wanted to save on harvest expenses.[43] The same held true in Canada. Often the state prisons in Michigan and Wisconsin sold twine across the international border, and more commonly it was smuggled into Canada for willing farmers wanting to pay less than the prices for the Canadian commercial twines. Never big wheat-producing states, Michigan and Wisconsin did not have laws against selling their prison twine out-of-state and thus needed to sell their stocks wherever possible. Minnesota was always the greatest prison twine producer and also sold outside the state, and along with Wisconsin and Michigan very aggressively marketed its product throughout the region.[44]

As mentioned earlier, Canadian officials had also decided to use convict labor to produce an inexpensive binder twine. Soon after the Minnesota State Prison opened its twine mill, administrators at the Ontario Central Prison in Toronto added a twine plant to their other prison workshops, although it only stayed in business for a few years. In 1894, a similar plant was established at the Kingston Penitentiary — a federal correctional facility in Ontario, which was greeted with enthusiasm by farmers across Canada in hopes of acquiring less expensive binder twine.[45] That kind of competition worried cordage companies, especially since the government advertised the prison twine with government-printed circulars instead of paying for newspaper ads, which sparked cries of injustice and unfair business tactics. The minister of justice, David Miller, then conducted a thorough investigation of the prison operation in 1900 and reported to Parliament that the Kingston plant was developed "for the purpose of giving employment to a number of the convicts, and so enable them to earn, at least, a portion of the cost of their maintenance, and, to that extent, relieve the public treasury from what would be otherwise a necessary burden." Thus it was far more about "suitable employment" than any kind of "unfair competition" with private industry, and he confirmed that the prison was involved in no kind of "ring, and no combination of any sort" with manufacturing or retailing its twine. Miller likewise declared that the Kingston plant was no political ploy, "established by the Conservative government in order to control the price of twine," like some industry officials were accusing it of being, and assured that the prison mill was being run "in a business-like way and upon business principles."[46]

At times the cordage industry's concerns proved to be valid. In 1894 a looming shortage of twine in the Prairie Provinces sparked a special shipment of Kingston Prison twine to be sent to Manitoba. The penitentiary even sent a representative to deliver the special shipments, "in time to prevent a shortage," as one local newspaper put it. The twine was said to be "made with results very favorable to the Government article" and "raised to the merits . . . of the Plymouth brand." The shipments arrived to avoid "a stringency, and no time will be lost by dealers handling twine in availing themselves of a sufficient supply to meet the demand in their immediate vicinity."[47] On the other hand, in 1896 there was a surplus of twine, and one industry official suggested that all twine made at the Toronto Central and Kingston prisons be used solely for exporting out of the country.[48] In the spring of 1903 the *Edmonton Bulletin* ran an article about one of the dominion government's circulars for an "unprecedented offer" allowing farmers to buy Kingston binder twine "at cost." And by the 1910s, the prison plant would also sell large stocks of twine on credit to farmers.[49] Another circular a few years later advertised that farmers could buy the more expensive manila twine from the Kingston prison at below market prices, and it would be sent f.o.b. (free on board), offers that private industry simply could not match.[50]

Worse, even penitentiary twine made in Canada at times was improperly tagged, as complaints in 1901 showed.[51] The issue had even come to the attention of Prime Minister Wilfrid Laurier when farmers were outraged by the fact that the Kingston twine they were getting had less footage per pound than stated on the label and that they were being unfairly charged for it.[52] This prompted the department of justice to order customs agents to seize quantities of twine in 1904.[53] Later that year Parliament added an amendment to the General Inspection Act, signed by King Edward VII, that required manufacturers to label how many feet per pound of twine there was in every ball.[54] Some companies, however, found the new regulations unnecessary and annoying. A representative of the Consumers Cordage from Nova Scotia noted in a letter to his member of Parliament that it was more the "rascality" of Canadian farmers, and the government's "vexatious rules" that were "simply killing the prospect of selling Canadian twine . . . handicapped by our own Canadian trade." The company did not understand why it should be regulated for exporting its product abroad, either. "I cannot conceive how our government should dream it their duty to legislate for the consumers of binder twine in the Argentine, Russia, or Australia, or England either," the representative wrote. One of their customers in England called the Canadian regulations "the most absurd notion I have ever met with in the sale of twine."[55] Nonetheless, the labeling requirement was mandated in the Sale and Inspection Act of 1920, but did specify that twine manufactured for export "need not be so labeled."[56]

That it was an illegal trade means that it is impossible to know just exactly how much twine was smuggled into Canada. But Ottawa's reaction to the situation clearly shows that it was a significant enough problem to warrant a great deal of debate on the subject and to enact and enforce stiff inspection and customs policies to keep the US prison twine out of the country. By 1925 the country employed forty inspectors throughout Canada instructed to "assist customs officials with regulations regarding imported binder twine." Still, a Canadian representative of Plymouth Cordage wrote the Ministry of Agriculture that in his company's "twenty years here" it had always considered twine inspection to be an "extremely important matter" and hoped that any changes in the ministry would "not have the effect in the slightest degree of letting down the bars to unscrupulous importers."[57]

The industry's concern centered on the fact that Canada's Inspection and Sale Act, which took imported twine off the "free list" and imposed duties on the product, had no specific provisions pertaining to prison-made twine, causing officials at Brantford Cordage to insist that the government hire a "special inspector" just for that. The request caused a bit of a heated back-and-forth between government and industry officials. A representative for Agriculture responded that such a request was not really feasible since his ministry did not have the authority to "interfere" with the Department of Customs and Excise. "We find this amazing," Brantford retorted, "since for nearly thirty years your department has been doing inspections." According to the ministry, Agriculture officials only worked "in perfect harmony" with customs agents and did not do their own border inspections. In March 1925 Brantford complained that "illegal importations" of prison-made twine were still coming into Canada. Clearly irritated, Agriculture could only respond by reminding the company that the law pertaining to twine imports was administered by the Department of Customs and Excise and that "all further references should be made to officers of that Department."[58]

Apparently it was Customs and Excise that was at the root of some of the problem. One industry memo stated that "all twine manufacturers agree" that forty "inexperienced" inspectors "going about the country inspecting binder twine . . . can do incalculable harm."[59] Worse, reports surfaced in 1926 that "charges of irregularity" and "laxity" by "certain customs officials" was why contraband twine was entering Canada. One trade journal reported that "prison-made twine is claimed to have been imported into this country contrary to customs regulations which prohibit the import of prison-made products" — some of which was being illegally imported by 'farmers' organizations." The journal asserted that there had been no problems in this regard until three years earlier when the "full-time inspector of binder twine" died and his duties then were divided among seed inspectors and other employees instead of being assumed by a full-time replacement.[60] This problem represented the larger problem that Canada had in those years of regulating economic activities, especially ones that required funding for increased border inspections. Perhaps government officials viewed twine imports as less important than other controlled goods. The problem, however, apparently continued for the next few years, as the Canadian Council of Agriculture, the United Grain Growers Ltd., and the United Farmers of Manitoba (all from Winnipeg), made official requests directly to the Minister of Agriculture to "tighten the regulations under which binder twine is sold."[61]

Parliament responded in 1928 by enacting a new and improved Binder Twine Inspection Act. Although nowhere does the act specifically cite contraband penitentiary twine, it makes hidden references to it by referring to how all bales of twine (six balls to a bale) had to be "labeled with the name and address of the dealer and the number of feet of twine in the bale marked or stamped thereon." To ensure quality, all twine was to have a tensile strength of not less than sixty pounds, and any with less or not properly labeled or sealed could be seized by the inspector who could issues fines of a thousand dollars to dealers involved in selling illegal twine.[62]

The measures seemed to have worked, since there were no complaints registered past that point about illegal penitentiary twine coming into Canada. During World War II, however, fiber for binder twine again became strictly regulated to ensure sufficient supplies for the making of naval ropes for the war effort and for farmers to harvest their crops to help feed the Canadian and British forces. The Department of Munitions and Supplies established orders on the use of hard fibers, especially that no "java fibres" would be used for bedding, upholstering, tying twines, and even "skipping ropes or any toy or plaything" during the war, adding a further rule that "no person shall use binder twine for any purpose except binding or tying agricultural crops."[63] Importing illegal twine into the country apparently was not a problem then.

By the 1950s and 1960s the demand for binder twine crashed with the rise of combine harvesters ("combines") that cut and threshed grain crops without the need for tying the cut stalks into sheaves. At the same time, some farmers started baling their hay crops, which the cordage industry saw as an opportunity to continue manufacturing and selling twine (somewhat different than binder twine, but made of the same fiber commodities). As one memorandum explained:

> Baler twine is a new cordage development created by the invention in 1938 of the automatic hay baler which bales hay, straw, and other fodder directly from the windrow and displaced the old stationary baler which used wire or steel ties. The development was an immediate success and farmers in increasing numbers have adopted it. . . . The need for baler twine rose accordingly. Binder twine, on the other hand, has decreased and is decreasing in use, occasioned by the development of the modern harvester combines which dispense with the item.

Nonetheless, Canada kept a 20 percent tariff on imported baler twine to protect Canadian cordage companies, which was needed, as one official explained, "due to the increasing number of combine harvesters which are replacing mechanical binders, our binder twine sales are decreasing."[64]

The story of illegal binder twine shipments into Canada adds a lesser-known angle to the broader picture of borderlands contraband. It perhaps does not represent criminal smuggling in the same way that other contraband products did (or have been written about), but it was another example of illegal activity that the Canadian government was forced to address. In that way, the government followed customary protocol and international law in "preventing counterfeiting [and] smuggling . . . with all readiness" and by creating "its own criminal law and its own customs law for itself."[65] Likewise, there was not much the United States could do to help since there was no federal law preventing state penitentiaries from selling twine outside their states or stopping Canadian farmers from smuggling in US prison-made twine. As one authority on international policy wrote, Canada, as "the injured state," could have asked for US assistance. Similar to the experience with Prohibition, which aggravated these borderland tensions, the fact "that export of contraband may [be] legally permitted by one state but may be prevented by another" made such a request difficult, and probably not worthwhile, to pursue.[66] Or as Itty Abraham and Willem van Schendel provocatively have asked in their essay "The Making of Illicitness," "What about trade that is authorized by the receiving country but not by the sending country, or vice versa?"[67]

Perhaps more important, the story of contraband twine illustrates in another way, as Abraham and van Schendel have advanced, how "illegal networks" connect "states and markets in a variety of ways," and how "state definitions of what is illicit are situational." They argue that these kinds of networks are the most successful in international borderlands — "spaces formed by the intersection of multiple competing authorities," and where "cross-border linkages are maintained, manipulated, and developed."[68] At that point, the contraband twine issue represents another factor in the hardening of borders between the United States and Canada in the late nineteenth and early twentieth centuries, and advances the thesis promulgated by Jeremy Adelman and Stephen Aron of how such examples of nation-state policies in North America "turned borderlands into *bordered* lands."[69] The Canadian government in the end broke the linkages of illegally imported twine, but it was changes in agricultural technology and economics that ended the demand for binder twine, and hence illegal twine, in the long run. As Josiah Heyman and Howard Campbell show in the Afterword here, illegal twine is an example of how "the life-cycle of some controversial issues" can be short and nonescalatory.[70] But for the first few decades of the twentieth century, many grain farmers did what they could to get cheap twine to bind their crops.

CHAPTER FOUR

Twilight of the Tequileros

Prohibition-Era Smuggling in the South Texas Borderlands, 1919–1933

George T. Díaz

Between 1919 and 1933, South Texas saw the rise of organized groups of smugglers. During this period *tequileros*, mounted ethnic Mexican liquor smugglers, supplied Mexican liquor to thirsty American markets. United States law enforcement, however, saw tequileros' armed forays into the United States as transgressions to American sovereignty and resisted them with deadly force. Conflicts between American law enforcement and tequileros made Prohibition one of the bloodiest decades on the border. Despite this era's violence, liquor smuggling in this period was interethnic in nature. Anglo bootleggers and ethnic Mexican tequileros cooperated to profit from the circumvention of unpopular federal laws. Although Anglo bootleggers and ethnic Mexican tequileros both participated in violating American laws, US law enforcement took a much higher toll on tequileros than on their Anglo counterparts. American law enforcement's war on tequileros was so successful that by the end of the 1920s, it had effectively ended tequilero forays into South Texas. American authorities' victory over tequileros proved hollow, however, when more sophisticated and more violent gangs of smugglers took their place.

Bars across the nation gave their last *legal* calls for drinks near midnight on January 16, 1920. Almost immediately, however, it became clear that many Americans did not agree with the teetotalers. Illegal bars, moonshiners, and bootleggers filled the niche that Prohibition created. Although Prohibition remains one of the country's most interesting and colorful eras, serious academic scholarship in the field remains lacking. Most books on the subject deal with temperance groups' long battle to pass Prohibition

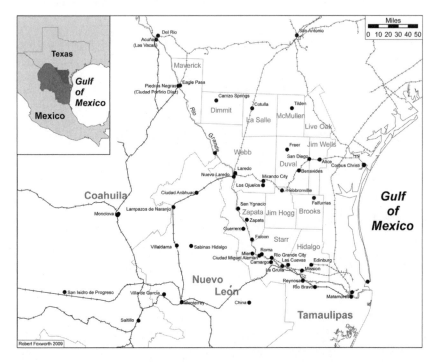

Figure 4.1 The Lower Rio Grande borderlands, circa 1920.

rather than the thirteen years the country was dry. The books that do examine this period are dominated by sensational accounts of the murders wreaked by mobsters such as Al Capone, or dwell on Prohibition politics. Moreover, much of the scholarship concerns the Northeast or Midwest and neglects other regions. Specifically, few scholars have examined Prohibition on the US-Mexico border.[1]

Although US Prohibition aided the rise of transnational trafficking across the US-Mexico border, few books or articles examine this period's impact on border history.[2] Most articles on Prohibition on the border are strictly informative in nature, notably, C. L. Sonnichsen and M. G. McKinney's "El Paso — From War to Depression."[3] James Sandos, one of the first scholars to seriously consider smuggling in the borderlands, has made serious investigations into drug trafficking's role in northern Mexican separatism during this period.[4] Robert Buffington's research has shown how US federal policy on Prohibition created rifts with local borderlands city governments.[5] Gabriela Recio's article "Drugs and Alcohol: US Prohibition and the Origins of the Drug Trade in Mexico," does an excellent job of revealing how contemporary trafficking along the border can be traced back to this period.[6] This chapter aims to contribute to the small body of scholarship on Prohibition and illicit trade in borderlands history by examining how state bans and interdiction efforts transformed smuggling from a low-level activity into a highly profitable professional criminal enterprise.

This chapter also enters into conversation with Elaine Carey's, Holly Karibo's, Dan Malleck's, and Marcel Martel's chapters and other transnational studies of vice and illicit trade by examining how borderlanders negotiated state law with their community values.[7] Prohibition made alcohol effectively illegal in the United States, yet most borderlanders viewed the consumption of liquor as licit. The United States' "noble experiment" to end the consumption of liquor within its borders marked the triumph of decades of Waspish nativist activism. The largely ethnic Mexican Catholic population of the South Texas borderlands, however, had few qualms about consuming alcohol. Moreover, as this chapter will show, many borderlanders accepted and celebrated certain groups of liquor smugglers as folk heroes.

Prohibition created a boon for contraband Mexican liquor in Texas. Ethnic Mexican entrepreneurs filled this demand by loading their pack animals with illicit spirits and journeying north to American markets.[8] Mounted smuggling forays south of the border had occurred as early as the mid-nineteenth century, when Mexican smugglers trafficked American consumer goods to avoid onerous Mexican tariff laws.[9] Armed smuggling forays north of the border, however, were new to South Texas. Although ethnic Mexican tequileros were initially successful in crossing the border illegally, making significant smuggling runs some seventy miles within US territory, American federal and state forces succeeded in effectively ending tequilero treks toward the end of the decade. Mounted US Customs inspectors, US Border Patrol, Texas Rangers, and county law enforcements' mounted patrols and their bloody engagements with tequileros effectively ended the smuggling of liquor across the border. Still, illegal liquor trafficking did not end with the tequileros. Traffickers merely abandoned horses and mules in favor of more discreet smuggling using cars and trucks. Bootleggers made highways the preferred avenue for transporting contraband liquor. Although the state may have succeeded in ending tequilero forays, a new, more effective, and violent form of smuggler came to take their place.

Prohibition came grudgingly to South Texas. Laredo, Texas, the largest town in the region, voted against Prohibition in 1919.[10] Laredo's ethnic Mexican Catholic majority was ill-disposed to accept moralistic Anglo legislation against alcohol. Unlike many Americans, the vast majority of

Figure 4.2. Texas Rangers with three hundred quarts of tequila and thirty-seven seized animals. Northwest Duval County, November 22, 1921. (Courtesy of the Center for American History, University of Texas at Austin; Roy W. Aldrich Papers, CN 11800)

Tejanos saw nothing wrong with having a drink. Proximity to alcohol in neighboring Mexico made Prohibition almost impossible to enforce. Whatever ethnic Mexican borderlanders may have felt about Prohibition, the region became a center for liquor smuggling from Mexico into major Texas cities. While national Prohibition did not take effect until January 17, 1920, numerous provisions made the country officially dry long before that time.[11] In April 1917, Congress passed the War Prohibition Act that outlawed the use of grain for the production of beverages with alcohol content above 2.75 percent. Furthermore, the Ten-Mile Zone law forbade the possession of alcohol within ten miles of military facilities. These laws, however, would not keep the people of Laredo or the local soldiers of Fort McIntosh from drinking smuggled alcohol. On January 5, 1919, a local newspaper commented how strange it was not to find any smugglers in court that Monday when so many were usually arrested over the weekend. Rather than naively believe that no alcohol was brought into the country, the writer attributed the anomaly to smugglers being "very much on the *cuidado*" (or being very careful).[12]

Cuidado or not, Prohibition ushered in a particularly bloody era in smuggling along the border. On the night of May 8, 1919, mounted Customs inspectors Robert Rumsey, John Chamberlain, and three Immigration inspectors came across four suspects crossing the Rio Grande by boat southeast of Laredo. The officers readied their weapons as they hid in the brush and waited for the suspects to land on the American side. According to newspapers, smugglers answered Rumsey's call to halt with bullets. A smuggler's bullet struck Immigration Inspector Hopkins, killing him instantly. Two other Immigration inspectors were wounded in the exchange, one fatally. When the smoke cleared, two officers had been killed and four smugglers were dead. Rumsey killed two smugglers in the battle and walked away unscathed. The dead liquor smugglers had been well armed. Each carried a rifle and sidearm. Smuggler Dorotéo Prado was even found holding a US Army automatic pistol in his dead hand.[13] The May 8, 1919, shootout was among the first of many violent confrontations between smugglers and US law enforcement officers during Prohibition.

Violent conflicts between US law enforcement and ethnic Mexicans during the Prohibition era stand out because, prior to Prohibition, both groups lived in relative peace. Central South Texas, or La Salle, Webb, Zapata, Jim Hogg, and Duval counties, escaped most of the interethnic violence that occurred in the lower Rio Grande Valley the previous decade. The Mexican Revolution, which broke out in the fall of 1911, did not stay in Mexico, but spilled north of the border. American residents in El Paso could see the fighting across the Rio Grande in the spring of 1911. Late in April 1914, soldiers loyal to Mexican dictator Victoriano Huerta put Nuevo Laredo to the torch rather than surrender the city to Constitutionalist forces. Although Huerta's soldiers attempted to dynamite the international bridge, and a few shots were exchanged across the border, the worst was yet to come.[14] In early 1915, Anglo authorities discovered a manifesto allegedly written by Mexican and Mexican American revolutionaries intent on reclaiming the US Southwest. The Plan de San Diego, as the document came to be called in honor of the Texas town in which it was supposedly signed, called for a "Liberating Army for Races and Peoples" comprised of ethnic Mexicans, African Americans, Japanese, and American Indians to attack and kill Anglo men over the age of sixteen and form an independent republic.[15] The plan, coupled with *sediciosos'* (seditionists) cross-border raids in the lower Rio Grande Valley that summer, sent shock waves among Anglos. Texas Rangers and Anglo vigilantes struck back against any ethnic Mexican they perceived to be a threat. Hundreds of Tejanos lost their lives in the counterinsurgency.[16]

Still, the violence that scorched the lower Rio Grande Valley did not spread to central south Texas. Although revolutionary violence affected the region, Texas Rangers and other law enforcement officers did not terrorize ethnic Mexicans of the area. American law enforcement's atrocities against ethnic Mexicans did not spread to central south Texas, because sediciosos' raids did not spread there either. Moreover, Laredo's interethnic elite may have helped prevent the worst abuses from spreading to the region. Laredo had a different ethno-racial experience than other borderland communities in the region and greater Southwest. While the infusion of "white" capitalists to the border during this period led to Anglo land-grabbing and racial violence in the lower Rio Grande Valley and much of the Southwest, this did not happen in Laredo. Rather than colonizing Laredo and demanding that area residents assimilate, newcomers largely assimilated into the borderland community. Laredo escaped becoming an internal colony for several reasons. Unlike communities in the valley such as Brownsville, which Anglos created after 1848, Laredo existed as an ethnic Mexican settlement prior to the border. "White" immigrants who settled the valley came in such numbers that they displaced many of the region's ethnic Mexican population, but such was not the case in Laredo. In Laredo, wealthy and middling Anglo and European immigrants quickly intermarried with local Tejano elites, and created a less racially dichotomous class of *gente decente*. In Laredo, class was a greater focus than race. Incoming wealthy Anglos and, more important, Catholic, French, and Italian, immigrants intermarried with already established Tejano elites, creating a multiethnic elite caste. Although this caste could be seen as more "white" than the working-class ethnic Mexican majority, elites' interethnic makeup did not allow for the violent racism that characterized Anglo–ethnic Mexican relations at the time. Moreover, ethnic Mexicans composed the majority of Laredo's population and controlled most of the city's public offices, including city hall, throughout most of this period.[17]

Tequileros' operations were simple, clever, and effective. Typically, tequileros operated at night in groups of three to five men, although some reports indicate that tequilero parties could swell to some twenty individuals.[18] Mexican nationals seem to have worked on the supply side of the operations and relied on Tejanos as guides, support, and possibly as go-betweens with Anglo bootleggers.[19] A group of tequileros captured in La Salle County on September 21, 1921, for example, claimed to have acquired their 550 quarts of tequila in a small town in Nuevo León some seventy-two miles from the border.[20] If what the tequileros claimed is true, then they managed to cross over a hundred miles of territory between their pickup in Mexico and their capture in the United States without being detected. Because of the difficulties in crossing so much terrain, it is likely that most tequileros operated closer to the border. Tequileros often worked out arrangements with local ranchers to cross through their land. In exchange for a few bottles of tequila, *rancheros* would leave a designated opening, or *falcete*, in their fence for smugglers to cross. Consisting of nothing more than simple links of barbed wire that were hammered in such a way as to allow for easy removal and repositioning, falcetes provide silent testimony to smuggler/ranchero amicability and cooperation.[21]

Tequileros used horses, mules, and donkeys in their operations. Horses carried the smugglers, while mules and donkeys served to convey their contraband cargoes. Tequileros were adept at packing their draft animals. A skilled packer could fit about fifty protectively wrapped bottles on a mature mule or donkey.[22] Tequileros' animals were themselves well trained. Mules and donkeys traveled single file and could journey without tequileros' guidance along familiar paths. Trained draft animals could also wait for their handlers at watering holes or home-in when separated from their masters.[23]

Typically tequileros' work consisted of transporting liquor across the Rio Grande into the United States. The agave plant from which tequila is derived flourishes throughout Mexico, but was primarily distilled in Jalisco in the southern part of the country.[24] Tequileros did not produce alcohol, but purchased it in Mexico to smuggle into the United States. Rather than sell the liquor themselves, it seems that tequileros often sold their liquor wholesale to bootleggers who then worked distribution.[25] Trafficking liquor could be quite lucrative. An apprehended group of tequileros claimed that they planned to sell their liquor to bootleggers for $2.50 a bottle. Given the men had 550 bottles of tequila, they could expect to have received $1,375 for their work. Divided by the number of tequileros in the party, each smuggler could have expected to receive $137.50, less their costs.[26] Had their venture been successful, the tequileros would have made over $5,000 by contemporary standards.[27] Whether tequileros and bootleggers worked together as part of a larger international trafficking organization, or in tandem independently, is unknown, but together they worked to supply contraband spirits to the United States.

Identity and Community Perception

Perceptions of tequileros varied greatly. United States law enforcement saw tequileros as criminal smugglers and armed invaders. William Warren Sterling, a Texas Ranger who fought against tequileros, called them "freebooters" who "would not hesitate to kill anybody who happened across their trail."[28] Maude T. Gilliland, a longtime resident of South Texas and the daughter and later wife to a Texas Ranger, wrote that tequileros were "unbelievably ruthless and cruel . . . Mexican bandits."[29] Perhaps to justify their actions against them, many Texas Rangers and mounted Customs officers held the belief that the sediciosos of the Plan de San Diego had returned as tequileros during Prohibition.[30] Some tequileros of the Prohibition era may have been former sediciosos, but just how many cannot be verified. Ethnic Mexican borderlanders had an entirely different view of tequileros. The *corrido*, or Mexican folk ballad, "Laredo" tells of smugglers as individuals who "were not criminals," but men who had "distinguish[ed] themselves in that famed world war."[31] Indeed many Mexican Americans in the area had fought for the United States in World War I, and it is reasonable to assume that some returning veterans became tequileros.[32] Mexicans and Mexican Americans both rode the South Texas brush country with sacks of tequila. Leandro Villarreal of the famous corrido "Los Tequileros" presents a striking contrast to the image portrayed by US law enforcement. In the corrido, two professional tequileros, Gerónimo and Silvano, cross the Rio Grande into Texas and decide to add another man to their party to increase their numbers. Leandro initially refused because he was sick. According to Villarreal family history, Leandro was not a professional trafficker like the other men. Years later his sister recalled that Leandro was young, only about eighteen years old when he died, and he had never smuggled before or otherwise broken the law.[33] Leandro, like most rural Tejanos, had only a few years of elementary education. He made some money from a little billiard hall he operated across the river in Guerrero, Tamaulipas, but not enough, apparently. Times had been hard for Leandro since his wife died, and the money he could make helping Gerónimo and Silvano would help raise the three children his late wife left him. What Gerónimo and Silvano told Leandro to persuade him out of his sick bed is unknown but leave it he did. When the trio came across the *rinches*, a derogatory term for American law enforcement, he was the first to fall.[34] Leandro Villarreal's story shows that tequileros were more than the armed brigands that US law enforcement made them out to be. Not all of them were hardened traffickers; some were young men from rural backgrounds trying to get by.[35]

Given their knowledge of the South Texas brush country and their ability to pack and drive animals, it seems that most if not all tequileros were ethnic Mexicans from the region's rural areas. Some were professional smugglers and others were novices. Tequileros may have resorted to violence at times, but in the eyes of the community they fought honorably. It seems unlikely that tequileros were former sediciosos who turned to

Figure 4.3. Leandro Villarreal as he appeared on his wedding day. (Photo courtesy of his granddaughter, Blasita Bluhm)

liquor running to continue their resistance to Anglo authority. Tequileros behaved very differently than sediciosos. Sediciosos attacked the Anglo establishment by striking at railroads, Anglo land grabbers, and US soldiers.[36] Tequileros, however, did not seek to engage the state and acted more like opportunistic entrepreneurs who saw liquor running as a good way to make money. A few tequileros may have been desperate men who could kill indiscriminately, but most seem to have been prudent businessmen who avoided confrontation and turned to violence as a last resort. Whether they intended it or not, tequileros' smuggling and battles with US law enforcement fell into the ethnic Mexican tradition of resistance to Anglo racism and American incorporation. Tequileros' manly actions in fact and song added to the *machista* culture of the border. Their courage, real or imagined, is enshrined in lore as examples of masculine honor. They are history and also legend.[37]

Tequileros did not just traffic liquor illicitly into the United States, they took things back, and what they took back was very different from the goods they smuggled in. Whereas contraband liquor flowed north, American foodstuffs and manufactured consumer goods passed south around onerous Mexican tariff duties. The ease of evading national tariffs and the demand for certain necessities created a moral economy in which some forms of illicit border trade were accepted.[38] Mounted Customs inspectors discovered new shoes and clothing among the belongings of three tequileros they killed in early April 1920.[39] Other common goods smuggled south included tobacco, sugar, flour, and bolts of calico. It seems that tequileros exchanged their liquor for these goods rather than sell their liquor for cash.

What tequileros did with the goods is difficult to discern. Tequileros of the Prohibition era may have trafficked consumer goods for sale in Mexico, like the great nineteenth-century smuggler Mariano Reséndez, or may have simply brought these goods back for their families.[40] Tequileros operations also may have coincided with various festive occasions. Texas Rangers of the era believed that a genuine "Christmas trade" existed.[41] It stands to reason that borderlanders consumed more alcohol on the holidays, and thus tequileros may have worked to fill that demand. Aside from the demand for liquor, tequileros may have also been motivated by desires back home. Tequileros were known to return from their sojourns with consumer goods, and it is possible that the clothing and shoes they brought back could have been meant as holiday presents.[42] Still, although it is reasonable to assume that some tequileros may have trafficked to purchase presents for loved ones, it may be overly romantic to assume that most tequileros smuggled to buy gifts.[43]

If borderlanders left their community as tequileros, but returned as merchants, were they smugglers or businessmen? It is doubtful their role in their community somehow changed depending on whether they were crossing north or south of the Rio Grande. Still, the way that the United States and Mexico viewed these same individuals did change if they were coming or going. United States Customs forces viewed tequileros as smugglers when they took their contraband booze north, but American law did not view these same men as smugglers if they carried licit American goods back to Mexico with them. That American law enforcement engaged and at times killed these morphed merchants on their return trip had more to do with these same men's actions as tequileros than their lawful transportation of licit goods south. Similarly, Mexican law enforcement may not have attempted to prevent the flow of liquor north into the United States, but did seek to curb these same individuals from evading Mexican tariffs on consumer goods they trafficked south. For example, late in September 1929 Mexican authorities expressed concern over one Jorge Rodríguez of Laredo who made his living smuggling liquor into the United States and fraudulently introducing clothes and textiles into Mexico.[44] In the complicated world of business on the border, the difference between licit and illicit trade was relative to what you carried as you crossed the border from one side to the other.

Violence

Between May 1919 and August 18, 1922, US law enforcement agents operating in South Texas had six encounters with tequileros which left ten smugglers dead and another ten wounded.[45] A typical encounter occurred in southeastern La Salle County, some forty-five miles from Cotulla. For months lawmen had received reports of cattle and horses being stolen from outlying ranches and suspected tequileros as the culprits. A party of Texas Rangers, mounted Customs inspectors, and county deputy sheriffs on patrol for the alleged offenders trailed and engaged a group of tequileros they found camped on September 12, 1921. Officers killed the reputed leader of the group in the exchange of bullets without suffering any loses. Area newspapers reported that officers seized 550 quarts of tequila and captured nine men and fifteen horses in the encounter. Authorities speculated that they came on the tequileros as they were waiting to rendezvous with bootleggers who were to collect the alcohol and transport it north by truck. Officers jailed the surviving suspects, and they remained in jail because they were unable to pay their thousand-dollar bond.[46]

Prohibition provided a boon for tequileros but also contributed directly to their decline. Prohibition created a market for illicit liquor that entrepreneurial borderlanders were only too happy to fill, but US state forces fought against this trade violently. Traffickers and *contrabandistas* did not seek violence. Rather their objective was merely to smuggle and make a profit. Smugglers were not "primitive rebels" or "social bandits" but circumstantial business persons or opportunists.[47] Tequileros did not issue revolutionary proclamations or try to right perceived wrongs.[48] They did not resist Anglo oppression as much as they circumvented federal laws for personal gain. Tequileros tried to avoid the state, going so far as to ride for days through miles of thorny scrubland so as not to engage it in pitched battles. During Prohibition, tequileros could scarcely avoid confrontation because the US government sought to engage them. In the aftermath of the Plan de San Diego, federal, state, and county law enforcement in South Texas viewed tequileros with a greater wariness. Some tequileros of the Prohibition era may have been former sediciosos, but even if they weren't they knew to fear the rinches who killed so many ethnic Mexicans the decade before. Knowing the danger, tequileros armed themselves and resisted apprehension with force because they likely felt it was the only way to save their lives. With armed tequileros fearful for their lives and mounted lawmen determined to stop their "armed invasion of the United States," it is not surprising that shootouts took place.[49]

Despite Texas and federal law enforcement officers' view that tequileros were desperate men who killed at whim, tequileros are alleged to have murdered only one rancher in the thirteen years of Prohibition. On June 28, 1923, a young Anglo rancher went missing. Gregg Gibson's father knew that groups of tequileros traveled through their ranch in Duval County outside Alice on their journeys north, and he suspected the worst. Law enforcement officers discovered Gibson's body the next day. Some claimed that fleeing tequileros shot him in the back to steal his horse.[50] At least three books by former Texas Rangers and their family members point to Gibson's murder as an example of tequileros' savagery, but tequileros may not have been as ruthless as Ranger reminiscences insist.[51] Gibson may have been patrolling his ranch armed in search of smugglers and found them. Even if tequileros had shot Gibson in the back, his case is the only one like it discovered in this period. Prohibition in South Texas may have been a violent time, but when blood spilled it spilled hot, not cold.

The stalking, ambush, and murder of the three smugglers in "Los Tequileros" is the exception that proves the rule. The corrido "Los Tequileros" is based on the deaths of three smugglers at the hands of American law enforcement on December 18, 1922. On December 17, 1922, a group of Texas Rangers and mounted Customs inspectors patrolling the Jennings Ranch in Zapata County came across suspicious tracks. Early the next morning they began tracking them. The officers followed the trail for twenty miles and were in Jim Hogg County, when they came on the smugglers at about 2:00 p.m. It was rough country, hills, rocky canyons, and arroyos. Perched on a hilltop, the officers looked down at their quarry. Ranger Captain William Wright had fought smugglers before: he knew the coverless canyon edges offered no protection from the Winchester and high-powered Mauser rifles tequileros often carried. Rather than engage the smugglers, he prepared an ambush. Wright and one of his men stationed themselves on the western side of the path, two took positions on the eastern side, and the rest of the officers hid in the southern end to block any retreat and "flush the game" to the barren northern ridge where they would be cut down.[52]

Wright's ambush worked exactly as planned. The officer guarding the southern opening fired his Winchester, driving the three smugglers to where Wright and the others waited. Smugglers ran pell-mell into the bush, and others took to their horses, trying to escape. When the shooting ended a few moments later, the three "Mexicans" were dead. A dead smuggler was found holding two ends of a broken rifle; a bullet had cut the stock in half.[53] After counting the bottles of tequila, the officers dashed them against the ground. For good measure, they lit the pile, and a long blue flame reached into the darkening sky. The officers camped there that night; the smugglers' uneaten lunch became their killers' supper. Gerónimo, Silvano, and Leandro were left where they fell until "a coroner came out and said they were dead."[54] After the match-light inquest, officers buried them in shallow graves.

Ranger historian Walter Prescott Webb quotes Ranger sentiments over the deaths starkly. In an unsigned dispatch to a Ranger captain a recently bloodied private wrote, "The other day we run on to some horsebackers and one of them thought he would learn me how to shoot, so I naturalized him — made an American citizen out of him."[55]

Texas Rangers' reputation for violence and racism against ethnic Mexicans is well known, but the bloodiness of this particular incident must be considered. Anglo newspaper articles on the incident described the killings with malicious glee. The *Laredo Weekly Times* headlined, "THREE SMUGGLERS KILLED . . . Captain Wright and Inspector Smith . . . Rid Country of Three More Booze Smugglers."[56] Other than saying that officers "rid" the country of the three smugglers, the paper went on to say that the tequileros had "bit the dust" under the Rangers' guns.[57] The probable reason that the *Laredo Weekly Times* took such relish in describing the deaths of the tequileros is revealed in a headline on the same story from the *San Antonio Express*: "First Victory over Border Gang since Death of Customs Inspectors."[58]

On August 19, 1922, three months before the killing of the three tequileros, bootleggers murdered Mounted Customs Inspector Robert S. Rumsey. Customs officers Rumsey, Frank Smith, and Will Musgrave were returning from an arrest of two smugglers when they passed two suspicious cars one mile west of Mirando City in eastern Webb County. The officers pulled the suspects over. Rumsey exited his car and was approaching the suspects when a tall, heavy-set man shot him. The first bullet hit Rumsey in the stomach, knocking him off his feet. Two more shots stuck him, hitting his left cheek and right leg. Officers Musgrave and Smith emptied their guns before the killers in the car fired on them, pinning them down. Rumsey's murderer stood over his dead or dying body and stripped him of his gun. The killer rushed back to his car and sped away, leaving the two officers to return Rumsey's body to his widow.[59]

Officer Rumsey's loss greatly affected Laredo. Rumsey was born in San Antonio but was raised in Laredo. He had worked at Fort McIntosh near Laredo and served as a Texas Ranger before becoming a Customs inspector. Rumsey had also married Maria Herrera, a local ethnic Mexican

Figure 4.4. Mounted
Customs Inspector Robert
Stuart Rumsey Jr.
(Photograph courtesy of
the Archives, U.S. Customs
and Border Protection)

woman and had started a family with her. Over the course of his life, Rumsey had walked the streets of Laredo and, we can assume, made friends. At the time of his death, he was an officer of the state, perhaps a brutal one, but also a Laredoan. Newspapers carried stories of his life, exploits, and death for weeks. Rumsey's murder particularly affected law enforcement officers. Mounted local police escorted his funeral procession. Texas Ranger captain William Wright publicly remarked that the "customs service has lost its best inspector."[60] Privately, Wright's response to learning of "his friend's" death was more visceral; he reputedly "jerked out his pistol and exclaimed 'Wish I'd a been there, boom, boom.'"[61]

Captain Wright had not been there to help Rumsey in August, but Wright was at the killing of the three tequileros in December, and so was Frank Smith, the mounted Customs inspector who had taken Rumsey's body back to Laredo. Rumsey's murder was undoubtedly on the minds of many officers at the time. Wright and the other men could have felt that justice was slipping away. Then they came on the three tequileros. In their minds, perhaps the officers thought that these were the same men who killed Rumsey. Or maybe it was simple revenge? Wright planned the attack well. The officers surrounded the smugglers on all sides, preventing any escape. They flushed the tequileros and cut them down in the crossfire. It was a slaughter. None of the men killed that day were found to be suspects in Rumsey's murder, but his death was likely the main reason for their killings. James White, a deputy officer at the time, verified this in a letter to a friend when he stated, what "started the Rangers . . . killing Tequileros was the murder of Rumsey."[62]

Mounted Customs inspectors and Texas Rangers responded to Rumsey's and other officers' deaths at the hands of smugglers by shooting first and asking questions later. Between 1922 and the end of Prohibition in 1933, mounted US law enforcement officers engaged horseback liquor runners in fourteen clashes that left nine smugglers dead.[63] Because most of the confrontations occurred in isolated rural locations, the exact number of clashes may be underreported. The state's war on smugglers took such a toll on tequileros that corrido writers remembered it a generation later. The 1970s-era corrido, "Pistoleros Famosos" begins, "On the banks of the Rio [Grande], from Reynosa to Laredo, there are no more bandits and no more smugglers. This is how the gunfighters are being wiped out."[64] The song goes on to list the names of the fallen, including Silvano [Gracia], of the corrido "Los Tequileros," "killed treacherously by the cowardly Rangers."[65] Dimas de León, Generoso Garza Cano, the del Fierro brothers, and one or two Americans, "all these brave men have been betrayed and killed."[66]

Tequileros stood little chance against the concerted power of the state. The most they could do was gather in larger armed escorts for better protection. On a Sunday evening in late September 1922, four Customs officers patrolling near Benavides in Duval County encountered a band of forty-five armed tequileros.[67] The large body of tequileros scared Customs forces into retreating, but state forces would not be dissuaded. In response to the Customs inspectors' rout, the *Laredo Weekly Times* advocated using US Army cavalry units to hunt down tequileros in order to prevent the "armed invasion of our territory."[68] Although no cavalry units are known to have taken the field against tequileros, the state did escalate its firepower in its campaign against them. In late 1922 and early 1923, Texas Rangers and Customs inspectors received Thompson 0.45 and Browning 0.50 caliber submachine guns. Brownings were too cumbersome to use on mounted patrol, and the ineffectiveness of Thompson submachine guns at longer ranges and in thickets minimized their usefulness. The guns nevertheless offered a profound psychological advantage to officers over the more poorly armed smugglers.[69] One night in early January 1924, a party of eight mounted Customs inspectors and Jim Hogg County sheriff deputies used one of their new Thompson submachineguns in an engagement against

Figure 4.5. Silvano Gracia, of the corrido "Los Tequileros," as he appeared shortly before his death. Note the fine clothes, which indicate his financial success in his profession and the gun he wears at his hip. (Photo courtesy of his grandson Carlos Gracia)

approximately fifteen tequileros near Hebbronville. No officers were reported injured in the clash, yet officers believed they had succeeded in wounding several smugglers. Law enforcement seized sixteen horses and more than 1,650 quarts of liquor in the confrontation.[70]

Attrition and the ever-increasing incorporation of the region eventually ended the era of the tequilero. They died in ones and twos. Some were wounded and others were thrown in jail. Mounted Customs inspectors, Texas Rangers, and the Border Patrol's campaign against tequileros wore them down. Texas Ranger captain William W. Sterling put it simply: tequileros "had to be dealt with as foreign enemies, not as ordinary domestic bootleggers."[71] The last five years of Prohibition saw only six reports of smugglers crossing overland through the brush in the counties adjacent to Laredo. Area law enforcement officers last reported encounter with tequileros took place in Jim Hogg County in February 1927. Mounted Customs inspectors killed one smuggler and captured seven hundred bottles of whiskey and six horses in their final skirmish with tequileros.[72] Future years would see the occasional horseback liquor smuggler, but the golden age of the tequilero came to an end six years before the repeal of national

Prohibition in 1933. Another, more successful and violent type of smuggler would come to fill the gap that tequileros left behind.[73]

Bootleggers

Bootleggers succeeded tequileros as the preeminent liquor traffickers of the Prohibition era. Unlike tequileros, who were ethnic Mexicans that operated in rural areas on horseback, bootleggers were mostly, but not exclusively, urban Anglos who used automobiles. Rather than cut through ranches where mounted law enforcement agents patrolled, bootleggers used the state's road system. Consequently, bootleggers were able to supply a much larger network than tequileros. Whereas tequileros' animal-powered operations could only supply local borderlands markets, bootleggers drove their contraband cargoes of Mexican liquor to demand centers in San Antonio, Corpus Christi, Houston, Dallas, and beyond.[74] Although a certain rivalry between tequileros and bootleggers may have existed, both groups were known to work together. English language newspapers of the period used the term *bootleggers* for alcohol smugglers in general, but U.S law enforcement did designate bootleggers as Anglos who smuggled liquor by automobile and tequileros as "horseback" liquor smugglers.[75]

Although the state seems to have placed a greater emphasis in combating tequileros, bootleggers took a greater toll on American law enforcement's ranks. Bootleggers killed two of the three officers who died in confrontations with liquor smugglers in South Texas during national Prohibition. Bootleggers killed Mounted Customs Inspector Robert Rumsey on August 19, 1922. Bootleggers also ambushed and murdered Prohibition Agent Charles Stevens on the San Antonio highway near Pleasanton on September 25, 1929.[76] Bootleggers killed more officers than tequileros because they could see the officers who pursued them. Unlike tequileros, who operated in dense cactus and mesquite thickets, the roads that bootleggers trafficked along provided a clear view to shoot. Cars also concealed bootleggers' hands, allowing them the opportunity to draw their weapons on approaching officers. Tequileros certainly shot at officers when confronted, but, surprisingly, tequileros operating in the Laredo area failed to kill or even wound a single law enforcement officer in the years between 1919 and 1933. In contrast, mounted American law enforcement officers killed nine tequileros and wounded at least a dozen more.[77] The reason for this disparity is more complicated than Texas Ranger Captain Sterling's explanation that drunken tequileros were no match to the "superior skill of the American rifleman."[78] American law enforcement's victories over tequileros are best explained by their use of surprise. Texas Rangers, mounted Customs inspectors, and the Border Patrol tracked tequileros and picked the moment to engage them. Mounted officers rarely came across tequileros by accident. Rather, officers on patrol would search for tequileros' trail and then stalk them.[79] Just how law enforcement/tequilero firefights occurred is unclear, but corridos' description of officers as "cowardly" has its basis in fact.[80] Officers tracking tequileros could have their guns drawn when they made their presence known. They could also choose to engage at an advantageous moment. Law enforcement officers tracking horseback liquor smugglers could get ahead of their targets and lie in ambush, as the Texas Rangers and mounted Customs inspectors who killed the three tequileros on December 18, 1922, did.[81] Thus it is not surprising that the balladeer in the corrido "Los Tequileros" comments that the only way the rinches can "kill us is by hunting us like deer."[82]

Because of their greater violence and use of modern equipment, borderlanders viewed bootleggers negatively. Tequileros' packing and driving of trains of animals through the brush country took a certain skill and hardiness that Tejanos esteemed. Bootleggers in contrast simply hid alcohol in cars and drove. Such was the disdain for bootleggers in the local ethnic Mexican community, that Tejanos eulogized officers who combated them in song. The 1920s era corrido "Capitán Charles Stevens," honors the life and death of Prohibition Agent Charles Stevens. Unlike the corrido "Los Tequileros," which described American law enforcement officers as rinches, Stevens's corrido describes him nobly. Stevens is described as "a man" who had "eagle eyes" and who in life was known as "the panther."[83] In contrast to the law enforcement officers in "Los Tequileros," who are described as cowards, Stevens is described as a brave man who "fought gallantly and without fear."[84] Stevens was a real person. Charles Stevens was a former Texas Ranger captain and had served as a US Customs agent in Laredo. At the time of his death, Stevens worked as a US Prohibition agent. In late September 1929, Stevens and two other officers were returning from raiding stills in Atascosa County when they spotted a woman on the roadside who seemed to be signaling someone with a spotlight.[85] Stevens pulled over and decided to take the woman in for questioning. Several men sprang from behind the foliage and riddled Stevens's car with shotgun blasts. The buckshot tore through Stevens's torso, killing him. Although the other officers returned fire and may have wounded two of the assailants, the killers escaped.[86]

The corrido's positive representation of Stevens is attributable to several factors. He did not kill ethnic Mexicans through ambush, like the Customs agents and Texas Rangers who killed the three tequileros on December 18, 1922. Tejanos' honor of Stevens through song shows that relations between Anglos and ethnic Mexicans at the time were not always contentious. Not all American law enforcement agents were rinches. Some, like Stevens, could be seen as brave and honorable. Moreover, Stevens did not work against tequileros, but rather against primarily Anglo moonshiners and violently criminal bootleggers. Locals seem to have despised bootleggers. The border ballad "El Automóvil Gris" (The Gray Automobile) captures bootleggers' greater tendencies toward violence. Unlike songs about tequileros, which celebrate their valor against rinches, the members of the Gray Automobile Gang are the "hand that squeezes, that assaults, that kills and robs."[87] Bootleggers were a different breed of smuggler than the tequilero. Tequileros were rural folk who were criminals in the eyes of the state but not necessarily the people. Ethnic Mexicans saw bootleggers as less honorable than the tequileros they succeeded. Corridos praise tequileros as folk heroes who defy unpopular laws and die fighting racist state authority, but do not cast bootleggers in the same light. The bootlegger in "El Automóvil Gris" is a self-serving decadent gangster, who could be seen "drunk . . . smoking fine cigars, drinking cognac, sherry, beer to the sound of merrymaking."[88] He even claimed to have enjoyed himself in Paris. Joe Hobrecht, Stevens's alleged murderer, fit bootleggers' image as gangsters. One newspaper published a mug shot of Hobrecht where the clean shaven "dapper youth" could be seen with his dark hair slicked back and wearing a suit and tie.[89] Bootleggers, a new class of criminal on the border, were amongst the first borderlands smugglers to extend their illicit trade networks beyond their regional communities. The singer in "El Automóvil Gris" boasts of his business in Matamoros, San Antonio, Laredo, and Belén. Bootleggers were amongst the first modern traffickers along the US-Mexico borderlands.

Traffickers' sophistication and scale increased as Prohibition wore on. The single largest alcohol seizure in the region occurred in early February 1927, when mounted Customs inspectors discovered 471 pints of whiskey and 170 five-gallon cans of alcohol cached under sacks of cabbages in a railroad boxcar. Officers waited for E. M. Stevens to pick up his bill of lading and arrested him. The car had been destined to Fort Worth, Stevens's city of residence. Stevens paid his two-thousand-dollar bond and was released. For more than a year the case was deferred until April 1928, when the Federal District Court sent Stevens to the federal penitentiary at Leavenworth, Kansas, for two years.[90] Nor were traffickers' schemes limited to the ground.

A colorful article that appeared in the Laredo newspaper in January 1931 mentions a "mysterious rider of the night skies" haunting the heavens over the border.[91] An unnamed "unimpeachable authority" is cited as telling the paper that the phantom flier was suspected of running liquor from Mexico to Kansas City by following airmail beacons at night.[92] Although somewhat laughable, the article may not have been far from the truth. As early as 1922, Laredo's Custom collector Roy Campbell considered using an airplane to scout along the river for smugglers.[93] A Customs air service could also pursue airborne bootleggers. American law enforcement intercepted airborne bootleggers on five different occasions between September 1, 1928, and the end of Prohibition in 1933. Mexican law enforcement captured two Americans outside Nuevo Laredo in early January 1932. The Americans' presentation of a flying certificate signed by Orville Wright failed to get them released or their plane "Low Money King" returned.[94]

As was the case with cars, horses, and mules, airplanes seized in liquor arrests in the United States fell under section 3062 of the *Revised Statutes of the United States*, meaning that such articles employed in smuggling became the possession of the Customs Service. Thus, the apprehension of an airborne rumrunner in Ohio in February 1932 provided federal agents a plane to pursue airborne smugglers. Border Customs officers put the seized plane to good use. In May of that year a Customs pilot chased an airborne smuggler 250 miles before forcing him down in McMullen County. The agent discovered more than 120 gallons of Mexican liquor in the plane and arrested the pilot, an American World War I ace. Nor was this the only documented case of airborne pursuit. Five months later, Customs agents observed another plane crossing the border between Laredo and Eagle Pass and gave chase. The pursuit ended 150 miles later when the officer flanked the flyer and aimed a rifle at him. It seems that the Customs pilot did what no German could. Customs officers caught an American ace credited with eleven kills behind the stick and found more than eighty gallons of alcohol in the plane. Successes in the air were such that Customs established a regular aerial patrol between Laredo and Eagle Pass.[95]

Conclusion

National Prohibition and US antismuggling efforts gave rise to violent professional smugglers and helped transform the border into a criminal space. American law enforcement viewed tequileros as the successors to the sediciosos of the Plan de San Diego and waged a bloody war of attrition against them. United States border securities' mounted patrols effectively ended the era of the tequilero, but bootleggers and other more sophisticated smugglers rose to take their place. Bootleggers took a greater toll on US law enforcement and likely smuggled more than tequileros. United States efforts to prohibit alcohol not only failed but contributed to the development of organized international smuggling rings and a greater degree of violence on the border. Violence marked Prohibition in South Texas. At least twenty-five persons died and another nineteen were wounded in smuggling-related confrontations during the era.[96] The border experience with Prohibition suggests that government bans not only fail to prevent the introduction of prohibited substances, they contribute to organized crime and violence on the border. Smuggling has a long legacy on the border, and, more and more, a handful of scholars are working to illuminate this underexamined aspect of borderlands scholarship. Aside from informing readers how this ongoing phenomenon occurred across Prohibition-era South Texas, this chapter suggests that state laws cause borderlands to become sites of professional smuggling.

PART TWO

Consolidating National Space

CHAPTER FIVE

Detroit's Border Brothel

Sex Tourism in Windsor, Ontario, 1945–1960

Holly Karibo

On March 14, 1950, the *Windsor Daily Star* published a report on prostitution and vice in the city of Windsor, Ontario, titled "Probe Heat Hasn't Cooled Off Joints."[1] With language that ranged from outright condemnation to voyeuristic intrigue, the author "reported" on what was happening after-hours in the Ontario border city: "The 'devil himself' lacks the persistency, defiance, the outright gall of bordell[o] and bootleg operators. Up until an early hour today, despite the heat exerted through a full-blown probe of vice in Windsor, prostitutes and bootleggers plied dollars from their customer list."[2] The author explained that, while no worse than the situations found in cities such as Detroit, Chicago, New York, and Toronto, "the open defiancy [*sic*] displayed in Windsor's tenderloin districts still goes unchallenged by cities of comparable size." In the small Canadian city, "keepers of bordellos hawk their fare in every bar; their prostitutes hustle on their own hook, give their lush earnings to procurers, who are known in the trade as pimps." The author characterized the trade as "a battle of wits" with "prostitutes and bootleggers vying for the payroll cash made available by the automobile industry and suckers from Michigan and Ohio."[3]

In the early postwar period, local newspapers regularly published stories about the growing vice economy in the city of Windsor. As "Probe Heat" demonstrates, contemporary articles highlighted the increasing accessibility and visibility of prostitutes and their clients in the city, and the increasingly international nature of the sex trade. In effect, *Star* reporters were articulating concerns over the growth of a cross-border sex tourism industry that developed as the Second World War came to an end.

Between 1945 and 1960, thousands of people entered the city of Windsor in hopes of securing employment in the booming auto industry. The city's position as a bordertown, when combined with social and economic changes brought about by World War II, fostered an environment that promoted the growth of the sex trade, particularly prostitution. As a result, cross-border "sex tourism" developed, which included an extensive network of bars, hotels, and bawdy houses that catered to the American market. This unofficial industry did not go unfettered, however, but instead came under increasing attack by middle-class residents and the police. Thus the city of Windsor proves to be a useful case study for considering the social tensions that developed in Cold War Canada, as well as the ways in which borderlands shape identities in relation to, and outside of, the nation as a whole.

Canadian and American men and women were instrumental in shaping the sex trade in Windsor, and their interactions produced a cultural space in which sexuality was exchanged as an international commodity. In her study on tourism in Niagara Falls, Karen Dubinsky argues that places have a sexual, as well as political and economic, dimension. Consequently, when places become commodities — which is what tourism is about — sexual images and meanings abound.[4] This study contends that "sex tourism" is not only the act of traveling to a different geographical location for the purposes of sex, but that sites of sexual tourism necessarily develop a local infrastructure that supports the commodification of sexualized leisure. Central to the growth of the Windsor sex trade were people working in related industries, as for example, bartenders, cab drivers, convenience store owners, and even policeman, who functioned as intermediaries between the prostitutes, pimps, and their clients. Unlike Niagara Falls, the tourist industry in Windsor was an unofficial one, based not on legally sanctioned marriage, but on illegal forms of "vice." Rather than an expression of sexual normativity, then, sex tourism developed in Windsor as an interaction between liminal peoples, ones separated from the mainstream of society by particular sexual interactions.[5] Thus a focus on the sex trade in the city builds on the work done by scholars such as Dubinsky and Dan Malleck by examining unofficial forms of cross-border tourism along the US-Canada border.[6]

An examination of "vice" along the US-Canada border necessarily engages with notions of licit and illicit. In *Illicit Flow and Criminal Things*, Itty Abraham and Willem van Schendel argue that how one defines illicitness (and by extension, vice) is fluid and determined by competing discourses in which the state is but one actor.[7] In building on Abraham and van Schendel's work, this chapter further contends that the licit/illicit binary is too simplistic to capture the lived experience of those who inhabited or visited the border cities of Windsor and Detroit. For example, the sex trade in Windsor, though illegal, drew in many individuals from various backgrounds. Some were attracted to it because of its illicit status; some accepted it as a legitimate industry in Windsor; and Windsor police officers often turned a blind eye despite its illegal status under federal, provincial, and municipal laws. Though illegal, then, prostitution was far from suppressed in Windsor in the early postwar period. Instead, various communities competed to determine its place in the local political economy. Thus this chapter will explore what brought men and women to Windsor for commercial sex, and how the competing notions of licit/illicit were negotiated within the border city.

This chapter begins by examining the historical development of Windsor as an industrial border city, demonstrating the working-class, masculine roots of its workers and residents, and the way this shaped the leisure culture of the pre–World War II period. It then explores the growth of sex tourism after the war, arguing that it developed as a white, working-class phenomenon, and that its integration into the broader vice economy was facilitated by proliferation of legal bars and blind pigs (speakeasies), hotels, gambling dens, cab drivers, and policemen willing to ignore the trade. This section also highlights the interconnected nature of race, class, and gender in the cities of Windsor and Detroit, noting who was able to cross borders for sex, and who was required to provide these services. As the Cold War intensified in the 1950s, however, so too did public outrage over illicit leisure activities, especially the influx of American sex tourists. Consequently, the third section of this chapter examines the regulation and temporary suppression of prostitution in Windsor, situating its decline within deteriorating economic conditions in the city and the increasingly conservative social climate of the Cold War period.

Industrialization, Migration, and the Growth of a "Sin City"

The social geography of Windsor during the first half of the twentieth century helped lay the foundations for its eventual reputation as Canada's best-publicized "wide open town."[8] Though the history of Windsor as a European colonial settlement dates back to 1749, it became a major Canadian city only in the early twentieth century. It was not until 1854, when the Great Western Railway reached the city of Windsor, that it became the chief center of population in Essex County.[9] In fact, the railroad laid the foundation for the subsequent industrial growth that would make the city the busiest crossing point between Canada and the United States.

Windsor's close proximity to the burgeoning industrial powerhouse of Detroit made its development seem almost inevitable in the early twentieth century. In 1904, the Ford Motor Company, in order to gain Imperial trade benefits, moved its Detroit-based operations across the river and into the surrounding Canadian border cities of Windsor, East Windsor (later Ford City), Walkerville, and Sandwich. With the onset of industrialization sparked by World War I, Ford became the predominant industry in the region, and by the 1930s, the border cities merged politically into a single community with a population of more than 100,000.[10] By 1939, 65 percent of those employed in the newly amalgamated city worked in the thriving auto industry.[11]

Windsor, as a one-industry town based on automobile manufacturing, had a boom-and-bust economy. During the "auto boom" workers had a fairly high standard of living. The city was in the vanguard of the technological and cultural changes that made up the second industrial revolution and was far ahead of the rest of Canada in developing welfare capitalism and employer initiated benefits for workers.[12] Since wages were higher in auto manufacturing than in many industries (with the exception of the skilled trades) Windsor gained a reputation as a lucrative place to live. However, while hourly wages remained relatively high in comparison to other industries, seasonal layoffs meant that the annual income was actually quite low.[13] As a result, throughout the first half of the twentieth century, the population of Windsor remained fairly fluid, with people coming and going according to the economic ups and downs of the Ford and Chrysler companies.

Workers came to Windsor from across the nation and the world. The first major influx of migrants occurred in the 1910s, and was mainly comprised of members of the so-called "New Migration."[14] Among the newcomers were Ukrainians, Poles, Russians, Yugoslavians, Hungarians, Germans, Finns, Scandinavians, Italians, Greeks, and Syrians.[15] The population of Windsor increased dramatically during these years, from 15,198 in 1901, to 23,433 and 55,935 in 1911 and 1921, respectively.[16] Although this remarkable increase was not limited to Windsor, its position as a border city attracted a particularly transient population. Between 1911 and 1929, there was a large movement of unattached male workers into the city, including European immigrants without families, single men from Canadian farms, and Chinese railway workers in search of new employment.[17]

Many migrants also came to the city as a way of gaining access to the

United States. As a consequence of the US Immigration Act of 1917, which was designed to reduce the number of "undesirable" immigrants, especially from Central, Southern, and Eastern Europe, many came to Windsor with the hopes of eventually crossing the border.[18] Similarly, Anglo and French Canadians in the first decades of the twentieth century, drawn to the industrial cities of Michigan, used Windsor as their departure point. Between 1900 and 1930, four out of five Anglo Canadian migrants who passed through Windsor settled in the city of Detroit.[19] Thus, in the first half of the twentieth century, many of those who entered Windsor did so with the intent of eventually crossing the border. The large population of single, unattached male workers, when combined with this cross-border fluidity, helped lay the foundations for the movement of people in the vice trade that followed World War II.

The high number of male migrants moving into the city encouraged the growth of traditionally "male" leisure activities, including drinking, gambling, and prostitution.[20] In his examination of working-class "manhood" among autoworkers in the early- to mid-twentieth century, Steve Meyer identifies three elements central to rough working-class male culture, namely "fighting, womanizing, and boozing."[21] Windsor developed a strong working-class community, featuring many of the masculine "vice" activities that often accompany industrial growth. The city's reputation as a "wide open town" was solidified in the 1920s, as Prohibition in both the United States and Ontario encouraged a massive bootlegging operation between Windsor and Detroit. When public drinking houses were legalized in Ontario in 1934, Windsor assumed a central role as a boozy town along the border. With forty-three legal drinking establishments between the years 1934 and 1947, Windsor had many more drinking spaces than the nearby Ontario bordertowns of Sarnia and Niagara Falls combined (which only had six and twenty-three licensed drinking rooms, respectively, over the same period).[22] Thus, after a long day of work in the Ford factories, the large number of male migrants who moved in and out of the city could regularly patronize the many watering holes available in Windsor.

For the Windsor-Detroit region, World War II brought an increase in economic optimism, followed by another surge in population. In the early 1940s, the need for heavy industrial goods skyrocketed, and the auto industry was poised to take advantage of this growing demand. Consequently, the city of Detroit became an industrial powerhouse, leading the United States out of the Great Depression. In Detroit, and subsequently, Windsor, Ford converted its assembly lines into mass producers of military hardware, including airplanes, tanks, and other war machines. Notably, between 1940 and 1947, manufacturing employment in Detroit increased by 40 percent.[23] Similarly, though 10,928 men left Windsor to fight in the war, many more people came in hopes of securing employment in the defense industry.[24] In 1942, 74 percent of those employed in the city of Windsor worked in the automotive industry.[25] By 1950, Windsor's residents earned more on average than workers in any other Canadian city, with weekly earnings averaging $52.50.[26] The economic optimism produced by World War II encouraged thousands of people to enter the region during the 1940s, driving Windsor's population up to 105,311 in 1941, and 120,049 in 1951.[27] As Windsor's industry and population grew, so too did its reputation as a "boomtown." This reputation played an important role in promoting the growth of vice industries in the years following the second World War.

Sex Tourism: From Local "Problem" to International Attraction

In the post–World War II period, Windsor's vice industries developed into a complex cross-border sexual economy. Following the war, the growth in sex tourism in Windsor was enabled by a number of contradictory social factors including, on the one hand, the rising disposable income of many North Americans, a rapid expansion of international tourism, and mobility aided by the increasing affordability of cars, and on the other, a society deeply concerned with the perceived social dislocation caused by years of war. Within this environment a white, working-class sex tourist industry developed, one that both reflected and challenged the social codes and mores that developed as North Americans grappled with these contradictory circumstances.

Migration, aided by increased mobility afforded by automobiles, played a key role in the growth of sex tourism in Windsor, as both women and men traveled from other cities, states, and provinces to participate in the trade. Significantly, the majority of the women arrested as "inmates" and "keepers" of bawdy houses between 1940 and 1955 were born in cities other than Windsor. According to a *Windsor Daily Star* article, "Many of those found practicing the 'oldest profession' in Windsor have come here from Quebec, the mining districts, and other parts of the dominion where boom conditions do not prevail."[28] Another *Star* report similarly explained that "prostitutes are attracted to Windsor because they hear of it as a sort of boom town. . . . The city also, because of the fact that industrial wage earnings is [sic] high . . . attracts women of loose morals."[29] The article quoted a doctor who claimed that, "Last week we jailed a couple [of prostitutes] who had been in town just a few day," and that, "when asked why they had come to Windsor, one frankly remarked, 'Green fields.'"[30] The search for "greener pastures" was cited in numerous news reports and was an important explanation for the growth in "out-of-towners" working in the city's vice trade. According to the arrest records, women came to Windsor from all parts of Canada, from Vancouver to New Brunswick, suggesting that Windsor's reputation was national in scope.[31]

While women came from various regions in Canada, and occasionally from the United States and United Kingdom, French Canadians were overrepresented within the police registers. In fact, they accounted for as much as one-third to one-half of those arrested between 1944 and 1955.[32] In the early postwar period, the *Star* was filled with articles about French Canadian prostitutes and pimps living and working in the city. The large presence of French Canadians in Windsor was, in part, the result of a crackdown on vice in the city of Montreal. In response to accusations of police corruption and laxity in the city's enforcement of "moral" offenses, the Montreal Police Department enacted vigilant antivice campaigns against prostitution and gambling rings. The crackdown came into full effect in July 1946 and included raids on brothels and rooming houses.[33] Significantly, 1946 was also the year with the highest number of arrests related to prostitution, which again totaled 281.[34] A *Star* article explained that "the fact that the majority [of prostitutes in Windsor] . . . hail from Montreal is said to be due to the fact that 'the heat' is on the latter Metropolis, although Montreal has always been the out-of-town vice market's chief source of supply."[35] And though Windsor was a farther distance to travel than cities such as Toronto or Hamilton, it was on the railway line, making it relatively accessible from Montreal. Given Windsor's booming vice economy, many women and men looking to get out of "the heat" may have felt the extra distance was worth the travel expenses.[36]

The gendered nature of labor in the region affected the growth of sex tourism in a number of ways. First, the predominantly male labor force meant that women were greatly limited in their employment options. At the end of World War II, women were forced out of defense work, which was particularly devastating for women living in industrial cities such as Windsor.[37] Consequently, by 1951, women accounted for only 23 percent of people (officially) employed in the city.[38] In order to make ends meet, many women had to look for other forms of employment, and prostitution may have proved to be a viable option for some. Second, the elevated numbers of employed men provided a large market of potential customers. High weekly earnings meant that many of these men had a disposable income that could be spent on various "leisure" activities including drinking, gambling, and prostitution.

To this end, the structure of Windsor's sex tourist industry reflected the fact that it emerged within a male-dominated economy. Most women worked for male pimps, and often had to give a large percentage of their earnings over to them. According to police records and news articles, the average price for sexual services was five dollars, and women often had to give most of this over to their pimp.[39] Though there were a few cases of women being arrested as "keepers" of bawdy houses, more often than not women were arrested with a male figure. It was not uncommon for this person to be her husband, further complicating the relationship between sex workers and their "bosses."[40] Soliciting in Windsor most often happened in hotels and bars, such as the Blue Water Hotel and Ambassador Hotel, where men and women would mingle in co-ed drinking rooms (against the regulations of the Liquor License Board of Ontario). Other times, pimps or "middlemen" would direct Americans to various brothels throughout the downtown core. Thus, though women were the primary workers within Windsor's sex trade, men often played "managerial" roles and were central to facilitating cross-border business.

Starting in 1943, the number of American sex tourists traveling to Windsor increased considerably. By the mid-1950s, more than 2.5 million vehicles passed though the tunnel or over the bridge into Windsor during any given year, making it the busiest crossing point between the two countries.[41] Obviously not everyone crossed into Windsor for sex, or even stopped in the city, but a portion of these travelers did come to enjoy the "wide open town." Again the police records provide important insight into who was coming to Windsor for sex, and where they were coming from. In 1940, everyone listed as a "found in" of a brothel was a resident of Windsor. However, by the end of the war, the numbers had changed substantially. In 1946, for example, more than 50 percent of the men arrested in raids on bawdy houses were American residents. This was compared to the mere 23 percent who were residents of Windsor.[42] Americans would continue to comprise the majority of arrests as "found ins" until 1955.

As may be expected, the majority of American tourists came from Michigan, and specifically from Detroit and its surrounding suburbs. What is more surprising, perhaps, is the distances other men traveled to come to the city. Visitors from states such as New York, Wisconsin, Kentucky, Pennsylvania, North Carolina, Texas, and California were among those arrested. Though it is difficult to determine if these men came to Windsor for the primary purpose of visiting the brothels, what is evident is that at the very least many American men made sure to indulge in the city's "services" while they were in the area. By 1946, this rise in American tourists prompted Windsor magistrate Arthur Hanrahan to assert that the city was destined to become a "border brothel for Detroit."[43]

The intersections of race, class, and gender in Windsor's sex trade provide important insight into the various "borders," both literal and metaphorical, that shaped the sex tourism industry in the city. Significantly, the Windsor sex trade was very much a white, working-class phenomenon. The men and women arrested for prostitution-related offenses were almost always reported to hold blue-collar jobs, as, for example, laborers, assemblers, waitresses, and domestics.[44] Given the industrial nature of many southern Ontario and Midwestern cities, this is not wholly surprising. What is more significant, perhaps, is that with exception of three women, everyone arrested on prostitution charges during this period was listed in the registers as "white." This is astonishing given that Detroit's African American population more than tripled during this period, from 9.2 percent of the total population in 1940 to 28.9 percent in 1960.[45]

Though an in-depth examination of Detroit is beyond the scope of this chapter, it is nonetheless important to acknowledge some of the push factors that encouraged white, working-class American men to cross into Canada for a night or weekend of fun. Detroit was a highly segregated city in the early postwar period, with black and white communities literally divided by Woodward Avenue, which ran north from the Detroit River. As one contemporary study of Detroit points out, by the early 1940s, the city was suffering from an "acute housing problem, racial discrimination, and national and religious antipathy." These issues were exacerbated by municipal housing policies that marginalized African American residents to particular "substandard" areas of town, which were underfunded and over-policed.[46] The city's vice districts were similarly segregated by race, with Hastings Street serving the late-night desires of black Detroiters, and Cass Corridor catering to the wiles of low-income, white residents.[47] Racially segregated social clubs, blind pigs, pool rooms, and restaurants catered to the various communities in the city. For example, one former resident characterized Hastings Street as "part-carnival side-show, with hard-drinking dudes and loud street ladies, and part close community, with people who looked out for each other."[48] Though the city had a vibrant nightlife, racial tensions were building in the early 1940s and came to a head in the Detroit race riots of 1943. Significantly, the riots followed a confrontation between black and white men at the beach on Belle Isle, an island park on the Detroit River, demonstrating the violence that could ensue in spaces where leisure crossed racial lines. The bustling city of Detroit, then, was also marked by substantial social and racial tension that furthered the divide between black and white working-class communities.[49]

The racially homogeneous character of Windsor's sex industry raises the questions of what borders were being crossed by sex tourists and who could cross them. Clearly, though crossing the national border enabled white men to traverse sexual, moral, and legal boundaries, it did not offer men of color the same possibility. Interestingly, though the connection is tentative, it is important to note that the number of American tourists in Windsor began to increase in 1943, correlating with the riots that took place in downtown Detroit. The Windsor sex trade, then, represented a form of "white flight," wherein white Detroiters could enjoy the comforts of white, male privilege without the overt challenges to this position that took place in the racially charged city of Detroit. Sex tourists necessarily reasserted the "white" nature of American citizenship by freely crossing the Detroit-Windsor border and engaging in socially stigmatized, yet tacitly accepted, leisure activities.[50]

A number of other factors likely played a role in attracting white American men into the Canadian city for sex. Sex tourism, scholars argue, is fueled by exoticism and fantasy, and is based on the perceived differences between sex workers and their clients. While this has most often been analyzed in relation to white, First World men who exoticize dark-skinned, "native" bodies in the developing world, this insight can also be applied to the sex industry in Windsor.[51] In the case of Windsor, for example, the fact that many of the prostitutes were not only Canadian, but *French* Canadian, may have added to the allure of the city, and may have served as a clear marker of difference between the "tourists" and the "locals." Windsor was in a unique position — it was different enough to elicit interest from neighboring Detroiters, but geographically close enough to make it a convenient destination for a night of fun. As one *Star* article satirically put it, "You see [Windsor] is so much closer to Detroit than Michigan is."[52] Just as Americans today travel to Windsor for the casino, Cuban cigars, full-nudity strip clubs, and prostitution, Americans in the postwar period were drawn to the alluring and exotic vice industries across the river.[53]

On a material level, the exchange rate during the 1940s was favorable to Americans. On average, between 1943 and 1946, the American dollar was worth $1.10 Canadian. While this fluctuated between $1.0025 and $1.08 over the next decade, the American dollar remained consistently stronger than the Canadian dollar until 1952.[54] Significantly, this pattern correlates with the record of arrests for prostitution charges, which begin to rise in 1943, and decline rapidly after 1952.[55] Windsor offered white, working-class Americans an opportunity to literally travel to another country without the high costs that often accompanied other tourist excursions.

The geographical location of the various brothels demonstrates the centrality of the cross-border business. Windsor did not have an "official" red light district, but instead, the bawdy houses operated openly in the downtown core. The *Star* regularly published the addresses of the brothels, which were most often located on streets such as Almer, Mercer, Pitt, Chatham, and Tecumseh. One *Star* article even reported on a brothel on Goyeau Street, "within half a block of the police station."[56] Significantly, these streets were not only in the downtown center but were also within close proximity to either the bridge or the tunnel that connected Windsor and Detroit. American tourists would not have to travel far once they crossed the 5,160 foot tunnel that separated the two cities. Once across, they often met men and women waiting on the Canadian side handing out business cards and directing them to particular bawdy houses. In an interview with Patrick Brode, Jim Ure, a retired Windsor police detective, recalled how one madam recruited clients: "One of the most famous bawdy houses was right behind the arena at 359 Brandt [Street] . . . that old gal she had business cards and maps and everything. I can remember such a line up there on weekends, they would go in and pay their money and they would have to wait out in the street with their chit, and then they would be called in."[57] Contemporary sources make similar points. One *Star* article reported, "Early Saturday a squad led by Sgt. Tom Smith made investigation at 173 Aylmer [Street] when they discovered a 'tout' directing traffic to that address."[58] In 1948, when two Detroiters pleaded guilty to being in a disorderly house, they explained that they "had come across to Windsor on Saturday night and had been approached by a man who took them to the [bawdy] house on Elliott Street."[59] Clearly, attracting the American clientele was a high priority for those working in Windsor's sex industry, and the open recruitment began from the moment they crossed into the city.

The sex trade in Windsor can also be identified as a tourist industry in that it was accompanied by a host of other people and businesses that catered to and benefited from the American market. Hotels owners, bars owners, and taxi drivers all provided important services to aid in the growth of the sex industry. The Blue Water Hotel, for example, was known for its "wide open" nature, a reputation earned in part because it was located next door to a bawdy house. Undercover LLBO inspectors kept detailed reports on the activities of the bar, which ranged from co-ed parlor rooms to open sexual solicitation. For example, between March 8 and March 17, 1951, Inspector Brown made six unannounced visits to the hotel and was very alarmed by what he found: "known prostitutes" and men sitting together at tables in the parlor room. Throughout the six days of visits the inspector noted that "conditions were very bad," with the women's licensed room "filled, both afternoon and evening," with prostitutes.[60] A few years later, at 11:25 p.m. on October 2, 1957, Inspector Smith entered the Blue Water Hotel to find many patrons "staggering" who "appeared to be intoxicated." In the "ladies and escorts" room, he found a noisy bunch of intoxicated patrons, staggering about and singing in a "racous manner" [*sic*] to the poorly played piano.[61] In hotel barrooms like that of the Blue Water Hotel, Canadian and American men and women could meet, enjoy drinks together, and solicit sexual services without any trouble from the establishment's owners.

Local and national papers ran articles about the multifaceted vice economy in Windsor, giving detailed accounts that often read as a "how to" guide to the "underworld" of the city. According to a 1950 *Maclean's* article, "For a $2 ride in and out of the compact streets of Windsor's business section any cab driver would point out which of the dingy rooming houses, pool rooms, and tobacco stores along Pitt, Sandwich, Assumption, and Pelissier Streets, behind whose false front you could get a girl, buy a drink, or place a bet."[62] Similarly, a 1950 *Star* exposé on prostitution in the city explained, "the mere mention of 'where can I have a good time' widens the eyes of virtually every taxi driver in Windsor. He has a contact with the brothels." It continued, "He'll take you to any one of the 50 brothels in the city where women are typed like brands of whiskey. Some good, some bad. You get what you pay for."[63] In classic muckraking style, the author described his various attempts to solicit prostitutes in bars and hotels, explaining that it was an easy task in each. He explained, "We visited nine joints, including three hotels. It was the same story in each, except that when we delved into the close-to-the-[Detroit] river spots things became a little rougher."[64] These reports demonstrate that the sex industry was necessarily tied to other forms of vice within the city, and even "legitimate" businesses had a difficult time turning their backs on the profit to be made off of American tourists. The closer to the border, the "rougher" the businesses got, suggesting again that much of the vice business was conducted in places expedient for Americans. Thus the sex tourism industry catered to its white American clientele, providing convenience, affordability, and accessibility just a short car or bus trip across the river.

The Decline of Sex Tourism

Sex tourism in Windsor declined almost as quickly as it developed. The beginning of the end of the postwar industry can most easily be identified as the establishment of a police inquiry that began in March 1950. The high-profile inquiry was aimed at cracking down on laxity in the Windsor Police force in regards to their handling of vice. However, the inquiry did not occur spontaneously but, instead, had its roots in a decade of public protest over vice in the city. The reasons for the rapid decline, then, must be understood within the context of broader social forces shaping the Windsor region in particular, and North America in general. When the "booming" economy leveled off, Windsor's days of rapid growth came to an end. Yet this economic decline also occurred within an increasingly conservative social atmosphere, which had dire consequences for the sex industry along the border. As the Cold War intensified in the late 1940s and early 1950s, not even the border was safe from the moral politics attempting to mold "proper" citizens across Canada and the United States, and the vice industry in Windsor became one of its targets.

The economic conditions that initially allowed for the development of a sexual tourist industry were in decline by the mid-1950s. By the end of the early postwar period, automation had become the standard in the auto industry, displacing thousands of workers across Canada.[65] This was especially devastating for residents of a city whose main source of employment was in automobile manufacturing. As the number of jobs declined, the population of the city began to shift from the center of the city into the peripheral suburbs of South Windsor, Sandwich East, and Riverside. In 1945, 85 percent of the people in Essex County lived in the City of Windsor; by 1956, the city contained only 65 percent of the population.[66] With "boom" conditions and jobs disappearing, many of those who came to Windsor to make money in the sex trade no longer had a reason to stay. Further, as the Canadian dollar began to strengthen, cross-border excursions into Windsor became less desirable for those whose job prospects were looking bleaker and bleaker. Thus the economic conditions that allowed for the rapid expansion of the sex industry immediately following World War II virtually disappeared by the end of the 1950s.

Yet economic conditions were but one factor affecting the decline of the sex industry. This can also be attributed to the shifting social climate of the postwar period. Throughout the course of the 1940s, residents of Windsor became more intolerant of the vice districts. This can be seen, to a large extent, as a by-product of the general moral atmosphere in Cold

War North America. Scholars such as Adams, Gleason, Iacovetta, and Valverde have been instrumental in identifying aspects of Cold War Canadian and American culture that were particularly hostile to people who deviated from social "norms" defined around the white, middle-class, nuclear family.[67] Sexuality was of particular interest in the postwar period and became a marker signifying "normality" or "abnormality." Consequently, the sex industry in Windsor, which stood as a blatant affront to Cold War moral politics, provoked residents to rally against it and the growth of what they termed "sex perverts"[68] coming to "their" city.[69]

In the mid- to late-1940s, the *Star* was filled with editorials and articles that emphasized the frustration that many middle-class citizens felt with the influx of sex workers and their customers, and the reputation the city attained as a result. Throughout the early postwar period, the concerns cited in the newspapers were generally centered on issues related to the moral and physical health of the nation and reflected nationalistic rhetoric about the safety and security of the country. For example, according to a 1944 article entitled "Venereal Disease: A Challenge to Leadership," prostitution had the potential to destroy all that was good about Canadian society, including the strength of the individual, the nuclear family, and the church. The article explained that "by permanently closing houses of prostitution and cleaning up undesirable places which facilitate the meeting of healthy and infected young people, Venereal Disease will be sharply reduced."[70] It continued, "The continuing threat of Venereal Disease is a tremendous challenge to church and home. The *moral sector* can reduce V.D. . . . IF the moral fibre of the nation is strengthened . . . IF individual character is fortified . . . IF the sanctity of marriage is upheld . . . IF, above all, the moral wisdom of the ages is applied in the practical, daily issues of personal community and national life in Canada."[71] Venereal disease, and by extension, prostitution, was presented as an element weakening the central tenets of a liberal democracy and destroying the institutions that were supposed to be at its foundations, including the church and family.

Linked to fears over crumbling morals was the problematizing of "transience." As argued earlier, the city of Windsor had a long history of relatively fluid populations, and the sex tourist industry was centered on the migration of Canadian and American men and women. This became a concern in the postwar period, as it was seen as undermining the sanctity of the stable, nuclear family. In a *Star* article focused on VD, the author asserts that transient peoples such as prostitutes and carnival workers were a major problem because they brought disease into a community. According to the article, of the prostitutes that traveled to Windsor to take up the sex industry, many were "unaware of [VD] infections" and some had been only "partially treated,"[72] making them a risk to local residents. The author further explained that traveling people such as "the hangers-on and camp-followers of traveling shows" also put a community in danger. According to the article, they "constitute a grave menace to the cities where they travel. I do not refer to the acrobats and others who must maintain a high level of physical fitness, but to the concessionaires."[73] The connection between carnival workers and prostitution was the mobility involved in their occupations. Importantly, this "instability" was portrayed as necessarily linked to immorality. The above quote also demonstrates that the difference between a healthy body and a "diseased" body was to a great degree a moral one. Issues of morality had strong class undertones, as acrobats were necessarily healthier than the lower-status concessionaires. This suggests a difference between skilled work and unskilled work, which can be linked to "legitimate" and "illegitimate" industries. Prostitution then was a form of "illegitimate" work wherein "outsiders" threatened the safety and security of residents of Windsor.

Prostitution was also dangerous because it attracted "transient" American men into the city for sex. In his study on drinking in the Essex and Niagara regions of Ontario during the interwar years, Dan Malleck argues that American drinking tourists occupied the realm of the "other," and that residents and liquor regulators felt that "this 'other' had to be carefully watched: he or she was morally suspect, potentially socially dangerous, and brought a degree of lawlessness to the province."[74] Similar language was found in postwar concerns over Americans coming to Windsor for sex. For example, in 1941, the *Star* ran a report about a man who kidnapped a fourteen-year-old girl from Windsor and took her across the border. The article stated that the girl went missing from her Windsor home, was "locked up in a Detroit hotel room for several days," and was "indecently assaulted" by her kidnapper.[75] Interestingly the article explained that the man, Leo Thompson, was a Canadian citizen, but that he had been "in Detroit on and off for 12 years."[76] He is also described as frequenting the "Blue Water Hotel," which suggests he regularly consumed alcohol in Windsor, and perhaps engaged in prostitution. In this narrative Detroit becomes a haven for sexual predators who intend to prey on the Windsor community and to use it as a place to unload their "delinquent" sexual desires. As one 1946 editorial explained, "Windsor is a bad spot for sex perverts, because in addition to the local rash of perverts, there are the ones who cross the river from Detroit seeking greener pastures on this side."[77] While bar proprietors, pimps, and cabbies may have welcomed the influx of vice-seeking Americans, many residents of the city saw it as a major problem. Consequently, the mobility that characterized the sex trade came under attack in Cold War Windsor, and local residents became increasingly intolerant of "deviant" outsiders.

As the rate of sex tourism increased, so too did the middle class's concern over the vice trade. By the end of the decade, however, these concerns had a new focus: the safety of the youth in Windsor. Prostitution was seen to not only threaten the family structure but to have its gravest affects on its most vulnerable members, the children. Fears over youth and sex were not new to the period, as campaigns against white slavery and subsequent child campaigns had long established a problematic link between youth and prostitution. However, in the postwar period, there was a renewed concern over delinquency among "teenagers," and this concern played an important role in rallying citizens against the sex trade.[78] Citizens expressed fears that the sex trade was drawing "undesirable" characters into the city, endangering the welfare of children and teens living in the city. According to a 1944 *Star* article, "When two teen-aged boys were found in a Windsor disorderly house, the incident lighted a fire of civic indignation that may flame into the biggest drive against houses of prostitution ever launched in the district."[79] The following year, the city enacted an educational campaign to "warn parents and children of the dangers lurking in the presence of sex perverts, curb cruisers, and other undesirable characters."[80] In 1946, thousands of women, including members of the YWCA, and Roman Catholic and Protestant churches, joined together in a militant drive to eliminate sex crimes in the city. This resulted in a meeting between the *Windsor Daily Star*, the Police Department, and the mayor to organize a campaign to eliminate "curb cruisers, sex perverts, and white slavers."[81] As the sex tourism industry expanded in the city, so too did the militancy of the antivice campaigns in Windsor. In 1948, in an attempt to dissuade men and women from participating in the sex industry, the *Star* began a campaign in which it published the names of those arrested for prostitution-related offenses. By 1950, the public and the papers had successfully highlighted the "problem" of vice in Windsor, attested by the fact that even national magazines such as *MacLean's* and *Saturday Night* published articles on vice in the city of Windsor.[82]

The loud public demands to eradicate vice in the city were met by the 1950 Windsor Police Inquiry. According to *MacLean's*, in March 1950, "Magistrate J. Arthur Hanrahan sentenced bootlegger Joe Assef to six months in jail and plunged the city of Windsor, Ont., into two weeks of explosive investigations of vice-ring activities in what has long been Canada's best publicized 'wide open town.'"[83] Over the next six months, the *Star* was filled with articles about the inquiry and corruption in the police force. On September 14, 1950, Attorney General Porter released a report by provincial inspectors Frank Kelly and W. H. Lougheed, which proved to be a strong denunciation of police work in Windsor. It called for twenty-four-hour morality policing, an increase of fifty police constables, and an immediate end to the vice trade in Windsor.[84] As a result, Police Chief Claude Renaud and Deputy Chief W. H. Neale "resigned," and the city set about to enact the recommendations of the report.

By the end of the 1950s, the antivice campaigns were successful at drastically reducing the sex trade and eliminating sex tourism from the city. According to the 1959 *Annual Police Report*, "The number of complaints received during the past year concerning so called vice have been very few. Bawdy houses are non-existent. The method of operation of prostitutes has changed drastically and they no longer operate from a house except in very isolated instances. The few prostitutes left in the City use automobiles, motels, or hotel rooms in order to carry on their activities and the same accommodation is not used more than once."[85] While it is likely that the *Annual Report* exaggerated the extent to which the police had been successful at eliminating prostitution, it does suggest that the moral and legal campaigns to eradicate prostitution were relatively successful by the end of the 1950s. The report also indicates that most of the women working in the sex industry had actually left the city, no doubt encouraged by a combination of economic, legal, and social barriers. By 1960, the city that was once "Canada's best publicized 'wide open town,'"[86] was transformed into a city that any Cold War crusader would be happy to call home, at least temporarily.

Conclusion

The 1940s and 1950s proved to be a dynamic period in the history of the Windsor-Detroit borderland, particularly in relation to sexuality. Windsor's booming, male-dominated economy, when combined with its position as a bordertown, enabled the development of an extensive sex trade industry. As a result, the city gained a reputation that was international in scope, drawing both Americans and Canadians into the city for the purposes of sex. For a few brief years, then, Windsor's sex tourism industry was able to withstand the social, moral, and legal regulation brought about by the Cold War. Through their participation in the sex trade, women and men necessarily crossed social, legal, and national borders, creating a unique sexualized space. However, bordertowns do not function exclusively outside of the scope of national laws, politics, and identities. This is best demonstrated in the strong, and relatively successful antivice campaigns that developed in response to the sex tourism industry, as well as the racial lines that determined who could participate in the trade. Windsor, therefore, proves to be an important case study of the ways in which bordertowns function both outside of, and in relation to, the power dynamics and politics of the nation(s) as a whole.

The history of a border is necessarily an intimate one, as people grapple with and negotiate its implications on very personal levels. A focus on the city of Windsor demonstrates that, because of their fluid nature, bordertowns facilitate the exploration of "deviant" sexual identities and their expressions to a greater degree than cities farther embedded within national boundaries. Since borders are both literal and metaphorical, they have the ability to challenge the social codes deemed to be at the "heart" of a society, and yet, at some level, must always answer to these codes. It is significant to note that, though efforts to eradicate prostitutes and sex tourists from the city of Windsor were fairly successful by the end of the 1950s, the triumph was short lived. Today, Windsor has regained its reputation as a "Sin City," due again to the high number of Americans that partake in the city's various vice industries, including drinking, gambling, and sexual recreation. Therefore, the study of sex tourism in postwar Windsor has important implications for current border politics in the Windsor-Detroit region, but also for the politics of sexuality along the US-Canada border in general.

CHAPTER SIX

Official Government Discourses about Vice and Deviance

The Early-Twentieth-Century Tohono O'odham

Andrae Marak and Laura Tuennerman

In 1917, Jewell D. Martin, superintendent of the Sells Indian Agency in southern Arizona told his supervisor that Tucson "is not a fit place for Indian girls to work after returning from boarding schools . . . [since] many of them do not have the moral stamina to withstand the temptations to which they are subjected."[1] Two years later, Janette Woodruff, a Bureau of Indian Affairs (BIA) field matron, remarked that almost all of the Tohono O'odham girls under her supervision attended the Catholic fiesta in honor of San Francisco de Xavier (Saint Francis Javier) in San Xavier del Bac Mission about nine miles southeast of Tucson. She allowed them to do so only after the "sisters very kindly fitted up a room to keep the girls that had no parents there over night."[2] Across the border, Mexican education inspector Gustavo A. Serrano argued in 1929 that the Tohono O'odham were "traditionally peaceful and probably more civilized than the average tribe" but were lacking in industry and did just enough to satisfy their needs. In spite of these perceived barriers, he believed that they could be turned into "good" Mexicans if the government invested in the proper educational and agricultural improvements.[3] It is worth noting that the focus of these different claims about the Tohono O'odham reflect the divergent preoccupations of elites on either side of the border: fallen women prone to vice north of the border and indigenous people and peasants who were "ignorant, rude, inefficient, violent, and beset with vices" south of the border.[4]

When we think of transnational vice in the US-Mexico border region in the early twentieth century, we often think of the passage of illegal or

Figure 6.1. Happy Tohono O'odham girls posing for a picture.
(Courtesy of the Department of Special Collections and University Archives, Marquette University Libraries)

semi-illegal goods — opium or alcohol during Prohibition — cattle rustling, or the passage of untaxed items across the border. Clearly, these were serious issues.[5] Nonetheless, in this chapter, we would like to examine the ways in which the US and Mexican governments engaged in programs to eliminate "vice" among the Tohono O'odham, a people who, as a result of the creation of the US-Mexico border in the nineteenth century, became transnational. Both the Bureau of Indian Affairs (BIA) and the Mexican Education Ministry (Secretaria de Educación Pública, or SEP) viewed the Tohono O'odham as backward, prone to vice, and in need of civilizing. Specifically, this chapter will analyze the practices that these governmental agencies engaged in to eliminate perceived vices among the Tohono O'odham as they first came into substantial contact with them, the BIA in the 1910s and 1920s, and the SEP in the 1920s and 1930s. In this way, as the introduction to this collection suggests, this chapter explores "official discourses about vice, 'deviance,' and illegal trade" at the level of their quotidian reality.

The fact that the Tohono O'odham's ancestral lands, the Papaguería (which was composed of southwestern Arizona and northwestern Sonora)

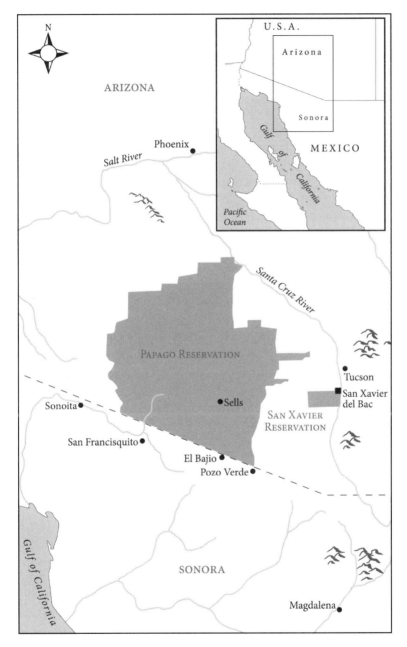

Figure 6.2. The Papaguería, the Arizona-Mexico borderlands that comprise the Tohono O'odham homeland.

spanned the border, added complexity to the situation. Many BIA officials stationed at the Sells Indian Agency viewed the Mexican denizens of the borderlands region to be as bad as or worse than the Tohono O'odham. For example, BIA field matron Woodruff argued that "the proximity to low standards [i.e., Mexicans] sometimes created a situation that was destructive to the general morality of the [Tohono O'odham] community."[6] The racial denigration of both Native Americans and "half-breed" (i.e., mestizo) Mexicans was part of a larger phenomena. Arizona had already passed antimiscegenation laws to protect "whiteness" in 1865 and again in 1913, forbidding the intermarriage of whites with blacks, "Mongolians," and Native Americans.[7] In addition, while there was "no clear racial order among monolithic groups labeled Anglo, Mexican, and Indian" and identity remained flexible and contingent, whiteness and ethnicity did matter. For example, better off and lighter-skinned Mexican Americans, most of whom called themselves Hispanics and claimed direct Spanish ancestry, were often considered white and married into elite Anglo families to solidify their social and political position.

By the twentieth century, however, this path was becoming less and less available to upper-class Mexicans north of the border. Historian Eric V. Meeks remarks that the denigration of nonwhites was "built into the very identity of Arizona from its inception."[8] Mark C. Anderson, using political cartoons published in US papers during the Mexican Revolution (1910–1917), has unmistakably demonstrated in turn that the depiction of Mexicans as backward, racially limited, and morally decrepit was part of a much broader cultural understanding that Anglos had about their southern neighbors and was not just confined to Arizona.[9] Nonetheless, amongst progressive social workers, government employees, and missionaries "racist ideology was not expressed as hatred but rather as paternalism."[10] Susan Yohn argues that these missionaries were in fact "antiracists" because they understood that race and culture were socially constructed. Even so, "they believed their own mores and habits to be superior and expected their clients to be transformed."[11] In relation to Mexicans and Mexican Americans, social workers believed that they would be able to assimilate them, just not as equals. To assimilate them, Mexican culture and character would have to be corrected (using Anglo ideals of manhood and womanhood as blueprints), but given the assumed limited aspirations of Mexicans, they would maintain their current humble place in society.[12]

Further complicating matters is the fact that the US-Mexico border is of relatively recent construction. The present-day border between the two countries was not finalized until the completion of a boundary survey begun after the 1853 Gadsden Purchase (known as the Treaty of La Mesilla in Mexico).[13] Even the Gadsden Purchase did not stop filibusterers from attempting (and failing) to annex additional parts of Mexico to the United States.[14] However, the border remained porous and a source for the possible passage of undesirable people, ideas, and vices. On the US side of the border, BIA officials viewed the borderlands region as a source of trouble. For example, Superintendent Martin argued that it was necessary to provide telephone service to a proposed agency site in Indian Oasis in southern Arizona because "many stirring events may occur near the trouble zone of the boundary."[15] Martin repeatedly stressed that the border must be fenced to prevent Tohono O'odham cattle from either straying onto the Mexican side of the border (even though Tohono O'odham lands existed on both sides of the border) or being rustled by bandits.[16]

In addition, Martin wrote to Dwight B. Heard, local chairman of the Arizona Council of Defense, offering the services of up to three hundred Tohono O'odham riders to patrol the border and deter the incursion of possible Mexican raiders.[17] On the Mexican side of the border, the perceived threat was of a wholly different kind. Mexico's revolutionary and postrevolutionary leaders were in favor of continued US investment.[18] In fact, the overall amount of direct US investment rose during the 1920s as presidents Álvaro Obregón (1920–1924) and Plutarco Elías Calles (1924–1928) lead the reconstruction of their shattered nation.[19] While both were interested in increased direct US investment in the Mexican economy, they had two larger concerns. First, they worried that there would be a backlash against increased foreign investment, especially in light of the fact that the Mexican Revolution itself was brought on, at least in part, by Mexicans' resentment of foreign businesses and their negative political, cultural, and economic impacts.[20] Second, they were uneasy about the possibility that the incoming American capital would bring with it US cultural imperialism. This fear would eventually lead to the creation of a series of "frontier schools" meant to stem the tide of US cultural influences.[21]

The US-Mexico border was not the only border in the region. As described in the Afterword, "One of the challenges of this book is that we refer to more than one phenomenon by 'border,' including boundaries of political-legal jurisdictions and wider sorts of social divisions and edges, some but not all with distinctive geographic manifestations."[22] Here we consider both jurisdictional borders and social borders because BIA officials also viewed the liminal spaces between the Papago and San Xavier reservations and non-Indian communities (especially Tucson) as filled with a plethora of "vices." It was their job, they claimed, to protect the Tohono

Figure 6.3. The Calles regime funded infrastructure improvements aimed at modernizing Sonora and attracting nonindigenous settlers. (Courtesy of the Fideicomiso Archivos Plutarco Elias Calles y Fernando Torreblanca)

O'odham from these potential hazards. This was in keeping with the original intention of Indian removal and placement on reservations. William T. Hagan argues that when the United States adopted its reservation policy in the 1860s and 1870s, "there was almost unanimous agreement among the whites that this was the [N]ative American's best hope of survival." Indian and non-Indian mixing would be more detrimental than helpful, unless indigenous people were exposed only to those people approved by the government and thought to have the best interests of Indians at heart.[23] Tohono O'odham tribal leaders tapped into this trope at a meeting held in 1916 to petition the BIA to set up the Papago Reservation. For example, Benito Segundo, "governor" of Topawah argued, "It is well known that if white men come in here they are not our relatives and soon differences will arise between us."

Jose X. Pablo, a Tohono O'odham who would later work for the BIA, echoed these sentiments, suggesting that the Tohono O'odham "are asking for nothing except to be let alone to pursue their own way in peace without aid from the Government or anyone."[24] The BIA view that vice was rampant in Tucson was also reflective of a shift to a more "fluid definition of respectability" by working-class women in the early twentieth century that coincided with the rise in industrialization and urbanization. It centered

San Miguel Mothers' Garment Making Club.
1926.

Figure 6.4. Clubs such as this one, the San Miguel Mothers' Garment Making Club, aimed to acculturate Tohono O'odham women into mainstream society. (Courtesy of the University of Arizona Libraries, Special Collections; AZ520)

on newly arisen social settings such as co-ed high schools, dance halls, cars, movie theaters, and amusement parks, less parental supervision, and new depictions of sexuality in media and publications. Though middle-class ideas of respectability had not changed, the new working-class norms were accepting of some female sexual self-expression and assertiveness. Many adults felt that this new popular culture was creating confusion in the moral order and would result in eventual ruination.[25] Thus, as Heyman and Campbell discuss more fully in the Afterword, the conflict was not so much over what was legal and illegal, but rather over what was licit or illicit.

BIA officials felt that it was incumbent on them either to prevent Tohono O'odham women from taking advantage of such social milieus or to chaperone them if they did. Janette Woodruff reported, "There were delinquencies among the Indians as a matter of course. . . . White teachers tried to build up ideals, but the proximity to low standards sometimes created a situation that was destructive to the general morality of the community."[26] Woodruff and other field matrons repeatedly commented on their concerns about protecting the Tohono O'odham girls from exposure to potential vices in Tucson — making sure girls did not go unsupervised, did not accept gentlemen callers in their own rooms, and did not drink or attend wild dances.

Even though they did not physically isolate indigenous people through a reservation system, Mexican elites also were concerned about exposing them to mainstream society. Plutarco Elías Calles and his secretary of education, José Manuel Puig Casauranc, who favored the eventual assimilation of "Indians" into mainstream Mexican culture, argued that indigenous people had the same potential as anyone else.[27] They claimed that the *only difference* — and this deserves emphasizing, because even if it was true, it was a huge difference — was that Spaniards and Mexicans had persecuted them for the last four hundred years.[28] Based on his understanding of nineteenth-century Sonora, Calles argued that mestizos and whites had invaded indigenous areas and confiscated the most productive agricultural land, forcing indigenous people into isolated areas with less fertile lands and less access to irrigation.[29]

Puig had a more nuanced understanding of the problem than Calles. Like Calles, he believed that the indigenous races were mentally fit, well organized, and capable of elevating themselves to the intellectual level of their nonindigenous neighbors. Nevertheless, he asked that people recognize that the truth about Mexico's indigenous population lay somewhere in between the positive physical and spiritual characteristics attributed to them by famed anthropologist Manuel Gamio and other *indigenistas* and the negative characteristics of docility attributed to them by skeptics.[30] Both Calles and Puig viewed education as a bridge to ending indigenous exploitation, reintegrating them into mainstream society, and harnessing their labor to promote Mexico's economic progress.[31] Of course, to do so, the government would need to dispatch well-trained teachers to their isolated locales to introduce them to modern civilization, serve as examples, and provide them with the proper training.[32]

Now that we have briefly laid out the "vice" problem, the ways in which it was connected to ideas of Indianess, and how elites in both the United States and Mexico situated the "redemption" of indigenous people, it is time to examine the particular circumstances of the Tohono O'odham in the early twentieth century before investigating the actual implementation of the antivice campaigns aimed at the Tohono O'odham on each side of the border.

Prior to the settlement of large numbers of Europeans in the Papaguería, the Tohono O'odham engaged in seasonal migration between winter villages and summer desert settlements where they practiced subsistence farming, hunted, and foraged.[33] They also engaged in migratory wage labor and communal cattle raising. By the early twentieth century, men increasingly took part in the local wage economies as mineworkers, ranch hands, and cotton pickers. Women followed suit by migrating into non-Indian areas to work as domestic servants.[34]

Each village was largely an "autonomous political unit" based on extended kinship relations. A council, led by a "keeper" that kept his position of power only so long as he had the respect of the local community and was able to forge a consensus, governed each village, ranging in population from twenty to three hundred.[35] This proved to be important because, on both sides of the border, government officials tried to work through village leaders, assuming that they had the right to make decisions on behalf of their constituents. Also important was the fact that around the time that each government began its antivice assimilation program, land was set aside for the Tohono O'odham on each side of the border. The US government created the 2.75 million acre Papago Reservation in 1916.[36] It covered much of southern Arizona. Just over twelve years later, the Mexican government set aside 7,675 acres in Pozo Verde. Both governments were acting in response to Hispanic and Anglo encroachment onto Tohono O'odham lands.

Antivice in the United States

Now, beginning with the United States, it is time to turn to the actual implementation of the antivice programs implemented by each government. After setting up the Papago Reservation in 1916, the BIA's official policy promoted vocational training of the Tohono O'odham so that they could eventually assimilate into mainstream society (though not as equals). This move mirrored broader national trends.

In the United States, at the turn of the twentieth century, there was an increased focus on publicly funded education for all children. This expanded to include compulsory school attendance in almost all states by 1900 and a growth of high school attendance overall. With the passing of the Smith Hughes Act of 1917, there was also more interest in — and funding of — vocational or manual training for working-class youth. One force behind this was growing concern over a diversifying population. As the country was flooded with immigrants, especially those coming from countries not commonly represented in the middle class, civic leaders faced concerns about how to best Americanize and acculturate these newcomers.

Policymakers saw education as a major mechanism for achieving these goals. This was true both for boys — who were viewed as future workers and citizens — and for girls, who were viewed as "moral" and the social conscience of the nation.[37]

The proper acculturation of women was especially important. For those who still believed in eugenics, feminine virtue and chastity was the key to racial purity.[38] For nearly everyone, women in the US West and Southwest were viewed as genteel civilizers and helpmates. As Elizabeth Jameson notes, "Women were to shape national morality from the privacy of their family hearthsides, leaving public action to men."[39] This belief ran through many areas of nineteenth-century reform and well into the Progressive Era. Women as municipal housekeepers was a common theme among urban and political reformers. Indeed, there was an entire group of women's suffrage supporters who argued that women should vote because they were more moral than men and would thus improve politics.[40]

On the Papago Reservation, officials likewise organized the assimilation program by gender. This program also reflected the realities of rural life. In 1910, 95 percent of Native Americans lived in rural areas and 75 percent were engaged in agriculture.[41] Accordingly, a BIA agency farmer trained the majority of men to "modernize" their agricultural production, transforming their seasonal "two-village" system into one that focused on the intensive cultivation of monocrops for the market.[42] To do so, BIA farmer A. M. Philipson held an annual Papago Indian Farmer's Institute at the San Xavier Day School. The institute featured specialists on horticulture, forage crops, and livestock from the University of Arizona in addition to local county government officials. The program was aimed at "the general improvement of farms, farm products and live stock on the reservation . . . the marketing of any products they may have to sell and the purchasing of any thing that may be needed in large quantities."[43]

Other Tohono O'odham worked under one of their own, Jose X. Pablo, to manage better their tribal livestock.[44] Although their jobs were to increase productivity in the agricultural and stock sectors of the local economy, the written record suggests that they spent much of their time attempting to overcome Tohono O'odham resistance to schooling and assimilation (which would, if things went according to plan, eliminate their vices). Philipson started his career with the BIA in the Tucson area at the Tucson Day School before moving on to become the agency farmer. In 1916, he asserted that the BIA had set too high of a standard for Tohono O'odham assimilation. He argued that there were two underlying reasons for the inability of the Tohono O'odham to assimilate rapidly. First, many of their parents were "almost devoid of civilization," and as a result, "the majority of them [the students] are very, very backward and very slow." Second, most students did not attend school until after the fall harvest and left again in March "to go back to their ranches with their parents."[45] In other words, while many parents valued the schools and sent their children to them, they prioritized the maintenance of their preexisting patterns of subsistence.

As agency farmer, Philipson had the task of enforcing agency regulations that required parents to enroll their children in BIA schools or be tried by an Indian judge (appointed and/or approved by BIA officials). The local superintendent argued: "Physical disability is the only excuse for these children not enrolling" at boarding schools in Yuma, Phoenix, Riverside (in California), or at local mission schools. The threats — including jailing (where they would be forced to engage in hard labor, usually for the agency farmer), fines of up to ten dollars, and sending their children away to boarding schools without the parents' consent — used to convince recalcitrant parents gives some suggestion to their reluctance to comply. In one case, the Indian judge's own sons were arrested and held overnight for failure to attend school.[46]

Philipson and Pablo engaged in more direct "antivice" work. For example, Philipson intervened in numerous instances of Tohono O'odham getting drunk. In one case, Philipson discovered that, in spite of Prohibition, some of the Tohono O'odham were purchasing lemon-extracts from a Chinese vendor and getting inebriated. Superintendent T. F. McCormick tasked Philipson with rounding up the men because "as long as they were drunk they deserve being punished." In another case, Philipson brought Antonio Robles before the Indian judge because Robles claimed he could neither remember where or from whom he purchased the alcohol that resulted in his arrest for public drunkenness. The judge sentenced him to ten days of labor under Philipson's watch.[47]

Surprisingly, even the BIA's farmer was engaged in antivice work aimed at potentially fallen women and matters of the home. For example, Philipson intervened in the case of Maria and Jose Juan, who had a common-law marriage and a nine-month-old daughter together. Jose had been staying out late, and when Maria accused him of seeing another woman, Jose kicked her out. Maria turned to Philipson in hopes that he could make Jose support her financially. Philipson, with the help of the local Indian judge, did her one better and managed to convince Jose to let her return home but demanded that they "secure a marriage license and be legally married."[48] In another case, BIA officials tried to force Lupa Lohenia to marry (probably because she was pregnant, though the record never says so explicitly), even though they were uncertain as to whom she had been dating. After local officials arranged Lupa's marriage to Joe Blain, one of several men who she had been dating, Lupa approached Philipson to see if he could get her out of the arranged marriage by arranging for her to go away to the Sherman Institution in Riverside, California. He refused to accept her application.[49]

Interestingly, while Philipson was minding to Tohono O'odham vices, he had issues of his own. The record is unclear as to exactly when Philipson became a widower — an efficiency report filled out by his boss in May 1920 listed Philipson as married even though, as we will see below, he had accepted female boarders in February of that year. In March 1921, Philipson wrote to Superintendent McCormick in hopes of receiving a favor. Because his request reflects the social values of mainstream society (or at least the potential undermining of those social values) as well as those that the BIA was trying to impose on the Tohono O'odham, it is worth quoting at length:

> I would like to ask a favor of you for my own personal protection relative to the Donsemore Sisters occupying part of my quarters since Feb. 19. I did not think of it this way at the time or I would have asked it then before permitting them to come in here. You can see what a position it places me in, knowing what I told you about my domestic affairs. I have absolutely no way of denying any charge that might be brought against me for allowing strange women to occupy my private rooms. Now the favor I ask is this, Please write me a letter or order dated Feb. 19, 1920 directing me to allow these women to occupy the rooms they are occupying. Such an order from you will, I think, put me in the clear before the court should an attempt be made to sue this charge against me. I do not know that anything of the kind will be attempted, but in case it would, I want to be on the safe side.

There is no way to tell for sure, but it seems apparent that Philipson had invited female boarders into his home prior to the death of his wife. Philipson feared it becoming public that he had done so of his own accord.

The issue of potentially fallen women and vice, which given their job description would have seemingly been tangential to agency farmers and stockmen, was of central concern to agency field matrons. BIA field matrons were part of a much broader trend of the professionalization of social work during the Progressive Era. Initially many of the individuals working with the poor, recent immigrants, and Native Americans were volunteers or untrained professionals. Missionaries (in the case of the Tohono O'odham, both Presbyterians and Catholics), charity workers, and others often were motivated by compassion to perform "good works." Over time, even among missionaries and volunteers — and certainly among professional social workers — however, there was a shift toward viewing charity work as a science. This included a move toward efficient, professional standards.[50] It also moved many reformers to demand more involvement from the state — in addition to the private sector — with a growing focus on social justice and social welfare.

This did not mean that workers were able to move completely outside of their own culture and moralities; most remained bound to their middle-class sensibilities. Neither did it mean that they demanded equality for their clients. Instead, they insisted that they receive more acceptance, tolerance, and understanding. Most important, it was accompanied by a shift toward viewing social problems (i.e., vices) not as the result of individual moral failing but rather as having societal causes that could be addressed and fixed.[51]

One of the major tools that the matrons used to overcome Tohono O'odham vice was civil (that is legally sanctioned by the state) and monogamous marriage. In an astounding 1917 report, Superintendent Jewell Martin suggested "it would be immeasurably better even for the girls to be sent back to the Papago desert to become wives on the desert farms and ranches than to run the risk of falling prey to the half-educated young Indian men who are in and around Tucson and . . . who do not as a rule wish to marry because they can have more spending money without a family to support."[52] The fact that Martin was willing to give up any chance at assimilating a Tohono O'odham woman, the bedrock of BIA assimilation efforts, in exchange for protecting her from the vice of unassimilated Tohono O'odham (and one would guess Mexican) men is suggestive. In this sense, BIA policy (or at least the people who put it in action) vis-à-vis marriage favored a view of women that was in many ways conservative and traditional, focusing on Americanization specifically by pushing gendered norms and expectations that favored marriage and the protection of moral virtue rather than women's rights or independence or vocations or careers.

Field matrons arbitrated domestic disputes, offered marital advice, and undertook a wide variety of efforts to safeguard the moral character of the young women they worked with. BIA matron Mary Doyle, a Catholic nun, for example, reported on a young girl named Maria whom she directly supervised for two years. Maria had "lax morals" and had ended up in court. However, with time and supervision Doyle reported: "There has been a vast improvement in her since she has resided with us. For some time after she came here people regarded her with great coldness and disdain; but she has raised herself in their estimation to a remarkable degree by her edifying conduct and quiet, pleasing manners. She is employed in domestic work and sewing, and has lately taken up the study of music."[53] The types of behavior that field matrons considered appropriate were consistently discussed in their reports, where they worried about protecting women from "influences." Those included women of bad reputation, men, and drink.[54]

While matrons worked to preserve the girls' good names, the matrons faulted white employers for not protecting Tohono O'odham as well as they should. Matrons reported their interest in finding suitable homes for working girls "where their environments will be of an inspiring nature, rather than in places where the living conditions do not tend to promote their best interests."[55] Records report of tensions with employers who did not provide the proper supervision of their maids. Outside housing was a particularly contentious problem since employers could not properly supervise girls living outside the main house during their time off.[56] This particular conflict with employers suggests that the matrons were more concerned with moral issues, particularly with protecting virtue, than they were with meeting employment needs.

The matrons' focus on protecting Tohono O'odham women from vice is particularly seen in the strong focus on Anglo-style marriage as the best long-run solution to most problems. Matrons often reported on their attempts to get girls married and to discourage informal marital arrangements, often described as "living in the Indian way." Ruth Benedict, a famous anthropologist who studied at Columbia University with Franz Boaz, noted that Tohono O'odham parents arranged the marriages of their daughters. This process of searching for a proper mate often involved years of careful scrutiny as the parents searched for a boy with a reputation for hard work and a family with whom they wanted to create bonds of reciprocity. Generally, after the parents proposed the potential marriage to the boy's relatives, the boy would come to the girl's house and spend four nights there. If things went smoothly, then the girl would leave with the boy and take up residence with him in his parents' house. Only after they had had several children would the couple move out and build a house of their own. Perhaps most important, Tohono O'odham men were allowed to have more than one wife, and the parents of girls often preferred to marry their younger daughter(s) off to the same boy on the grounds that if the marriage between the boy and their eldest girl was working out well, then there was little reason to take a chance with another potential spouse. Also of importance was the fact that if a couple "did not want to stay together, they could be divorced merely by deciding to separate." Younger siblings usually returned with the divorced girl to her parents' house, though older boys often decided to stay with the father.[57]

BIA officials worked hard to undermine the "Indian way." Matrons often aimed to move a couple into a legal union where they were living together or when children were involved. In some cases, this could be difficult, as in the case of a girl named Julia who was living secretly with a young man. While her father wanted the matron to compel them to marry, the courts did not want to grant a marriage license to a couple under the age of eighteen when pregnancy was not involved. The matron then appealed to her superior for help getting a license issued.[58]

In many other cases, the concern was over sexual exploitation of women and the solution was almost always legally sanctioned marriage. There are even indications in the records that superintendents were performing marriage ceremonies when a justice of the peace was not available, reinforcing the idea that bureau officials quite literally supported marriage.[59] BIA officials also worked to co-opt the sanctioning of Tohono O'odham marriage and divorce proceedings. Superintendent Martin noted that one Tohono O'odham leader, Mertias Hendricks, had been "dabbling in divorce business" and other things that "he had no right to do." Martin tried to convince Hendrick to become a BIA sanctioned judge, but when that failed, he appointed as judge "a returned student of the rather intelligent competent class, who can read and understand the regulations and to whom I personally gave careful and detailed instructions in his duties."[60]

Matron Woodruff also suggested that support of marriage from outsiders was both useful and necessary. In one letter, she recounted that

> one of the helpful attainments of civilization among the Indians, is when the Commissioner urges us to enforce the marriage law among them. Sometimes it is quite a task on the Supt. and employees to reason with some of them, and talk to them in a quiet way, and have them get married. I notice after they are married they seem so happy together, and are rather proud to think and know they are trying to start out in life right. Many of them come with their own free will and tell me they want to get a marriage license.[61]

Clearly, matrons viewed marriage as a sign of civilization and believed that individuals who embraced marriage were better off than those on whom it was thrust.

Although the reports of all of the matrons working with the Tohono O'odham showed evidence that they believed that civil marriage alone would solve most couples' problems and give them a proper moral grounding, none demonstrated this more clearly than Janette Woodruff. What perhaps frustrated her most was when she offered marriage as a solution to Tohono O'odham couples but was rebuffed. For example, when Frances Narcha had a child out of wedlock with "big Joaquin," Woodruff offered to have them married. Joaquin responded by telling her that they already were married in the Indian way. When Woodruff tried to press the issue Frances laughed at her. Woodruff tried on two occasions either to get the sheriff to take Frances and Joaquin to court and force them to get married or to bring the Catholic priest out to perform a ceremony in order to "make an example of them."[62]

Matrons also worked with the police and governmental officials to address immoral behavior. At times, they also looked to the girl's own family and community to take control of her. One matron wrote to a father about his daughter's bad conduct, describing her as "drunk, indecent, ugly and blasphemous." The matron suggested, "I think you are aware that your daughter, Carlotta Moreno, has been guilty of bad conduct recently. I regret to inform you that her deportment has become exceedingly bad, and it will be necessary to take measures to bring her to justice unless you, yourself, or other relatives can control her actions. . . . You are requested to take charge of her and KEEP HER AT HOME."[63] In this case, at least, family supervision was preferred to legal action. If family supervision failed, however, the matron suggested that local officials place Moreno in "an institution or prison."[64]

As an interesting counterpoint, there also seemed to be some expectation coming out of the Tohono O'odham community that matrons would promote morality among those under their supervision. Woodruff, in her report on working girls in 1927, noted: "Looking at the situation from another side, the Indians think I should stop the dancing and drinking among them. I can realize how the Indians feel to have their children come to town and be led away by the evil that is carried on in the village."[65] Moral protection loomed as a large concern for the matrons and for at least some of the native population themselves.

In the end, civil marriage was encouraged as an appropriate moral choice, fitting with larger societal norms. As such, it was seen as a step toward civilization for members of the Tohono O'odham. But perhaps most importantly, it was seen as a way of maintaining stability — social and economic — within the Tohono O'odham community. Civil marriage protected women and men from vice, and it provided for the financial support of women and children.[66]

Antivice in Mexico

The documentation of the SEP's attempt to root out the vices they believed were latent in Tohono O'odham culture is much less thorough than that of the BIA's similar program. Although Mexican local, state, and federal officials had been in contact with Tohono O'odham representatives on a regular basis at least since 1920, the Education Ministry did not make contact with tribal representatives until 1928.[67] In any case, it would be more correct to say that the Tohono O'odham made contact with the SEP than vice versa as BIA agency stockman and Tohono O'odham tribal member José X. Pablo approached SEP officials and told them: "We have always been thinking of Mexico, which is our true country. Hopefully someday our government . . . will place schools here in the frontier, very close to us so that we will not have to send our children to schools in Tucson or other American schools that are near the border." In addition, Pablo suggested that all of the Papaguería was "really Mexican" and that although the US government had been trying to assimilate the Tohono O'odham, they were in their heart of hearts truly Mexican as well.[68] This was quite a provocative statement coming from a man who spoke no Spanish and had worked closely with BIA officials for over a decade.

As mentioned earlier, Mexican president Calles believed that there was little difference between the oppressed rural masses and indigenous people, both of whom he viewed as backward, uncivilized, stricken by vice, but still redeemable. One indigenista captured this idea when he noted that "it is clear that the solution to the racial problem in Mexico lies in giving a better, a much better culture to the Indian, and not only the Indian, but to the mestizo as well, and the population in general."[69] According to Alexander Dawson, Calles and his education minister Puig "envisioned a uniform set of practices through which all indigenous Mexicans would come to enjoy the benefits of modern civilization and abandon their barbarous tendencies."[70] Of course, the border was a unique region. Given the federal government's increasing concern about the impact of US cultural imperialism in the border region, Pablo was assured of a rapid response.

In some ways, the attempt to modernize the Tohono O'odham was remarkably similar on both sides of the border. In Mexico (as in the United States), the Education Ministry focused on eliminating their two-village system, and the seasonal migration that came along with it, and modernizing their agricultural practices. Anywhere from four hundred to eleven hundred Tohono O'odham, depending on the season, were scattered across several small towns — Sonoita, San Francisquito, Pozo Verde, El Carrizo, Veracruz, and El Bajio — where they engaged in agriculture and raised livestock. The Education Ministry wanted them to relocate to more densely settled locations and practice modern agricultural techniques. One inspector argued that they got low yields from their crops because they failed to rotate properly their crops, planting only wheat and corn. What he probably failed to note (and likely chalked up to their laziness) was the fact that many of the "weeds" — including "squash . . . cotton, tobacco, gourds, [and] devil's claw" — in and around their fields were not only edible but part of the Tohono O'odham diet.[71]

The issue of settlement density was also a result of adaptation to local conditions. The head of federal education in Sonora, Fernando F. Dworak, however, believed that their living in dispersed settlements was a direct result of Tohono O'odham immorality. He argued that if modernization in the Papaguería were ever going to take hold, the Education Ministry would first have to root out their vices.[72] Elpidio López, Dworak's successor, echoed these beliefs. In March 1933, López tracked down a graduate, Francisco Domínguez, of Mexico's premier Indian boarding school and offered him a job as a teacher. According to López, Domínguez declined the job, preferring his tribe's "savage custom" of collecting firewood and selling it in the United States.[73] Of course, the aridity of the Papaguería coupled with the fact that the ejido that the federal government had given to the Tohono O'odham was some distance from the nearest town precluded denser settlement. The fact that SEP officials focused more on Tohono O'odham vices than local conditions says as much if not more about SEP officials than it does about the Tohono O'odham.

Education inspector David Torres Orozco, however, was not blind to these issues. He correctly noted that there was an additional underlying cause for the scattering of Tohono O'odham settlements: federal, state, and local authorities had long sided with non-Indians when it came to land and water issues.[74] In fact, the loss of Tohono O'odham lands had more to do with the Tohono O'odham's so-called savage customs than anything. BIA officials noted that firewood collecting could be potentially lucrative, with the average Tohono O'odham earning up to ninety dollars per year.[75] Another inspector noted that if the government gave the Tohono O'odham access to more land and, more important, more water, they could be transformed into "good" Mexicans producing for the market. He held out hope for the Tohono O'odham because they were, in his estimation, "probably more civilized than the average tribe" in Mexico, but also one lacking in industry, doing just enough to satisfy their needs. However, he estimated the initial necessary investment at ten to twenty thousand pesos, an amount that his superiors were unlikely to consider.[76]

Religion and Women

So what explains the differing focuses — potentially fallen women in the United States and "ignorant, rude, inefficient, [and potentially] violent" men in Mexico — on each side of the border? As noted earlier, both BIA and SEP officials tried to deal with the Tohono O'odham by talking first to tribal "chiefs" or "governors." For example, the BIA met with a gathering of the "leading Papagos of all parts of the country" before inaugurating the Papago Indian Reservation.[77] In Mexico, education inspectors and the heads of education in Sonora always went to confer first (and as far as the record shows, almost only) with supposed local Papago governors. The BIA, however, moved beyond working with just tribal leaders, implementing programs (especially those under the purview of the field matrons) that much more fully penetrated Tohono O'odham society. At one level, this was a matter of resources, and this is reflected in the scarcity of historical sources on the Tohono O'odham in Mexico. In many ways, the federal and state government were more ephemeral than real in the postrevolutionary period up to at least the mid-1930s. It is even possible that the early Catholic and Presbyterian missionaries in southern Arizona had more contact with the Tohono O'odham than did local government officials in northern Sonora. But this awaits further research.

The Mexican government's lack of funds and inability to penetrate into the daily lives of many of its rural citizens, indigenous or not, is further highlighted by the fact that the Education Ministry did have a program similar to that undertaken by the BIA's field matrons aimed at "modernizing" rural and indigenous women. The program's "intent was not to emancipate women and children but to subordinate the household to the interests of national development." The program focused on, among other things, introducing new "scientific" standards of nutrition and hygiene into the home.[78] Records fail to indicate the involvement of tribal women in the program. This does not absolutely mean that none were included, but it clearly reflects the government's inability to introduce the program in a systematic manner. Clearly, tribal requests for huge investments mirroring those made on the US side of the border served as a deterrent for Mexican education officials, who rightly feared that they could not compete with US resources. Nonetheless, the federal government had implemented this and other similar programs in other remote villages, so there must have been some other deterrents. As mentioned earlier, the Tohono O'odham use of a two-village system and the migratory patterns that went along with it also served as a deterrent. The Mexican government was unwilling to adjust its model of schooling to the exigencies of Tohono O'odham life, allowing them to continue their long practice of resistant adaptation.

However, a more significant deterrent to the government's antivice program existed in Mexico: the postrevolutionary regime's anticlerical program. Anticlericalism had been a part of the liberal state since Mexico's independence, but Calles's postrevolutionary government renewed its application with vigor. Stephen Lewis has argued that postrevolutionary anticlericalism was "sheer madness" because it attacked "Mexico's most compelling institution of national cohesion."[79] This is true, and its implementation was part of a systematic effort to replace the primacy of the Catholic Church with a strong central government, especially in light of the fact that the church and the government had many of the same transformational goals.[80] This battle was reflected in the Papaguería. After his first trip to the region, Inspector Torres Orozco suggested that the SEP confiscate the Tohono O'odham Catholic churches in the region and turn them into schools to compel them to support federal education programs.[81] The SEP, in conjunction with state officials, later sponsored a program of "saint burning" where government officials with aid of local supporters raided local churches, confiscated revered religious iconography, and then burned them. In 1934, teachers invaded the Tohono O'odham's most sacred church in Magdalena, seized the venerated statue of San Francisco Xavier, and burned it in the ovens of a local brewery.[82] In southern Arizona, on the other hand, the BIA generally worked closely with both Catholic and Presbyterian missionaries. Even as the field matrons worked to professionalize their work with the Tohono O'odham (and replace the role of the missionaries that preceded them), they became ever more accepting of allowing the Tohono O'odham to attend religious festivals. As one of our opening vignettes demonstrates, as long as the young Tohono O'odham women had the proper moral fortitude and, more importantly, were properly supervised, they were encouraged to attend.

Conclusion

It is clear that in both the United States and Mexico governmental agencies engaged in a variety of efforts to eliminate illicit activities and perceived vices among the Tohono O'odham as they first came into substantial contact with them, the BIA in the 1910s and 1920s and the SEP in the 1920s and 1930s. For reasons of politics, timing, and religious ideology each governmental agency focused on a different segment of the population and offered different solutions to eradicating vice. Indeed there were clearly divergent preoccupations of elites on either side of the border: fallen women prone to vice were the focus on those on the US side of the border, and indigenous people and peasants who were "ignorant, rude, inefficient, violent, and beset with vices" on the Mexican side of the border.

Nonetheless, though they defined their targets and tasks differently, the United States and Mexico had several striking similarities worthy of note. First, both sides shared a prevailing view that vice was a serious problem for the Tohono O'odham and for the larger nation that incorporated them. Second, and most important, both countries believed that the problem of vice could be fixed. Neither side choose to dismiss the Tohono O'odham as unsalvageable, to declare them biologically unfit and unfixable. Instead, as was the case with so many reforms of this era, both governments adopted a mixture of efforts aimed at protecting, disciplining, and educating the Tohono O'odham to bring them in line with the dominant culture of the day. On both sides of the border, the decision was made to push for acculturation — to bring the Tohono O'odham under the reach of the civil and moral codes of the day. As such, a movement into the mainstream — rather than the passing of laws to separate out and further restrict members of this tribe — was seen as the cure for all that ailed them. This suggests both a strong belief in the power of the existing culture and a willingness to believe that the Tohono O'odham could be successfully incorporated into that mainstream culture. Policymakers in both countries had firmly moved away from nineteenth-century views of vice as being intrinsic to individuals, a personal moral failing, to the more Progressive or modern view that there were both societal causes and cures for these problems. Clearly, some failings continued to be personal and moral, but even these, if approached correctly, might be fixed. In the eyes of government officials, the Tohono O'odham had moved from being permanently damned to being wayward children (or protocitizens) in need of guidance and redemption.

CHAPTER SEVEN

Crossing the Line

Transnational Drinking and the Biopolitics of Liquor Regulation in Ontario, 1927–1944

Dan Malleck

As several articles in this collection have clearly demonstrated, borderlanders often look warily across the line.[1] Yet such concern over the proximity to the residents and cultural differences of another country are not confined to those in the immediately adjacent communities. Elaine Carey has shown that even bureaucrats far from the border could understand concern about the infiltration of foreign ideas and individuals into the host country.[2] This wariness was not exclusive to drug enforcement officials in the United States. In 1935, Inspector Wilson Wylie of the Liquor Control Board of Ontario (LCBO) noted that the Embassy Hotel in Port Dalhousie was holding dances in a darkened room. This concerned Wylie, since any number of moral dangers could lurk in that darkness, and the proprietor could not adequately oversee the activities of his hotel guests. This darkened dance hall, Inspector Wylie noted, was an innovation from across the river — that is, from the United States.[3]

Wylie's statement held significant meaning to the officials at the central board office who were to read his report. "Across the river" lay danger, and it was not staying put. The porous border allowed such morally suspect and corruptive individuals access to the residents of the province. In the discourse of this cultural prejudice, Americans who crossed "the line" (as it was often called) would expect to be able to drink in a space with lax regulatory standards that offered opportunity for moral transgression and adventure, like those darkened dance halls. Such expectations presented a danger to the social stability of the province and a challenge to the liquor control authorities. It was the LCBO's job to control access to and consumption of liquor in the province, and its inspectors and administrators saw themselves as charged with maintaining public order in post-Prohibition Ontario. To the LCBO, Americans who crossed the line (literally and figuratively) were most likely going to cause trouble and would threaten the social order the regulators sought to maintain.

This perception of the dangers presented by a porous border informs our understanding of transborder interchange, expanding it from one of commodities (including material goods and commodified people such as immigrants and sex-trade workers) to one of ideals and values, which breach the border and infect the national body. The concern was both about Americans crossing into Canada, and Canadians crossing into the United States. In both instances, Canada — or for this study, Ontario — was in danger of being corrupted, weakened, and irreparably damaged. These ideas were not new. As Jeremy Adelman and Stephen Aron argue, the so-lidification of North American borders in the early- to mid-nineteenth century was accompanied by a rigidification of the notion of who was and was not part of the nation. Outsiders, stripped of rights of citizenship, and often defined ethnically, were at best tolerated within the nation-state. The metaphor of the porous border links with the metaphor of the body politic, and the values of the invader are the sort of corruption that a virus wreaks on a physical body. Unlike bacteria, which can be expelled from the body, a virus expands and mutates, and is always present, hiding until some physical weakness allows it to reassert itself. So when we look at how a regulatory agency and concerned citizens viewed the passage of every-day people — consumers, not criminals — across the border, we can learn quite a bit about their ideas about the ideal, uncontaminated body of their nation, and that of the corrupting invader. While the importance of the border has been studied in many contexts, in histories of liquor regulation it has generally been marginal, if you pardon the pun. With a few exceptions, much of the work that looks at liquor regulation in post-Prohibition Canada has tended to underplay the effect that proximity to the United States played on post-Prohibition liquor control.[4] While many acknowledge that illegal activities on both sides of the border were problems to authori-ties, and some have noted that the end of Prohibition in Canadian prov-inces placed pressure on American authorities, most have underplayed the actual influence the border had in shaping post-Prohibition liquor policy. This generalization excludes several chapters in the current volume, nota-bly by Marcel Martel and Holly Karibo, although specific work on liquor control remains limited. The most notable exception is Stephen Moore's interpretation of the role of the border in shaping US-Canada relations during the Prohibition and post-Prohibition period.[5] Moore observes that few decades were more pivotal in shaping US-Canada relations than the 1920s, and that during Prohibition this relationship was shaped by multiple meanings of the border: border as interface, border as opportunity, border as danger, border as refuge, and so on. While an excellent overarching examination of policy and attitudes at the higher levels, Moore's study does not consider the perception of the border and of those crossing it on the community level. In other words, how did the people who were living in the border communities perceive this border and those who crossed it? How did regulators, whose job it was to ensure that public drinking was done in a responsible and orderly way, view the border and those who crossed it? These questions are important because to look at the attitudes toward Americans at the borders is to understand more clearly the perceptions of right and wrong, proper and improper behavior, thereby facilitating an excavation, however limited, of the value system on which liquor regulation operated.

This chapter uses the records of the regulator, the LCBO, to examine perceptions of American drinkers and American drinking culture by central provincial regulators and borderlanders living in two Ontario communities. It spans the period from LCBO's inception in 1927 to the 1940s, when public drinking became the purview of a different board. These communities are Essex County, immediately south of Detroit and Lake St. Clair, with the Detroit River to the west and Lake Erie to the south, and the "Niagara Region," an anachronistic term I apply to the counties of Welland and Lincoln. These counties make up the geographic space bordered by lakes Ontario and Erie to the north and south, respectively, and the Niagara River to the east. Both regions were bounded on three sides by water, with one side a river across which lies the United States; while there were other border communities (east of Lake Ontario and in Northwestern Ontario), these were the most populous border regions between Ontario and the United States. This chapter is part of a larger project examining the transition from Prohibition to liquor control in Ontario communities from the LCBO's inception to the end of the Second World War, examining ideas of governance and biopolitics in shaping the ideals and practical activities of the Liquor Control Board.[6] While the records are predominantly state-generated, this research attempts to avoid the pitfall of "speaking like a state" by critically examining the work of the LCBO, and asking questions about how letters to the government reveal the way nationalism, citizenship, and the dangers of the border were represented and constructed.[7]

Ontario's Prohibition regime lasted from 1916 to 1927, ending when the Liquor Control Act (LCA) superseded the Prohibition-era Ontario Temperance Act, and the Liquor Control Board of Ontario replaced the Board of License Commissioners. Initially a three-person committee with a large staff, the LCBO was charged with managing the distribution and consumption of liquor in Ontario. In June 1927, the LCBO began to open its retail stores for liquor sales, and license restaurants, snack bars, and hotels for the sale of light beer — roughly 2 percent alcohol by volume, which was considered nonintoxicating — for public consumption.[8] In 1934, after facing years of demands from various sectors for beer by the glass and in reaction to the end of Prohibition in the United States, immediately before dropping an election writ, George Henry's Conservative government passed legislation permitting the sale of regular strength beer for public consumption. The Conservatives still lost the election, and Mitchell Hepburn's newly elected Liberal government (itself divided between drys and wets) was left to administer a vaguely worded but potentially radically permissive new law. The newly appointed chief commissioner of the board, Edmund Odette, a former member of the federal parliament from Tilbury, Ontario (near Windsor), was appointed as the sole member of the board. Despite fears and speculations that the new act and new government would usher in a much more permissive liberal approach to liquor regulation, the LCBO's new regulations remained conservative and significantly limited public drinking. While some speculated that beer would be allowed in public restaurants (thereby opening up a broad range of public drinking establishments), the LCBO under Odette permitted public consumption of beer only in hotel "beverage rooms," and beer and wine could be consumed in hotel dining rooms, but only with a proper meal. Beer and wine permits were also available for private clubs, religious or veterans' associations, steamships, and trains, but the main emphasis was on standard hotels. Ontario's temperance forces argued that the beer-by-the-glass provisions of the 1934 LCA would bring back the saloon with all the social trouble that entailed.[9] In contrast, the LCBO mandated that the beverage rooms would be cleansed of all the associations with the saloon: the board permitted no music, no singing, no game playing, no stand-up bar, no food beyond the occasional bowl of peanuts or chips. The board increased the number of hotel inspectors from six to twenty-one, and began the onerous process of inspecting and regulating the public consumption of regular strength beer in the province.

The LCBO's work, like post-Prohibition liquor regulation in other provinces and states, tapped into an emerging school of thought that saw liquor control to be a reasonable and more workable solution to the "liquor prob-lem" than absolute Prohibition, one that would place erstwhile damaging behavior under the scrutiny and care of the state. As Robin Room has argued, liquor control was an alternative school of thought to the more absolutist idea of Prohibition, an early form of harm reduction.[10] Under liquor control, government would oversee the distribution of potentially harmful products in a way that ensured the dangers of overindulgence were minimized. The most discussed form of liquor control had been the Gothenburg System of "disinterested management," so called because the government agencies that sold the products had no financial interest in their sale.[11] In the ideal disinterested management system, profit was not just a circumstance, as Robert Campbell characterized liquor control in British Columbia, it was anathema.[12]

As several authors have observed, liquor regulation in post-Prohibition Canada was driven by the effort to exorcise the specter of the saloon from the social landscape through various governmental interventions.[13] They argue that the common view of the pre-Prohibition working-class saloon was one infused with various types of immoral behavior, drunkenness, lasciviousness, prostitution, gambling, drug taking, and so on, that chal-lenged the fabric of society, what John Burnham called the "constellation of vice."[14] In Ontario, liquor control sought to remove those problematic influences, to isolate the practice of drinking from other deleterious behav-iors. So while Prohibition was widely considered to have failed, government control would chart a middle path, creating a controlled but permissive en-vironment in which citizens could consume alcohol.[15] These individuals, what I call "citizen-drinkers" were justified in doing this because their ac-tions were both endorsed by the state and controlled by it. The process is a clear representation of biopolitics, the state's dispersal of biopower that was both restrictive and permissive. Like many of the ideas explored by Michel Foucault, the idea of biopolitics, while often confused and confusing, can be a useful way of understanding the interaction between regulatory agen-cies and the individual. For the purposes of this analysis, I define the term *biopolitics* as the process of governing the relationship between individuals and their bodies, and therefore the process of the state entering into the very personal activities of the individual.[16] In the process of reconstruct-ing the citizen drinker, the government had to permit certain behaviors (consuming alcohol in public) while simultaneously restricting them (the spaces were controlled, the behavior was proscribed). The agency charged with overseeing and undertaking this biopolitical project, the Liquor Con-trol Board of Ontario, was motivated by both political and pragmatic idealistic ends. It had to construct a drinking system that reduced opposition while reducing misbehavior. These goals were simultaneously political and pragmatic: political, because the outcome of the bureaucracy's activities reflected both on its own social and cultural authority and on the government of the day; pragmatic, because the system had to function relatively well to allow drinking while discouraging illegality.

Since the Liquor Control Act was short on specifics about public drinking, it placed the onus on the LCBO to deploy the vision and construct the regulations. To understand the attitudes of the regulators, then, it is important to look beyond the actions and rhetoric of politicians, and to gather evidence about what was actually going on in the communities where the drinking was taking place. The vagueness of the act had a secondary effect: it allowed the LCBO to enforce rules subjectively, based on the needs and context of individual communities. For the most part, inspectors lived in the communities they regulated and provided insight and context for any range of activities or complaints that reached the central administration. Concerned with social order, the LCBO created and administered regulations that tapped deep into the heart of the nation-building project. As Philip Corrigan and Derek Sayer demonstrate, a key process in nation building is the normalization and naturalization of specific cultural presumptions and values.[17] This process renders other values *ab*normal and *un*natural. Liquor control aimed at controlling behavior of drinkers and the drinking environment, normalizing certain activities based on a fuzzy vision of social order that we might define as loosely bourgeois, while marginalizing other behaviors that veered from that norm and that, while they were often associated with working-class socialization, were certainly not limited to working-class establishments. In its control project, liquor regulation drew on notions of "self" and "other." These highly subjective ideals were never clearly stated; except for a few passages prohibiting "drunkards, gamblers or idlers" from beverage rooms, the LCA did not define a good drinker and a bad drinker.[18] That was left to the individuals enforcing the law.

Usually scholars define the "other" in terms of race, gender, or class, but it can be expanded to include less visible, but often more significant, values and differences. Without a doubt the board's officials employed notions of class, race, and gender in their analyses. Single women drinking with men in bars were morally suspect. Non-Anglo hotel proprietors needed to be watched carefully for "un-British" activities, including anarchism, communism, and during the war, Nazism or Fascism. Hotels and clubs catering to the working man had to be scrutinized more closely (though at times certain standards of cleanliness might be less vigorously enforced) than were the establishments catering to elite clientele. Yet in the nation-building project, nationality itself could be a defining characteristic. William Katerberg suggests that nativism was essentially the same thing in Canada and the United States: an act of ethnic exclusion and white supremacy.[19] Yet such characterizations ignore perceived differences between racially similar groups. As Linda Colley argues, identity among racially homogeneous people was pliable. After the British conquered French North America, the leaders of the Thirteen Colonies no longer saw themselves as British in contrast to the French "other."[20] The British, racially identical to Americans, now occupied the role of "other": a stereotype against which national value and sense of self is measured. Colley describes identity formation as deciding "who we are by reference to who and what we are not."[21] So, just as a woman in a bar, or a working-class man, or an ethnic minority might require more scrutiny than Anglo, middle-class men, so too did another group: Americans.

In the minds of borderlanders and key members of the LCBO the American drink tourist, and indeed Americans themselves, occupied the role of "the other" within the discourse of liquor regulation in Ontario. This "other" was morally suspect and therefore potentially dangerous to the social order of the province. Although the political and economic situation changed significantly from 1927 to 1945, the notion of the American as a distinct "other" with specific differences persisted. For the six years from 1927 to 1933, after which the Eighteenth Amendment was repealed by the Twenty-first, the Niagara and Detroit rivers were all that was stopping Americans from rushing across the border to satisfy their state-proscribed thirst. Then, after 1933, the border states became more liberal with respect to drinking laws. As a result, traveling Americans held a different set of expectations of the drinking environment they would patronize. These expectations, combined with Ontarians' perceptions of the United States as affluent but decadent, and heightened by the economic Depression of the 1930s, all combined to strengthen the perception of the American as a person distinctly different from the Canadian, and one of whom good Canadians should be wary. Yet, as Marcel Martel and Holly Karibo also discuss in this collection, the specter of the American in Canada was a complex one; people with various financial and social interests viewed their influence on the border in radically different ways. To beverage room owners, they were the source of much potential income, but also people who could lead the proprietor into temptation. To the LCBO and individuals complaining about the activities in certain beverage rooms, they were less law abiding, less morally controlled, and brought demands that could challenge the social order. They were certainly un-British. All of these were character traits that were contrary to the values on which the LCBO based its activities.

From the LCBO's inception, its members (local inspectors, central office staff, and commissioners) recognized the potential effect US Prohibition could have on the social fabric of Ontario. Reacting to concerns that American tourists would flood the border in search of the coveted water of life, in 1927 the board's first chief commissioner, D. B. Hanna, insisted that "people who come across the line for the purpose of indulging in 'a blow-out' will be disappointed."[22] And, of course, Americans came to Canada to drink. When the first liquor store opened in Niagara Falls, the second person to purchase liquor, a bottle of Old Crow Bourbon, was Joseph Powers, a steeplejack contractor from Cleveland, Ohio, more than two hundred miles away.[23] Moreover, one month after liquor stores opened in the province, Canada celebrated its sixtieth anniversary of Confederation on Friday, July 1, and the United States celebrated Independence Day on Monday, July 4. As many expected, it was a long, boozy weekend, with the newspapers reporting stories of rowdiness, car accidents, and other problems they associated with liquor consumption and the influx of thirsty Americans. It did not help that the Peace Bridge in Fort Erie Ontario had just opened, further facilitating the influx of Americans to the province.[24]

Yet the Liquor Control Act created a new income for the government, and the benefits of increased sale to Americans were not ignored. In its first report to the provincial legislature, the LCBO recognized its contradictory mandate in one telling sentence: "Ontario must not be made a beer garden for non-resident groups; at the same time the Board welcomes to Ontario and desires to give service to legitimate tourists and travellers from the United States and elsewhere."[25] Indeed, the proximity to the United States, and its thirsty population, could be a boon. As table 7.1 and table 7.2 indicate, the population of these Canadian border communities was a fraction of their neighbors' across the rivers. While it offered promise of economic success, such a large population might also place considerable pressure on the proprietors of beverage rooms to bend the rules to make a buck.

In the correspondence of the LCBO, hotel proprietors often made the case that they were hoping to bring American money into the province, but before the beginning of the Second World War these arguments generally had little positive impact, and indeed could be a basis for the board to distrust the motives of the applicant. Prior to 1933, the concern was to lure

Table 7.1 Population of US and Canadian Border Communities

	1920	1930	1940
Detroit	993,678	1,568,662	1,623,452
Buffalo	506,775	573,076	575,901
Niagara Falls, NY	50,760	75,460	78,029
Essex	102,757	159,780	174,230
Lincoln	48,625	54,199	65,066
Welland	66,668	82,731	93,836

Table 7.2 Border Communities Compared

	1920	1930	1940
Detroit	993,678	1568,662	1,623,452
Essex	102,757	159,780	174,230
Population of Essex as percent of Detroit	10.34%	10.19%	10.73%
Buffalo & Niagara Falls, NY	557,535	648,536	653,930
Niagara region	115,293	136,930	158,902
Population of Niagara region as percent of New York communities	20.68%	21.11%	24.30%

Americans into Canada. In 1928, an application from Windsor was denied because the hotel was close to the "Detroit Ferry Dock" and the previous owners had hoped that their hotel "would become a popular resort for Detroit people coming over as tourists, taking such rooms as guests and having liquor therein."[26] In 1932 Nellie McNamara was fined a hundred dollars and costs for advertising in a tourist guide that her hotel, the Ambassador Hotel in Windsor, sold "ale and beer" without noting that it was "light." The implication was that she was aiming such advertisements at thirsty Americans.[27] After 1933, the proprietors were more crucially interested in keeping people in the province. When arguing for permission to allow dancing in his dining room in 1937, Gordon Brisson, the proprietor of the Embassy Hotel in Port Dalhousie observed that "thousands of dollars are going to the American side," and he wanted to make his hotel "one of the finest places in . . . the Province."[28] Writing on behalf of his clients at Crystal Beach's Hebert's Hotel, barrister W. K. Brown noted that new customs regulations that required American tourists to remain in Canada for forty-eight hours before taking merchandise out of the country was hurting trade. He argued that by permitting Hebert's Hotel to have a year-round license, the board would permit the American visitors to remain longer and spend more money. He also noted that the hotel would cater to Americans who came to Canada in the winter time for "winter sports, such as ski-ing [*sic*], and snow-shoeing."[29] In spite of the Ontario government's growing interest in fostering tourism during the Depression and the board's own assertions that it facilitated tourism, these requests were unsuccessful.[30]

When directing its regulatory efforts to the border communities, the LCBO, then, was in an unenviable position. Its political bosses wanted to increase American tourism, the beverage room operators wanted to increase American customers, but the LCBO was charged with maintaining order, and the economic lure of increased tourism challenged that mandate. Its administrators were concerned about the potentially unreasonable and disruptive demands that American visitors would place on the hotel proprietors. Currying the favor of American visitors by bending the rules was not acceptable. Both before and after the passing of the Twenty-first Amendment and the enactment of the Liquor Control Act (1934), Ontario's beverage room proprietors saw the Americans as a viable source of quick income, while the LCBO continually challenged that impulse.

Prior to 1933, when Ontario was the more permissive polity, the board was concerned that Americans would come to the province in search of legal booze, thereby disrupting a (perceived) fragile but well-ordered social system. So the board looked at making sure that hotel owners did not fall into the trap set by the rampant thirst of liquor-hungry Yankees with a fist full of dollars. In 1929, W. S. Dingman, the director of permits, wrote the owners of the Pickwick Inn in Fort Erie, informing them that reports have been "latterly unfavourable, in that the manager's idea of a hotel seems to be largely to cater to drinking parties from the U.S and in consequence the place has been allowed to deteriorate."[31] When her application for a light beer license was investigated, the proprietor of the Sunset Inn in Essex said that the large quantity of liquor in her bedroom was for her friends who visit from Detroit.[32] General Inspector John Pitt recommended against a light beer license for the club house on Pelee Island because the place was "inhabited by Americans every summer" and had a reputation for considerable lawlessness.[33] In contrast, Mr. George Gulliver, the proprietor of the Ruthven Hotel, told the LCBO that he always sold only light beer, and "when Americans or anyone else comes in I always tell them it is light beer."[34] His insinuation was that Americans were the ones demanding the stronger stuff. He noted that he had experienced no problems so far.

Suspicions that American tourists would make questionable demands on hotel proprietors were not without foundation. One vivid example among many should suffice. In 1931, the proprietor of the Ravine Hotel in Essex County decided to try to circumvent the board's rules about public drinking of strong beer in order to attract conventions of Americans. The LCA before 1934 permitted visitors to purchase liquor to drink in the privacy of their hotel rooms, requiring them to purchase a visitor's liquor permit that was effective for thirty days. The Ravine Hotel's proprietor built a small three-room cabin near the main hotel, furnished it with a bar and several kegs and nine tourist permits. He then hosted a convention of Americans involved in the steel industry, suggesting that the three rooms could pass for the visitors "room" and the tourist permits were all that these visitors needed to drink as much as they wanted. The resulting chaos, reported by the Ontario Provincial Police (OPP) and complaining neighbours, included drunken joy rides along county roads that resulted in several accidents, including the death of a farmer's horse. The local OPP Inspector Elliott was incensed, arguing that the hotel simply did not have the sort of room to properly accommodate such large parties, and "I do not think that we should encourage or be a party to Americans coming over there for nothing more or less than a drinking bout."[35] After delivering a stern rebuke, the LCBO permitted the hotel to continue operating, with the express condition that such activities never happen again. The following year, 1932, the hotel hosted a convention from the Chrysler Corporation. Not surprisingly, it violated the same laws in the same way. What is surprising is that the proprietor was only severely reprimanded; he did not lose his license. It appears that no further problems ensued.[36]

The immediate effect of the end of American Prohibition on Ontario beverage rooms is difficult to discern, because it is complicated by the fact that a few months after the repeal of the Eighteenth Amendment Ontario expanded its liquor laws to permit stronger beer in beverage rooms. In spite of the new Liquor Control Act, from 1934 onward the bordering states were more permissive places to drink. Repeal, accompanied by a low rate of excise duty on domestic spirits and "the comparative unrestricted sale of alcoholic beverages in those States adjoining Ontario" increased problems of liquor law enforcement because now American liquor was being smuggled into Ontario.[37] The LCBO administration continued to be concerned that the American permissiveness (now clearly entrenched in state legislation) would not infect the well-ordered activities of the hotels that it licensed. With the bordering states permitting far more diverse activities in their drinking establishments, hotel proprietors in Ontario's border communities had to scramble both to draw in Americans and to keep Canadians at home.

Some of the board's concerns at the borders remained the same: they had to continue to curb the pressure of Americans' demands. In 1937, the proprietor of Fort Erie's Mather Arms Hotel applied for permission to have dancing in his dining room with the aim of catering to Americans. Inspector Wylie noted that "my experience of the conduct of over the river guests has been they have little disposition to observe the regulations of the [Liquor Control Act]."[38] Wylie was equally concerned about Crystal Beach, a resort town up the highway from Fort Erie that had a high proportion of American tourists and summer cottagers. He advised the board that it might be valuable to reinforce the rules at the beginning of each summer season, "in view of the American atmosphere that prevails at Crystal Beach and the possibilities of temptation to law infractions."[39] The proprietor of the Anglo-American Hotel in Fort Erie argued that since his was a border city, "many came across the river on Saturday and it was hard to make them believe they could not sing and have a good time, like they do on the American side of the river."[40] His argument fell on deaf ears. The proprietors of the Edgewater Inn, a persistently troublesome dance hall in Riverside, outside of Windsor, justified their sale of bottled beer on a Sunday by saying it was not sold to regular customers: "They were only accommodating their American friends," an unacceptable excuse in the board's opinion."[41] In contrast, Mrs. Emery of Emery's Corners outside of Windsor told the OPP in 1935 that "although they had many requests (especially from the American tourists) to sell beer on Sundays . . . they always followed the rules."[42] Here resisting the temptations of American tourist money was held out as an indicator of the proprietor's virtue.

In postrepeal Ontario, however, an additional concern was to keep impressionable Canadians from going to the United States to drink. Here the board and the proprietors agreed, though for different reasons. Proprietors argued that they wanted to keep Canadian money in Canada, while the board wanted to keep Canadians out of the perceived morass of degradation that they imagined could be found across the line. For example, James Briand, proprietor of the Venetian Hotel in Niagara Falls argued that he should be given permission to allow dancing in his dining room by noting that his clientele is made up of "the younger generation, and if they cannot indulge in dancing while partaking of their meals they will go to the American side and patronize hotels there."[43] U. G. Reaume, the inspector for Essex County, observed a similar problem of proximity to the United States when he reported that "there are a certain number of young people who are anxious for dancing and if it is not provided here they will, naturally, cross to Detroit where dancing is allowed in road houses [and] beer parlours up to two o'clock in the morning. It is a real situation here."[44]

Reaume's reference to road houses and beer parlors and the lateness of the hour at which the younger generation was allowed to drink (in Ontario all drinking had to stop by midnight, and some municipalities legislated earlier closing times), suggests that by being a little more flexible, the board would avoid an exodus of impressionable youth into the morass of immorality across the Detroit River. While it is possible that these arguments were economic in nature, it seems more likely, given the emphasis on youth, that the writers were concerned for the morality of young Canadians who ventured across the line.

The pressures from Americans involved more than just drinking; the appeal of the drinking establishment, represented in the stereotype of the pre-Prohibition saloon, involved associated activities of variously questionable morality. Some saw the American influence as central to this pressure. Responding to the board's directive that a slot machine had to be removed from his hotel, the proprietor of Niagara Falls' Maple Leaf Hotel explained "our American trade look[s] for a little amusement."[45] The board and many municipalities outlawed such devices, and hotel owners often expressed surprise that their machines were illegal. More often, however, the amusement sought by American visitors was dancing. While beverage rooms were not permitted to have music or entertainment of any kind, the board did allow proprietors to play background music in the dining rooms, which it emphasized needed to be "incidental" to the dining "and must not be used as a means of drawing trade."[46] Hotel proprietors quickly sought to exploit this apparent loophole, introducing small orchestras, nickelodeons, or simply a Victrola, to entertain their guests. The logical progression was to permit dancing. In the eyes of LCBO bureaucrats, this was a slippery slope. Yet the pressure from proprietors was intense, and eventually, recognizing the problem was not going to go away, the LCBO acceded to permit "dine and dance arrangements" under heavily restricted conditions, in establishments they determined to be most conducive to properly carrying out such activities.

The board's guidelines around dinner dances reinforced the idea that dining rooms were to be primarily for dining. A standard memo sent to proprietors to whom the board granted the "dine and dance" privilege stipulated that meals had to cost at least twenty-five cents; patrons had to be given a "food check," which would "be considered proof that [the guest] is entitled to utilize the privileges of the dining room, and to dance." The memo concluded by stating that "none other than bona-fide Dining Room patrons be allowed the privilege of dancing on the premises."[47] To reinforce the rules, Deputy Chief Commissioner Arnold Smith traveled to Windsor in 1935 to explain to local hotel owners the specific conditions they would permit around dancing in dining rooms. In spite of these board activities, and of persistent vigilance on the part of inspectors, proprietors continued to perpetuate many violations, modifications, and innovations on the dine-and-dance system. As indicated in the evidence above, a number of these transgressions were seen as the result of the pressures of the American guests.

Americans were associated with any number of potential misdemeanours. At Spain's Hotel in Fort Erie, described as serving "the toughest element" in the city, Inspector Wylie observed that the proprietor, an American, made little effort to enforce the board's rules, and that he "possibly has an American idea as to enforcement of law."[48] Several times inspectors indicated that they became suspicious when they arrived at a hotel and saw a large number of American license plates on the cars out front, because they could indicate immoral activities going on inside. It was not just that there were cars; the inspectors clearly indicated it was Americans that were the main problem. Similarly, in 1941 a correspondent complained of "a certain [moral] cloudiness" around the proprietor of the Edgewater Hotel in Riverside: "Why should she bring three blonde girls from Detroit to help on busy nights. Why does she not employ Canadian girls?"[49] The insinuation is that Canadian girls are acceptable, but blonde girls from Detroit were bad. The writer further notes that among the many violations of this hotel, the proprietor had "informed her doorman on no account to turn American tourists away on Sundays."[50] Serving beer and wine on Sunday was prohibited, but again the implication is that the American tourists are particularly dangerous. When the Willow Beach Hotel in Essex was raided by the Ontario Provincial Police, the constable found "five men and two women consuming beer. . . . The two women were girls, who resided in the city of Detroit, one of whom was eighteen years of age and the other nineteen."[51] Again, the inference was that the young Detroit women, be they underaged drinkers or "blonde girls," were morally questionable. Whether cars with American license plates, American girls in the beverage room, or simply American tourists, the mere presence of Americans suggested something unsavory was going on.

Similarly, the permeable border brought questionable American entertainment to Ontario. In 1937 Mrs. J. S. wrote to complain about the Arcade Hotel's employment of a group of American entertainers called "the Happy Hour Club" from Detroit. "Their dancing and singing is disgusting and is unworthy of being tolerated in any licensed hotel. I personally enjoy good clean entertainment but feel that such entertainment [as that] . . . should not be allowed. Also, why should American entertainers be allowed in our

Canadian Hotels?"[52] She was not alone. Inspector Wylie entered the Grand Trunk Hotel in Fort Erie and to his dismay found dancing and singing to the music of a piano, activities that were expressly forbidden. The proprietor of the hotel informed Wylie "that the conditions were due to the presence of a number of Americans who had staged a party."[53] In 1934, Chief Inspector John Pitt surveyed the state of hotels in Windsor and noted that "some are trying to emulate the American ideas with Music and entertainment."[54] Inspector Reaume reported in 1943 that the management of Windsor's upscale Prince Edward Hotel decided not to open the beverage room at all on Saturdays "so as to prevent fights, because on Saturdays many Americans cross over and sometimes cause trouble."[55] With Americans, then, came social disruption.

To the LCBO and wary borderlanders, Americans represented the dangerously seductive "other." The temptation to serve stronger liquor, the temptation to permit lascivious entertainment, the temptation to allow dancing in darkened rooms, the temptation for single men and women to mix and drink together, the temptation for social disorder, were often blamed on the presence of Americans. Onto this "other" were projected the negative qualities and tendencies attached to improper, socially disruptive drinking, the sorts of things that should be anathema to the proprietor of a well-run beverage room. Certainly, non-Americans could be troublesome, but observers often blamed transgressions on Americans; it is the idea that we (self) are okay but the problem is them (other). That is not to say that Americans were the single biggest threat, but they were the only identifiable social group consistently identified as problem makers. Beyond women (who had their own drinking space), ethnic minorities (many of whom had their own social clubs licensed by the board), and working men (many of whom were described as respectable), Americans were the group to watch.

Why did this perception exist? It might be sufficient to say that the "othering" of American drinkers was simply a representation of broader anti-Americanism in Canada. Certainly, during the Second World War some Americans' behavior was described as "un-British," but then again so were the activities of some Russians, Italians, and Hungarians. So a reductionist answer that explained this suspicion of American drinkers simply as a manifestation of British anti-Americanism, while tempting, is wholly inadequate. While the board and borderlanders who were complaining about hotels expressed suspicion of the American influence, proprietors, who were also usually native-born Canadians or naturalized British subjects, were doing their best to court American tourists. Commissioner Hanna's outstretched arms to American tourists in 1927 characterized a general sentiment that, simply put, American money was good. Indeed, during the Depression the Ontario government actively courted American tourists, to strengthen the economy of the province. Certainly if the government could do it, so could the hotel owners, right?

No. Herein lies the difference between government control and a wide-open system of sales: government control is expected to keep everyone honest. When we look at exceptions to the rule, the instances where Americans in Canada were welcomed or at least viewed as a positive and desirable element in the community, we see that they were *certain types* of Americans, at *certain times*. First, the board viewed favourably "high-class" patrons who acted the way the board wanted. For example, in 1938 Inspector Reaume noted that the Bellvue Hotel in Windsor "is enjoying a very fine business and [has] a very fine class of trade. A large percentage of its meals are to guests from Detroit."[56] Unlike the dancers in the dark in Port Dalhousie, these Americans were eating a proper meal, though they may also have enjoyed some dancing. A hotel that served a lot of meals was instantly elevated in the eyes of the board, because it was not simply courting the rowdy drink tourist. Similarly, Reaume explained that the Edgewater Inn's trade was mostly Americans, and the hotel "cater[s] to high class patrons and they specialize in high class meals."[57] Crystal Beach was similarly endowed with a high class of American clientele, notwithstanding the excursionists.

The second instance of acceptable Americans appears during the Second World War, when the importance of revenues from American tourists was connected to the war effort. Prior to 1939, hotel proprietors who argued during the Depression that they should be allowed to court American money usually found that their argument did not sway the board. In contrast, when war broke out the board's inspectors began to recognize the value of American money to the war effort. Courting the American dollar became a nationalistic effort to feed the economy of the nation at war, or at least to keep Canadian money at home. Niagara inspector Vern Buchanan argued on behalf of the proprietors of the Dwarf Village Inn, near Jordan, whose hotel was "a real attraction for American tourists . . . at a time when every effort is being made to attract American tourists to spend every dollar possible in this country."[58] When the owner of the steamship SS *Pelee*, which traveled from Sandusky, Ohio, through Pelee Island to Leamington, Ontario, asked for a beer and wine authority, Essex inspector Reaume agreed, noting that "the large percentage of customers would be American . . . we are making every effort to secure American money and this would be a good way to help the cause along."[59] American money was synonymous with helping the war effort.

Hotel proprietors who made similar arguments were generally more successful during the war than others had been earlier. Eva Bolus of Jordan's Dwarf Village Inn argued that her hope to expand and improve her hotel was a direct result of the Ontario government's publicity campaign to attract American tourists to the province.[60] As noted above, Inspector Buchanan seconded her arguments. The proprietor of Windsor's Bridge Avenue Inn asked for permission to allow dancing in the dining-room, noting that "we are losing so much good Canadian business . . . and we feel that at this time every bit of money should be spent in Canada."[61] This request was granted.[62] The proprietor of the respectable Royal Hotel in Niagara Falls asked to operate a music machine in his dining room in order to retain Canadian money "that otherwise would be lost to the Country" and to attract Americans who would "remain to spend money, chiefly foreign currency."[63] Other hotel proprietors made a similar request, with similar arguments, and were equally successful, but usually only during wartime.[64]

These exceptions to the morally corrosive American stereotype offer tantalizing suggestions of the reasons for the "othering" of Americans. Prior to the war, the LCBO saw Americans as dangerous because their high expectations and money would tempt proprietors to violate the regulations. "High-class" Americans, who came not just for drinking but also presumably to partake in other respectable activities, were beneficial. "High class" appears to be a euphemism indicating not just wealth but how that wealth was used — respectably, in bourgeois pursuits. But the American drink tourist, looking for a "blow-out," was a danger. The board insisted that individual profit must not become a priority. However, with the country at war, the influx of money was no longer simply a question of individual profit: it became linked to the national war effort. Money was no longer dirty, and the profit motive need not mean a challenge to core national values. The board still remained interested in regulation of behavior, but it seems to have been more willing to be flexible, if it meant drawing more American money in turn to support the war.

In both the instances of good Americans and those of bad, the salient quality is the very affluence of Americans. Not just money, but the temptation it caused, was the main concern of the LCBO. "High-class" American tourists stood in contrast to tourists whose money could corrupt the moral integrity of the province. Here American affluence could mean American decadence: the road houses and beer parlors in the United States suggested that. Decadence meant moral bankruptcy: as typified in immoral girls and the darkened dance hall. Moral bankruptcy, then, a contagious toxin, was a result of affluence: suggested in the proprietors' interest in breaking the rules to profit from attracting more American money. These images are persistent in the discourses that emerge from a close reading of the LCBO's documents.

Concern with American affluence corrupting Ontario's hotel proprietors informs our understanding of provincial liquor regulation's place in state building. The board's job was to modify behavior, to govern the retailers so that people would be forced to fit a certain type of conduct, the idealized conduct of a morally responsible Ontarian, the citizen-drinker. The LCBO was a biopolitical agent of normalization, viewing the behavior of a certain class of individuals to be correct, but not assuming that all members of that class, when liquored up, were going to act properly. The LCBO both permitted and restricted, altering the individual's perception of his or her body based on an often bourgeois notion of proper comportment and proper biophysical subjectivity. In this biopolitical, nation-building project, discourses of gender, class, and race/ethnicity were joined by a discourse of nationalism. Here the American "other" strikingly contrasted with the Canadian "self." This wariness of the affluent American constructed a distinct view of Americans as opposed to the ideal of Canadians, and of American influence as fundamentally corrupting. The Canadian emphasis of "peace, order and good government" contrasted with "life, liberty and [especially] the pursuit of happiness." As Adelman and Aron have noted, the consolidation of borders created new ideas of insiders (citizens) and outsiders (foreigners), and "the rights of citizens . . . were now allocated by the force of law monopolized by ever more consolidated and centralized public authority."[65] As one of the centralized public authorities, the work of the LCBO reinscribed ideas of worthy and unworthy individuals, with safe and dangerous tendencies, those to be protected, and those to be feared.

Typically, the notion of the "other" implies the negative characteristics that one group projects onto another and provides an idea of what the "in-group" saw as positive and negative traits. Here we see a blurring, in the words of correspondents to the board, of the tricky line between behaviors that were illegal but acceptable, what some label "licit," and those that were illegal and unacceptable (illicit). Licit activities of residents, warranting at best a slap on the wrist, might be reframed as socially dangerous illicit activities when undertaken by foreigners.[66] Central to the discourse of the American "other" was the notion of misdirected affluence. The image of the out-of-control drinker, who encouraged hotel proprietors to break the rules in search of economic prosperity, clashed with the belief in moderate drinking and an emphasis on social order. The board's concern with Americans crossing the line and spreading chaos indicates that Americans embodied, for the regulator, a serious social threat, caused by the very affluence into which the hotel proprietors wanted to tap (pardon the pun). This contrast in values, between moderation and excess, control and chaos, was reiterated by the images from American Prohibition. The daily newspapers saw stories of gangsters, rumrunners, and any number of unsavory activities across the line; these images remained part of the popular imagination long after 1934. The permeable, malleable border served to distinguish between the self and the other, but that "other" could too easily cross the border and infect the "self" with an un-Canadian toxin: social chaos. Conversely, the Canadian "self" could cross into the domain of the "other" with the same outcomes, facing disaster at the hands of the other. The metaphor of infection is quite apt since, as the growth in panic over transnational biopathogens illustrates, citizens returning from abroad can be carriers of infection, just as easily as can foreigners.

Yet what remains to be determined is whether this image of the corrupting American, which seems to have been strong in the everyday regulatory behavior of the LCBO's correspondence, was as influential over higher policy developments. On this issue we must be equivocal. Just as the LCBO had a bifurcated and often contradictory mandate, selling and controlling, so its relationship with the border was ambivalent. As noted earlier, in the first seven years of the LCBO's existence, while Prohibition continued across the border, the province benefited from a cross-border trade, and welcomed it, benefiting from the taxes on the trade. After December 1933 the illicit flow often went the other way, with Canadians heading to the United States to party. Nevertheless, the provincial government continued to benefit from the reopening of a massive wet market in the United States. So while Canadians traveled to the United States to tie one on, Canadian liquor flowed both to and in the United States. Although the LCBO's administrators, charged with the task of maintaining order, saw the proximity to the border as an additional challenge to its operations, we cannot conclude that the politicians viewed the border with such disdain. The American other was, after all, still a paying customer.

CHAPTER EIGHT

Selling Is More of a Habit than Using

Narcotraficante Lola la Chata and Her Threat to Civilization, 1930–1960

Elaine Carey

On April 27, 1945, Mexican president Manuel Ávila Camacho issued a presidential decree that waived constitutional guarantees in cases of narcotics trafficking and permitted the immediate detention of peddlers and smugglers in the Federal Penitentiary at Tres Marías without first being tried in the Mexican courts.[1] Moreover, he released a second decree to the minister of interior and to all police agencies throughout the country to arrest "public enemy number one": the infamous narcotics trafficker Lola la Chata.[2] In the United States, Federal Bureau of Narcotics (FBN) director Harry J. Anslinger received word from a "special employee" operating in Mexico about the pending arrest of this prominent criminal. Anslinger immediately passed this information on to the director of the Federal Bureau of Investigation (FBI), J. Edgar Hoover, as well as attachments that contained a history about la Chata, the results of her growing narcotics empire having become a concern for Mexican as well as US officials since the early 1930s.

Ávila Camacho's presidential decree followed by Anslinger's correspondence to Hoover highlighted the transnational threat of Lola la Chata's drug empire. She emerged as a dominant figure in the illicit narcotics trade during a time when women — particularly elite women of European descent — were portrayed as the victims of urban narcotics peddlers that allegedly swarmed to urban centers in the 1930s throughout the world. During the era of Lola la Chata, criminologists, policymakers, and international women's organizations tackled the emerging epidemic of narcotics

141

abuse — part of the international crime triad of white slavery (prostitution) and venereal disease — that victimized certain men and women and that threatened the nation on both sides of the border.[3] In this study, I situate La Chata as a representative and predecessor to the emerging popular culture manifestations of women in drug culture. From localized peddler to international trafficker, her role in the business of narcotics reveals that the trade offered just as many rewards to women as to men.[4] La Chata and women like her complicate the masculine constructions of the history of drugs. Her role disrupts the view that women always have been passive and naïve victims lured and tricked into drug trafficking by falling prey to the vices and whims of male peddlers.[5] She was not a victim, but rather an opportunist who became wealthy and well-respected in the informal economic and criminal underworld.

This study documents the thirty-year career of a female Mexican heroin peddler and trafficker and the efforts of police, government officials, and diplomats on both sides of the border to undermine her while using her to justify shifts in policy discourse. It is based on sources found predominantly in the United States, a fact that illustrates La Chata's transnational threat. Like her counterparts, whether male or female, La Chata threatened civilization since her involvement in illicit trade brought her wealth but also access to power. Although not a borderlander, she endangered Mexican and US societies since she ruptured the normative expectations of what it meant to be a woman and to be civilized by using limited and constrained forms of feminine power to become a transnational threat.[6] Like her mother before her, she used the space of the open street market — a feminine economic site — as the basis of her enterprise. She relied on her own familial relations and informal networks to circumnavigate structures of constraint placed on her because of her sex and class.[7] In turn, she, and her successors, repositioned the social reproduction and economic survival of the family within the illicit market. Moreover, she revealed her fluidity and flexibility when confronted with policy shifts as well as changes wrought by modernity. From her actions, she threatened Mexico by opening it to inspection and ridicule; Mexican officials found themselves mocked at international meetings. This scorn further translated into direct action whereby the FBN violated Mexico's national sovereignty by issuing demands and placing agents in the country.[8] Despite La Chata's threat and extension of influence, policymakers continued to view her femininity and her ethnicity as a potential site of weakness as they struggled to undermine her.

Selling Women: A Girl from La Merced

Lola la Chata — María Dolores Estévez Zuleta was born in 1906 and grew up in La Merced in Mexico City.[9] La Merced was known as a focus of danger that was notorious for its "quantity of thieves" and its poverty.[10] During La Chata's lifetime, La Merced grew due to an influx of migrants from the provinces and ever-increasing formal and informal economic activity.[11] It was, and continues to be, a place of stealing but also of marketing both legal and illegal commodities. Today, as in the early twentieth century, vendors plied crockery, food, clothing, live animals, and sex, but also lotions, potions, herbs, powder, spells, and other substances to help alleviate any human ailment. Young Estevez worked in her mother's food stall selling *chicharon* (pork rinds) and coffee. Later, her mother expanded to more lucrative markets: marijuana and morphine. At the age of thirteen, Estevez entered the trade working as her mother's mule running drugs from La Merced.

Young Lola and her mother were not unique to the buying and selling of marijuana. Women and men sold it in the streets for local consumption. Street-vending children, like Estevez, moved through the city with open and covered baskets that hid their wares (see fig. 8.1). The fact that parents induced their children to sell marijuana and other substances led to shock and outrage on both sides of the border.[12] Parents acculturated their own children into the life, ensuring not only that the practice of addiction but also selling passed from one generation to the next.[13]

Most likely, Estevez's work as a mule for her mother helped her to learn the local terrain of peddling, but she furthered her skills in part due to the Mexican Revolution. The chaos of war led to the migration of people in and around the nation. Estevez was no exception. Through her work as a mule in La Merced, she met Castro Ruiz Urquizo. With Ruiz, she went to Ciudad Juárez, where she learned the skills of transnational trafficking from one of the prominent trafficking families on the border.[14] Her time in Ciudad Juárez expanded her future career in both personal and professional ways. There, she gave birth to two daughters, Dolores and María Luisa.[15] Her daughters ultimately followed her into the trade, creating a business matriarchy, per se. Her education on the border ensured that her destiny did not remain localized in small-time peddling. Eventually, she made her way back to Mexico City, and like her mother, she too ran a stall that sold cheap lunches and that served as her legitimate business cover. From that stall in La Merced, Lola la Chata began to build her marijuana, morphine, and heroin empire in the 1920s.

Recent studies on the history of narcotics reveal that Mexico, particu-

Figure 8.1. A young man selling *carrujos* (bindles) of marijuana, ca. 1930. (Courtesy of México, DF, Placa de nitrocelulosa, Fototeca, Pachuca, Hidalgo, photo 70646 Casasola; reprinted in Ricardo Pérez, *Yerba, goma, y polvo: Drogas, ambientes, y policías en México, 1900–1940* [Ediciones Era, 1999], 26)

larly Baja California, had been a central transit port for opium destined for the United States beginning in the late 1800s and early 1900s.[16] The production of poppy in Mexico emerged with the arrival of a large Chinese population that settled in the Mexican states of Sinaloa and Sonora. Initially, the Mexican government viewed opium use and addiction as a problem unique to Chinese immigrants and bohemians. In 1917 Dr. J. M. Rodriguez proposed the creation of the Consejo de Salubridad General (Department of Public Health), and two years later the ministry focused on the abuse of alcohol, but also on the consumption of opium, marijuana, heroin, and cocaine, because the use of such substances was spreading across class and ethnic backgrounds.[17] In 1923, President Alvaro Obregón (1920–1924) prohibited the importation of opium (morphine and heroin) as well as cocaine. By 1925, President Plutarco Elías Calles (1924–1928) ordered the police department to arrest all users and dealers and deport foreigners engaged in the trade.[18] Despite those early efforts to stem the flow of drugs in and out of Mexico, Lola la Chata, operating in La Merced, became one of the people responsible for that growing accessibility to narcotics in the capital city.

La Chata went unnoticed for much of the 1920s, but in the late 1930s, she emerged in official documents in both the United States and Mexico. Her success, but also legal shifts, contributed to the growing interest of narcotic smugglers in the United States. In 1933, the Eighteenth Amendment to the US Constitution was overturned. With the end of Prohibition, the US government grew more concerned about another menace that was seeping across its borders from the south: narcotics.[19] US drug policy toward Mexico became more focused in the 1930s with the establishment of the Federal Bureau of Narcotics (FBN), housed in the Treasury Department in 1930.[20] Anslinger, the first director of the FBN, the predecessor to the Drug Enforcement Agency (DEA), became something of a celebrity spokesman on the decadence and decline of an America that was under attack from black, Latino, and Asian hordes who brought their vices to the teeming shores.[21] Anslinger could not, and did not attempt to, understand the Mexican view of narcotics or its efforts to stem the flow of narcotics trafficking and addiction.

In Mexico, with the end of the Revolution, the government began to act on its concerns about the rise of narcotics abuse in the cities. Like Anslinger, Mexican officials became increasingly concerned about the vices of foreigners, particularly Chinese immigrants, who were perceived as a threat to the nation.[22] The stereotype of Chinese as responsible for the increase in drug trafficking relied on xenophobic and femininized deviant discourses that painted them as a danger to the Mexican nation, very similar to those same arguments developed in the United States.[23] Beginning in the late 1800s, Mexican officials organized campaigns in northern states to boycott Chinese businesses, control intermarriage, and press for anti-Chinese legislation. Suspected ties to narcotics trafficking further fed anti-Chinese sentiment.

Despite the creation of a public enemy responsible for the introduction of opium and blamed for the rise in drug trafficking, by the 1930s, the chief of the Alcohol and Narcotics Service of the Department of Health, Dr. Leopoldo Salazar Viniegra (1938–39), realized that drug addiction and peddling were no longer minor problems associated exclusively among the Chinese, students, bohemians, and sailors. In 1938, Salazar published the results of a fourteen-year study on marijuana use. In "El mito de la marijuana" (The Myth of Marijuana) he argued that marijuana was less dangerous than tobacco, and he claimed that only in the United States did it provoke crime.[24] Concluding, he suggested that drug addicts should receive treatment rather than be treated as criminals.[25] A medical doctor rather than a criminologist, Salazar viewed addiction from a medical perspective. In turn, he viewed the peddler as the criminal rather than the addict.

Despite his differences with Anslinger over addiction, Salazar considered peddling and smuggling as part of a growing crisis that threatened the nation and complicated its relations with the United States.[26] Consequently, in the late 1930s and early 1940s, La Chata's growing success brought her unwanted attention from officials on both sides of the border that had potentially damaging repercussions on her business.

In Mexico City and the provinces, La Chata's mules covertly moved her heroin in little packets with religious stamps on the front or in the bases of yoyos. La Chata built an empire in the best way she knew how and one of the few ways open to women: through familial and sexual connections.[27] She married an ex-police officer, Enrique Jaramillo, whose auto mechanics shop served as a distribution center and whose police contacts provided invaluable networks. Although they were rumored to have allegedly divorced to suppress criticism, her "marriage" into the police force ensured other alliances with police, bureaucrats, and politicians whom she was able to pay for information and protection.[28]

Her relationship with Jaramillo contributed to her business, but Mexican and US authorities recognized him as a successful trafficker. Despite her sexual and familial alliances, La Chata's power made her unique compared to other women in the trade.[29] Both Anslinger and Salazar saw her as an equal if not superior trafficker and dealer to Jaramillo. Although both studied and analyzed her relationship to Jaramillo and other men in the criminal family, both drug warriors recognized her as a primary threat.

Despite her widely acknowledged ties to those in power, police and government officials arrested and imprisoned Lola la Chata seven times from 1934 to 1945. Whether in Lecumberri, Cárcel de Mujeres, or Islas Marías, she endured her prison terms in style. She maintained her own servants while in prison, and a woman came once a month to do her hair. Similar to Pablo Escobar, she hosted numerous visitors to the prison, many of whom asked for favors. Like any other "Godfather," she offered advice, assistance, and help to those in need. Like other prisoners in the penal colony Islas Marías, La Chata received conjugal visits, and her daughters visited her for extended periods of time. Differing from her fellow prisoners, she was reputed to have built a hotel and an airplane landing path so her daughters would find their visits easy and comfortable.

Figure 8.2. La Prensa coverage of La Chata's arrest. She is on the left in a *reboza*. The headline reads: "The End of Drug Trafficking in Mexico."

In 1957, police arrested Lola la Chata for the last time as she was pro-cessing heroin in her home.[30] Described in the press as a "famous inter-national narcotic trafficker," she had been captured after eluding police for two years. The raid took place in the early morning. She was arrested with her "cohort Luis Oaxaca Jaramillo" and ten servants described as her agents. In the search of her mansion, investigators found 29,000,000 pesos ($9,000, the equivalent of $72,300.00 in 2011) in cash, expensive jewelry, equipment, as well as firearms and ammunition. In an interview with the press while in jail, she made one statement, "Yes, I'll talk, but first question all the police agencies. . . . All they wanted to do was arrest me and get me out of the way. However, don't implicate any more innocent people. I am the only responsible one for narcotics traffic and business that I established."[31] Accepting the responsibility, she made a strategic — if not honorable — move of disassociating her deputies and agents from the crime. She challenged bourgeois concepts of the patriarchal family where the men dominated and protected the women. Once found guilty and sent back to Cárcel de Mujeres, she died in September 1959 of coronary failure. Despite her arrests, an estimated five hundred people, one-third of whom were rumored to be police, attended her funeral.

Folk Hero: Lola la Chata and Her Threat to Civilization

La Chata's success came during a time when officials in the United States and Mexico became increasingly worried about the impact of narcotics on national goals and on the dangers of narcotics and the behaviors, especially sexual lasciviousness, that such substances allegedly caused. Her reach extended from Mexico to Canada, exceeding those of many other narcotic smugglers, and her power proved effective in combating those who fought to undermine her.

In 1944, S. J. Kennedy, treasury representative in charge, requested information from Mexican officials about narcotics smugglers operating in Mexico. Mexican authorities informed Kennedy about one of La Chata's laboratories that also highlighted her connections to powerful men and her reach in Mexico and beyond. The lab operated in the basement of the Hotel Imperial in the northern industrial city of Monterrey. La Chata, Jaramillo, and Enrique Escudero, all successful traffickers, held interests in the lab, but so too did Gaston Vaca Cordella, the former chief of Sanitary Police and a local politician.[32]

In the same year that Ávila Camacho issued the presidential decree regarding drug traffickers and demanded the arrest of La Chata, Anslinger wrote to the Canadian chief of the Narcotics Division, Colonel C.H.L. Sharman, about her case.[33] When Mexican authorities issued an arrest warrant for La Chata, Anslinger warned Sharman that La Chata and Escudero would be traveling to Canada by car to transport heroin.[34] Ultimately she was arrested in a hideout in Mexico City. Despite her arrest, she fought the presidential decree. Special Employee Peña noted that US Treasury officials and Mexican officials were closely observing who supported La Chata. Peña wrote: "A close watch was kept by agents of the Federal Narcotics Police of the Department of Health and Assistance and by this office over people who tried to help her by using their influence with the authorities. This was done in order to keep check on possible connections between this subject and any prominent Mexicans who might have some interest in the illicit traffic of narcotics."[35]

Both Anslinger's memo to Sharman and Peña's letter to US Customs revealed the complexity of power that surrounded La Chata. Anslinger saw her threat as extending beyond her stronghold in Mexico City. The evidence of her laboratories throughout Mexico and in states that bordered the United States further contributed to the fear of her enterprises. As she emerged from a successful local peddler to a transnational trafficker, Peña acknowledged that she had powerful friends that facilitated her business. In 1945, Mexican officials did send La Chata to Islas Marías. Within a few years after her arrival to the island prison, however, she received a medical transfer that brought her back to Mexico City where she continued peddling.

Although Anslinger acknowledged that women profited from the sale of narcotics, he saw certain ones as vulnerable and in need of protection from dope dealers and addicts. Women served the social reproduction of the civilization. They acculturated the children into the family, the community, and nation through their child-bearing, mothering, and socializing of their young. Addicts pursued their own self-interest at the expense of their children and families. Their individual pursuits to feed their addiction and criminality disrupted their families, their communities, and the nation. Anslinger, who held racist and elitist discursive views of addiction as foreign and criminal, became particularly concerned about drug use and prostitution when he came across rich, Westchester County (New York) matrons who shuffled between their country club homes to Harlem for a fix. He further concocted an image for the public of a young "flaxen-haired eighteen year old girl sprawled nude and unconscious on a Harlem apartment tenement floor after selling herself to a collection of customers throughout the afternoon, in exchange for a heroin shot in the arm."[36] Once addicts, these especially vulnerable and weak women fell into the grip of prostitution, where these housewives and teenagers were prone to engage in miscegenation.[37]

According to Anslinger, narcotics abuse was one of the three horsemen of the apocalypse. The white suburban addict was to be pitied for her weakness. How could she, a lowly woman, stand against the communist, "oriental," African, and/or "Central American" conspiracy against the United States that plagued not just women as victims, but also men? In public, Anslinger liked to elaborate on the potential sexual connection between suburbanites and urbanites that seemed to cast women as victims. However, he recognized that women sold narcotics, but this too took on a sensational aspect that endangered "real" Americans.[38] When he addressed the Latin American woman in the trade, he cast her as the stereotypical Latina firecracker. According to Anslinger, with a sexy swish of her hips and a slip of a packet packed with heroin, a Latina dealer could intoxicate any good (white) American man with her womanly ways and her drugs.[39]

Despite the sexuality of the Latina that Anslinger used to titillate his audiences in the United States, Lola la Chata complicated his narrative of deviancy. In 1945 when Anslinger received a report about La Chata's attempt to flee to Canada, he circulated a report that described Lola la Chata as short, fat (180 pounds), with a "Negroid" complexion and features, and with gold-gapped teeth.[40] By describing her as "Negroid," Anslinger highlighted her danger that differentiated her from other Mexican peddlers and traffickers who many times were listed in documents as "white" or with a "dark complexion" by agents operating in Mexico.

In photos published in the Mexican press after her arrests, La Chata did not smile to reveal her gold-cap teeth, and she demurely covered her head in a silk *reboza* (see fig. 8.2). During her trials, she reiterated her Catholicism and devotion to good works for the poor. For Anslinger, who enjoyed titillating the crowds that came to hear him speak on the perils of drugs and foreigners who turned good men and women into addicts, a short, squat, religious, and grandmotherly figure seemed an unlikely seducer of men. Perhaps that was what made her all the more dangerous.

La Chata obviously was not a beauty, but her appearance drew considerable attention by men in positions of authority on both sides of the border.[41] Salazar wrote an open letter in 1938 to Lola la Chata and those who protected her. Opening the letter to the "White Lady" he seized on the concepts of beauty as an aspect of a culture of restraint. He wrote:

> I was certain that you, Chata, I mean, Lola were a young, beautiful, and seductive woman, and really I was worried about the time you would finally be brought to me and would try your wiles upon me in an effort to obtain my complicity because, and I tell you this very confidentially, I am susceptible to feminine charms. Later, I discovered — and you need not worry about me now — that you were not born under the sign of Venus

and further that the years, the sale of quick lunches, the drug traffic, police persecution — of which it must in all honor be stated has always been
cordial and affectionate — had inexorably rounded your figure.[42]

Both Anslinger and Salazar saw Lola la Chata's body and physical at-
tributes as a site of danger and obsession.[43] Her weight represented her
rejection of the feminine addict — the image of the heroin and morphine
habitué that was featured in women's magazine and soft pornography for
the elite classes. Her rounded body and face undermined the assumption
of authorities that she was a heroin addict — a fact she continually denied.
Her weight and ethnicity ensured she was no target for sympathy from
men such as Anslinger. Physically, she revealed that she was beyond a culture of constraint. Her physical appearance reflected her lack of control:
her gold-capped teeth displayed her vulgarity, while her chosen profession
depicted her immorality. She had constructed her own concepts of beauty
that would have been completely alien to Anslinger, though Salazar must
have been more accustomed to these representations.

For Anslinger, his description of her as "Negroid" reflected his supposi-
tions of her sexuality, her morality, and her potential threat. She embodied
the sexually lascivious black body that had to be restrained, but she operated and moved about freely.[44] La Chata's "blackness" further underlined her
deviancy and her threat to the United States. For Anslinger, her purported
ethnicity and her growing success further reinforced his view of the dangers
of heroin and the inability of Mexican authorities to control the growing
drug problem. In a memo to Henry Morgenthau, secretary of treasury, about
heroin and the need for aggressive control of the substance, Anslinger wrote:

> The dangerous nature of heroin from the social point of view overshad-
> ows its therapeutic importance; that the social dangers of heroin arise
> from the great reputation this substance possesses among drug addicts
> and from the illicit traffic which has arisen, its habit forming properties
> being much worse than those of other habit-forming narcotics; and that
> the effect of heroin is, in the main, to produce a change in personality
> characterized by utter disregard for the conventions and morals of civili-
> zation which progresses to mental and moral degeneration.[45]

Anslinger's fears regarding the narcotics trade and addiction combined
with his thoughts of Mexican justice grew to an obsession with a desire to
control not only smugglers but also those responsible for their capture. Although Mexican authorities lobbied the legislature to strengthen the penal
laws dealing with narcotics traffickers and peddlers, developed programs to

treat addiction, and sought to stem the flow of drugs in and out of Mexico, US officials constantly questioned Mexican assertions of success in the war on narcotics.[46]

To Anslinger, a woman like La Chata and others involved in the trade remained a menace to the United States. In his eyes, Mexican officials were weak when it came to dealing with traffickers and addicts. The FBN, in its attempt to control men and women like La Chata, continually issued demands that threatened Mexican nationalism and sovereignty. For instance, in 1947 the FBN requested a list of the names of all known traffickers in Mexico. Mexicans replied that they could not turn over the names of people who were under surveillance but could provide names of those that had been convicted of trafficking. One of which was Lola la Chata.[47] The list provided to the FBN by the Mexican authorities simply gave them information that they already knew. Thus Mexican authorities continually sought to outmaneuver Anslinger's efforts to undermine their own control.

In an attempt to undermine the Mexican narcotics trade, Salazar took a very different approach than Anslinger when engaging Lola la Chata. In his "Open Letter to the White Lady," Salazar recognized that her chosen profession may have contributed to her rounded figure, but he did not discuss her complexion or ethnicity. But, like Anslinger, Salazar viewed her as dangerous because of her physical rejection of elite masculine concepts of feminine beauty, morality, and restraint. Despite her trade and her wealth, she was neither the fallen woman nor the elite moral female crusader, which made her more threatening than the female addict to constructs of Mexican and US civilization.[48] Instead, she operated on the boundaries of cultural gendered expectations of both nations.

Although Anslinger and Salazar worried about the physical deviations from civilizing constraints, US Beat writer William S. Burroughs found Lola la Chata a fascinating character. Burroughs introduced one of Mexico's most infamous traffickers to US popular culture. Burroughs came to Mexico in 1949 to escape a narcotics charge in New Orleans. Accompanied by his wife and young son to the emerging leviathan of Mexico City, Burroughs, like other contemporary urban explorers, sought cheap drugs — and easy sex.[49] He found Mexico's ease with drug culture fascinating, though he — as well as other Beat writers — indeed misread the cultural meanings. While living in Mexico City, he became mesmerized by the infamous crime boss Lola la Chata.[50] As a character, she powers into his novels and short stories sometimes by the name of Lupe, Lupita, or Lola.[51] Burroughs specialists have questioned whether he actually met her or not, but his fascination with her continued for years.[52]

Unlike Salazar and Anslinger, Burroughs relished La Chata's deviations from constraint, and he found in these departures sources of power that were uniquely tied to the body. In *Cities of the Red Night*, Burroughs described a meeting between his protagonist Mr. Snide and Lola la Chata.[53] As Snide arrived at a warehouse owned by La Chata guarded by a "skull-face *pistolero*," he entered a room richly decorated like a "Mexican country estate." A feast had been prepared for the visitors: "platters of tamales and tacos, beans, rice, and guacamole, beers in tubs of ice, bottles of tequila, bowls of marijuana, and cigarette papers." He pointed out the table with the syringes and other "beverages" as well as the curtained booths for later encounters. Then his attention shifted to Lola. Burroughs wrote:

> Lola la Chata sits in a massive oak chair facing the door, three hundred pounds cut from the mountain rock of Mexico, her graciousness underlining her power. She extends a massive arm: "Ah Meester Snide . . . El Puerco Particular . . . the private pig," she shakes with laughter . . . And your handsome young assistants . . . " She shakes hands with Jim and Kiki, "You do well by yourself Meester Snide."
> "And you Lola . . . You are younger if anything . . . "
> She waves her hand to the table, "Please serve yourselves."[54]

Burroughs played homage to his dealer by admiring her power in the context of her body. In this setting, Burroughs described her as gracious because of her immensity in presence and power by elaborating on her massive figure and visibly displayed wealth. In the Beat subculture, he celebrated her deviancy as corporal and sexual. To Burroughs, she embodied a natural essence of Mexican culture; he described her as an Aztec earth-goddess who gave her special clients packets of heroin from between her massive breasts. Burroughs associated her breasts as a site that nurtured his addiction. She suckled her favorite clients to her, via a syringe. Her femininity and nurturing of her addicts was an integral part of her peddling. Similar to Anslinger, Burroughs's visions of her gender, but also her otherness, offered a potential site of weakness that led even junkies to consider the fragility of her power in the hopes of conquering her heroin franchise.

Like Burroughs, Salazar recognized La Chata's power and influence. Both acknowledged that she knew the desires and needs of her clients. Like any good business woman, she provided a hook — a day where all could be had for free, even for the police.[55] In examining her business acumen, Salazar recognized her intelligence and her hard work. He confessed:

This, I must tell you for your own satisfaction has not diminished my admiration for you. I consider you to be a perfect product of our time [mean and age]. For you, a drug addict is merely a good customer and nothing more. For me, he is an unhappy person dragged in the dust by civilization. As it is, you as a drug dealer have had better luck that those of us who are entrusted with incorporating the addicts into active, social, and living (people). You have accomplished a marvel — and this is a real compliment to your talent and ability — of knowing how to maintain your position and gaining always goodwill of the whole police force. You are a dispenser of graft, a national emblem. No one ever resists your bribes which, according to what I am told are very grand indeed. One thing is surely clearer, you, old in the custom know how the business can produce even if sometimes the demands are heavy and excessive, with a little more bicarbonate in the heroin and a little more pressure on the client, you are able to make ends meet.

In addition to your business ability, you have a very acute sense of psychology, you know the "when" the "how" and the "how much" of the bribe to be given; you know how to tell if the person involved has his teeth sharpened or not.[56]

Salazar's ironic admiration for her ability to know the needs of her clients as well as how to protect herself established that Lola la Chata embodied the portrait of a peddler who had matured in the highly competitive and politicized informal economic market.[57] She created a plague of addicts that Salazar struggled to help against insurmountable odds. Like many prostitutes and street vendors, she was an uneducated mestiza from an impoverished family and had few options in life. For many women in these circumstances, the future was limited to being street vendors, waitresses, maids, nannies, prostitutes, or traffickers. Having few opportunities available because of her class and ethnicity, she took those gendered constraints and developed them into a skill that was private but evolved into a public threat.[58] Narcotics abuse was and is solitary and private in contrast to the public nature of drinking that takes place in the cantina, bar, or pub.[59] Thus opium and its derivatives appealed to women of the late nineteenth and early twentieth century. In Mexico, habitués, elite female opium addicts, appeared as beautiful, lounging on satin pillows, with billowy smoke framing their perfectly made-up faces (see fig. 8.3). Their threat was private; they neglected their feminine duties of child rearing, sexually satisfying their husbands, preparing food, and maintaining the home. Their beauty may have stayed intact, but their addiction dis-

Figure 8.3. A Mexican narcotics habitué, ca. 1930. (Courtesy of México, DF, Casasola, Placa de nitrocelulosa, Fototeca, Pachuca, Hidalgo. Reprinted in Ricardo Pérez, *Yerba, goma, y polvo: Drogas, ambientes, y policías en México, 1900–1940* [Ediciones Era, 1999], 51)

Figure 8.4. Drunken women on a Mexico City street, ca. 1925. (Photographed by Tina Modotti. Courtesy of México, DF, Placa de nitrocelulosa, Fototeca, Pachuca, Hidalgo, Photo 35297 Casasola. Reprinted in Ricardo Pérez, *Yerba, goma, y polvo: Drogas, ambientes, y policías en México, 1900–1940* [Ediciones Era, 1999], 36)

rupted their families. Families easily hid, explained, and dismissed these disturbances. Lowly and poor *borrachas* (female drunkards), on the other hand, evolved into public nuisances. Artists, writers, and social workers documented their public shame. Borrachas transgressed acceptable gender boundaries to drink in masculine spaces — bars, cantinas, or streets. Like the borracha, La Chata differed from the addict because she resituated the private location of women's lives and traditional work into the public realm.

Opium addiction as a feminized and private past tied to race and gender evolved into a public act when it was peddled and trafficked. The marketing and selling of items represented a common and acceptable historical act of women, except that women were not to enrich and empower themselves from those acts. La Chata used feminine skills as a location to build a powerful enterprise. Food vending corresponded to a private skill common to all women at the scale of in-home production. Once women marketed an item, it too became a public act that gave the potential for danger. In-home food production or street vending of food products denoted the systematic survival of people on the brink of a culture of poverty. Drug peddling, however, permitted certain people, such as La Chata, to break away from that poverty by moving into the public realm while maintaining private business practices. The illegality of heroin, and to a lesser degree marijuana, required that it was more discreetly marketed and used than alcohol. Peddlers subtly created networks of distribution for these items. Even the ability to bribe the police became a form of manipulation that was common to women and, as Salazar suggested, La Chata had escalated this skill to a fine art.

The private and informal selling of narcotics was conducive to Mexican women's historical work.[60] Lower-class people, particularly poor mestizas such as La Chata, struggled to break out of the culture of poverty against insurmountable odds. The legal system, the Ministry of Health, and the police sought to keep women like La Chata restrained and marginalized. Sexism and racism further ensured that she would not rise above her given lot. La Chata realized how fragile those restraints were. La Chata recognized that police, judges, and politicians — those responsible to maintain order and control — were just as easily bought as the junky in need of a fix.

In her own neighborhood, known as a place of thieves and where everything was for sale, addiction, prostitution, and crime reinforced one another as international women's organizations and policymakers feared. Like prostitutes throughout the world, Mexican prostitutes used mind-altering substances that enabled them to perform their jobs.[61] Thus, as food items are sold to the local community, La Chata found a local market for heroin and marijuana in and around La Merced, a basic element of a successful business. As Burroughs wrote about his folk hero, La Chata sold "heroin to pimps and thieves and whores."[62]

Her ability to create and maintain a local market for her drugs created a domestic front for Salazar in his combat against narcotics peddling and smuggling but also a place to study those problems associated with addiction. La Chata and other peddlers who rose to prominence undermined Salazar's attempts to paint Mexico's drug problems as something associated with a minor portion of the population that could be medically treated. In international meetings, Salazar portrayed Mexico's drug problems as localized in a few areas. At the League of Nations' Advisory Committee on Traffic in Opium and Other Dangerous Drugs, Salazar stated: "In Mexico, the problem of drug-addiction is of minor importance. It only exists in the capital and in the port cities, and a few larger cities."[63] While la Chata was based in Mexico City, Salazar's Open Letter published in 1938 demonstrated that her threat was more insidious than he presented at international meetings.

Salazar's attempts to combat narcotics revealed a growing recognition of the impact of technology and gender in the trade. Although La Chata used traditional gendered forms of influence and power to build her empire, her location in La Merced and her ties to quick lunches and feminine skills became a central point for Salazar to criticize her. Like Burroughs, he too suspected that her gender and naturalness contributed to some weakness. He saw her as evolving into a small-time peddler who was being outmuscled by others in the business. Times were changing and Salazar's 1938 open letter seeks to place women like La Chata as slipping into history. He noted that her deputies, many of them men, would continue in her name, but he also noted that the trade was modernizing. He stated:

You are in spite of your popularity a factor of little importance in the vast network of drug dealing; your stay in the Penitentiary would only greatly increase the traffic therein, without really affecting the traffic outside as you would leave your deputies and temporary substitutes in change. Moreover and above all, there are your colleagues who, while they do not sell quick lunches, have airplanes at their disposal and descend from the clouds with their infamous cargo.[64]

La Chata's top two deputies included her alleged husband Jaramillo and her rumored lover and accomplice Enrique Escudero Romano. Her relationships with men ensured that her business moved beyond the borders of La Merced. Jaramillo, a well-known trafficker in his own right, maintained contacts and laboratories in the provinces, as did Escudero.[65] Men offered her protection, but they also surrounded her since they had a vested interest in her survival and continuation. Yet she was not their dupe. Instead she constructed and developed a criminal enterprise that served men. That did not mean that there were not other men that hoped to wrestle her market away from her. As in any business, she faced stiff competition. Her lovers and police agents protected her — as Salazar was well-aware of — but she was also victimized by them.

While men provided protection and their alliances became her alliances, Salazar's letter focused on La Chata, not her deputies, as a source of contagion that demanded to be controlled. While she could be victimized, he did not see her as a victim. In the documents, her male associates were not the basis of power, but her underlings. If and when she went to jail, Salazar knew that her business would continue as it had and it did. Instead, Salazar sought a point of weakness based on gender and modernity. Thus, while he congratulated her on her business expertise despite its femininity, he also expressed that her time was coming to a close. Like the middle-age woman who gazes in the mirror and fears the loss of her beauty and sexual viability, Salazar played on this ancient theme by noting that traffickers employed more sophisticated use of technology. How could an illiterate mestiza compete? In other words, he inferred, La Chata's time was coming to an end.

In 1938, Salazar's gendered and technological assumptions about La Chata's marginality were more hope than reality. La Chata developed from a local peddler to international trafficker during a time when traffickers were becoming increasingly sophisticated in their use of technology and networks.[66] Moreover, she continued to sell heroin, morphine, and marijuana, whether in or out of prison, for almost another twenty years, which lead to a growing crisis between Mexican and US officials who attempted to arrest and imprison her. They did so many times. Even after the presidential decree in 1945, she successfully fought a long-term prison sentence and continued to traffic and peddle for another twelve years: a testament to her ability to maintain networks of powerful friends.

Lola la Chata and those women like her defy the contemporary images of *narcotraficantes*, although the role of women in the trade continues to shock, surprise, and titillate.[67] Like her mother before her, she, and many women of her background, knew buying, selling, and creating a market, whether for food, sex, or narcotics. Using those few spaces within the economy left open to them, women like La Chata resisted the limitations that had been constructed for her. Although a large cadre of men assisted her in her narcotics empire, Salazar, Anslinger, and even Ávila Camacho acknowledged that it was hers. Her physical presence, criminal mind, and manipulation fascinated the narcotics warriors. She embodied a danger and a threat to Mexican and US societies since she ruptured the expectations of what it meant to be a woman. She was not an addict, but a shrewd business woman who recognized the demand for her product. More dangerous than the addict, her ability to bribe and manipulate the laws and those entrusted to enforce them showcased her danger. Moreover, her success ensured that even when she was taken off the streets her empire, or one like hers, would continue whether by the women in her family, her syndicate, or her competitors. As Lola la Chata predicted, "Selling is more of a habit than using."[68]

CHAPTER NINE

Preventing the Invasion

LSD Use in Canada during the Sixties

Marcel Martel

In 1967, during a conference at the University of Toronto, Donald Webster, who was associated with the American Schizophrenia Foundation, stated that using lysergic acid diethylamide (LSD) was "something like eating or making love, but you [had] to experience it yourself." If his audience welcomed his statement, opponents of the nonmedical use of LSD vehemently opposed it. However, Webster cautioned them that "while drugs may be shocking to the Puritan, it is quite in keeping with the times."[1] By alluding to the new phenomenon of using LSD for recreational purposes, Webster added his voice to those who believed that the world had entered a new era where drugs were freely used and moral judgments on drug users belonged to the past.

Reports on the use of LSD triggered fear among individuals, parents, social organizations, and government institutions that dealt with young people. These fears led to reports that LSD crossed the boundaries of legitimate use because users, often as young as sixteen, were using this substance without any medical supervision. The list of social actors who intervened in the debate was impressive because it included parents, media, industry representatives, scientists, physicians, public health officers, and politicians. The public debate in Canada over LSD raised the question of who had the authority to define what constituted its legitimate and illegitimate use. On the latter point, and despite their differences in terms of ideology, financial and human resources, and ability to shape the views of others, all these social actors strongly believed that they had the right to intervene in the debate and disseminate their views.

Convinced that their social and political responsibilites conferred on them a certain authority and consequently a right to intervene in the debate and express their views, these individuals and groups called for government interventions, some even suggesting jail terms for those who used LSD for nonmedical reasons. There was a sense of urgency that became an episode of moral panic due to media coverage and statements by "concerned" parents, politicians, and other social agents. They all agreed that the phenomenon of LSD use for recreational purposes came from south of the border. At least that's what many in Canada believed based on news reports and views expressed by health officials, law enforcement officers, and media pundits. This assumption was not new since previous scares, triggered by nonmedical use of drugs, were based on the belief that these substances originated from outside Canada, often in the United States. Given their growing feeling that an invasion was underway, opponents of LSD use for nonmedical purposes declared that the US-Canada border was porous and called for the government to regulate the movement of the drug. If it was impossible to stop the phenomenon, at least the government should prevent it from spreading.

This chapter explores the role that the US-Canada border played in the debate over the regulation of LSD use in Canada, as well as how references to the United States impacted the debate. Even though several studies have been published on Canada-US political and economic relations, there are few studies on how the United States played a role in the development of the Canadian drug policy.[2] Looking at how a state asserts its control over its borders raises questions regarding the meaning of border, state sovereignty, and constraints imposed on state sovereignty when a state willingly signs bilateral and multilateral treaties and conventions.[3] In the case of drugs, the Canadian government signed several international conventions and saw its ability to design its drug policy constrained by these international obligations.[4] However, Canadian proponents and opponents of drug use had specific views on the border and the role of the state. Ideally the border could shield Canada from this invasion, but in practical terms, this was very difficult since the border was seamless. At the time, the US-Canada border, which is 5,525 miles long, was relatively easy to cross. Nevertheless, there was the belief that the state could exercise its sovereignty and implement a policy that would deal with the issue. When a consensus emerged on the need for regulations, it quickly disappeared when it came to defining the best approach to restricting LSD use in Canada, especially among youth.

This chapter is also a case study of one province in particular: Ontario. Although nonmedical use of LSD was a North American phenomenon, and every province came under pressure to regulate it, Ontario exercised its political authority within the limits set by the Canadian federal structure. Despite these limits, and unlike other provinces such as Alberta and British Columbia, the Ontario governement promoted solutions based on a mixture of education, health resources, and prevention.

The Invasion Is Coming:
The New Phenomenon of LSD for Personal Use

In his presentation to coroners in 1966, Dr. Beatty Cotnam, an official from the Ontario Ministry of the Attorney General, quoted the New York County Medical Society as saying that LSD was "the *most dangerous* of all the under-the-counter drugs available today." Although Cotnam had been silent in the previous year on the issue of LSD when addressing this audience, this time he devoted a third of his presentation to the drug. He insisted on the dangerous effects of this drug by insisting that "L.S.D. produces bizarre-psychic effects with extreme and distorted sensations of color, taste, sight and sound to the point where there is a complete breakaway from reality while still conscious." Furthermore, the drug had a "disastrous" impact on mental health since "anyone who takes even one '*trip*' never looks at life in the same manner again." Following the description of the terrible consequences of LSD use on a person's health, Cotnam asked why anyone would try this substance anyway. In answering his question, he did not hide his strong bias on this issue: "This is part of a sickness in our society today. Many people are taking all sorts of substances . . . to escape from reality and seek new adventures in the unknown." Although the habit of taking this drug had become very popular in the United States, but not yet in Canada, Cotnam warned his audience that they should not take comfort in this fact. In fact, he told them to brace themselves for the worst because he believed that the phenomenon of LSD use for nonmedical purposes would migrate north.[5]

By warning his audience that the LSD use phenomenon would migrate north, Cotnam, probably without knowing it, repeated arguments used in previous debates over drug use. For instance, the director of Canada's Food and Drug Directorate reacted to reports on the health dangers associated with Morning Glory seeds being used by youth in the United States and Mexico. He tried to take comfort in the fact that this practice was not occurring in Canada (but for how long this would continue he couldn't say).[6] One of the characteristics of the drug debate in Canada was the assumption made by numerous individuals and groups opposed to the nonmedical drug use that the drug problem was an imported phenomenon, an argument that was similar to those disseminated in the United States.[7] Although demands by members of the social reform movement, and physicians' concerns about the short- and long-term impact of drug use on a person's health, played a role in the creation of drug laws in Canada, race and age factors had an impact as well. At the beginning of the twentieth century, anti-Chinese racist sentiments fueled the campaign for harsh drug laws in an attempt to rid the country of opium — and ultimately of Chinese immigrants — which led to the criminalization of this substance. According to opponents of opium use, Chinese immigrants, some of whom came via the United States, who had been attracted to Canada by the gold rush and the construction of the railway in British Columbia at the end of the nineteenth century, introduced white Canadians to the substance. Therefore, state regulatory powers were required to prevent white Canadians from using the substance. When moral entrepreneurs targeted marijuana some years later, factors such as the role of Canadian bureaucrats and actions taken by states, notably the United States, in enrolling the international community in the drug war against marijuana had an impact on the criminalization of the possession, importation, and exportation of marijuana in Canada in 1923.[8] At the same time, we cannot exclude statements by Canadian individuals and groups who constructed the nonmedical use of marijuana as a terrible threat because blacks and other nonwhite Americans brought the practice of marijuana use to Canada. According to these worried Canadians, it was these ethnic groups who introduced the nonmedical use of these substances to white Canadians.

With the publication of news reports in the sixties on the popularity of LSD in the United States, some Canadians believed that the country was about to experience a new drug invasion, as it had with opium and marijuana. Unlike previous drug scares, the race factor was absent this time, since LSD was not associated with any ethnic group in particular. However, the age factor remained part of the scare. As had happened during the opium drug scare at the beginning of the twentieth century, young people were the target.[9]

In concluding his presentation, Cotnam correctly predicted that more and more stories would be published about LSD in Canada over the next couple of months. If many news articles dealt with American stories, it did not take long for journalists to report on stories of LSD use in Canada. While there were no articles about LSD in Canadian magazines in 1965, this changed the following year, with the publication of three stories. Although by 1967 several studies had been published in Canadian magazines, most of them did not specifically focus on LSD. On the contrary, LSD was mentioned along with other drugs, including those prescribed by physicians, which were now used for recreational purposes. However, Canadians had access to American media, especially newspapers and magazines. In a study published in 1971 for the Commission of Inquiry into the Nonmedical Use of Drugs, known as the Le Dain Commission and appointed by the federal government, its author concluded that American news coverage shaped how English-speaking Canadians understood the drug issue. It was not the case with French Canadians because the language barrier did not give them an immediate access to American news stories. How did he come to this conclusion? According to his analysis, "more US periodicals than Canadian periodicals [were] read in Canada and the US periodicals feature[d] drug-related news more frequently than [did] the Canadian counterparts." For instance, news media covered Tim Leary's 1966 tour of American campuses and his promotion of LSD use. He added:

> If it is true that periodicals probably played a role in amplifying the marijuana phenomenon, the same holds good for LSD in 1966 and 1967 at least. From 1968 onwards, the almost uniform emphasis by the medium on the possible link between LSD and chromosome damage (defective babies, LSD and leukemia and cancer) may have had the effect of discouraging *potential* users. It is doubtful; however, considering the way society reacted to the tobacco-cancer scare, whether this medium had any major effect on *actual* users of LSD.[10]

Although drug use opponents blamed the media for inciting people (especially the "impressionable" youth) to try LSD, this premise raises the still highly debated question of the role of the media and their impact on public opinion. Do media reflect or influence public opinion? If public opinion in the sixties tended to blame the media for encouraging individuals and especially young people for doing drugs, we know that links between media, cultural phenomenon, and public opinion are very complex. We cannot identify the media as the only suspect in explaining why individuals tried licit and illicit drugs. Other factors such as peer pressure, parental behavior, class, gender, and ethnicity are intertwined. Drug opponents dismissed these considerations. They shared the belief that there was a direct correlation between the number of drug stories in the media and the popularity of LSD, and they took comfort in studies that supported their views.

According to a 1970 survey carried out for the Canadian Senate Committee on Media, 61 percent and 51 percent of the 2,254 Canadians who participated in the survey blamed television and newspapers, respectively, for an increase in what was described as "drug addiction." It is worth pointing out that only 28 percent of the interviewees identified radio stations as being responsible for the increase in "drug addiction." Furthermore, 54 percent of the participants stated that there were "too many articles on drug usage" on television. For newspapers and radio, the percentages were 45 percent and 21 percent, respectively.[11] The author of a study carried out for the Le Dain Commission on drug use and the media explored the link between media and drug use. He stated that the awareness of drugs and the drug phenomenon differed according to the relationship one had with them. Drug users learned about drugs through friends as opposed to nonusers who derived their knowledge from media. Although drug use opponents often blamed television and newspapers for inciting individuals, and in particular "impressionable" youth, to experiment with drugs, this study cautioned everyone against jumping to conclusions. The media were not responsible for spreading the use of nonmedical drug phenomenon. Awareness of all sorts of drugs came from different sources, although the media played a greater role in acquainting nondrug users with this phenomenon.[12]

Having started as a phenomenon affecting the United States, LSD use for recreational purpose migrated north and crossed the border. This was quite ironic, since Canada's relationship with LSD started after World War II. The government of Saskatchewan, and in particular its premier, Tommy Douglas, were committed to health reform and implemented the first publicly funded health care program in Canada. Premier Douglas was also concerned about mental health. Consequently, the government of Saskatchewan enabled psychiatrists, such as Abram Hoffer and Humphry Osmond, to pursue their research on mental illness and the use of chemical drugs. While funded by the Saskatchewan provincial government, they experimented with LSD, hoping to better understand mental illnesses. At the beginning of the 1960s, Hoffer and his team sought volunteers among students with no mental illness for testing the effects of LSD. In her study on LSD use in Canada, Erika Dyck writes that ads were included for recruiting volunteers in student newspapers at the University of Saskatchewan. It did not take long for these volunteers to encourage friends to take part in these sessions because they enjoyed "the psychedelic experience in the safe surroundings of the clinical observation room."[13] Some of these students and others learned how to make their own LSD and experiment, without medical supervision, with the properties of this drug and its ability to produce a euphoric state of mind and, for some, even a form of religious experience.

While Canada's relation with LSD dates back to before the 1960s, this was lost on the minds of those who woke up to the news that young Americans used the substance for pleasure. A sense of emergency grew once stories about Canadian youth, mostly young and white middle-class individuals, appeared in Canadian media. At first there were some positive stories about LSD use, such as articles in the *Globe and Mail* about how the substance helped alcoholic patients. In the October 1962 news article, Dr. Hoffer claimed that about half of his patients had recovered or had been sober. This positive assessment was similar to articles published by American mainstream media.[14] However, a drug conference held in the winter of 1967 in Toronto generated great concerns about the nonmedical use of LSD.

Called Perception '67, the drug festival was organized by the University College Literary and Athletic Society at University College in Toronto, Ontario. Participants could attend a variety of activities such as a performance from the New York rock group the Fugs and an exhibition by Toronto artist Michael Hayden called Mind Excursion that simulated a drug experience by using music, lights, and other special effects. For those who wanted to learn more about licit and illicit drug use, the organizers included in their program various panels featuring American beat poet Allen Ginsberg and Dr. Humphry Osmond among others.[15]

The invitation of Dr. Timothy Leary cast a shadow over the events when municipal politicians and Toronto newspapers expressed their displeasure over his presence as one of the panelists. The former Harvard university professor was a controversial figure since he had embarked on the promotion of the nonmedical use of LSD. He argued that individuals should experiment and discover by themselves their surroundings. In its editorial entitled "No Welcome Mat for Leary," the *Toronto Star* made a clear demarcation between what constituted legitimate and illegitimate use. LSD had a purpose: to be used in medical treatment. When Canadians, especially young ones, started using LSD for personal pleasure, the Toronto newspaper concluded that the practice was totally unacceptable because the drug was used without any proper medical supervision and for no health-oriented reasons.[16] As Elaine Carey illustrates in her chapter in this book about American officials using foreign figures in their antidrug campaigns, the *Toronto Star* used a similar tactic by insisting on the fact that Leary was a foreigner who would turn young Canadians into drug users.

Federal officials from the Immigration Department reassured concerned Torontonians by not allowing Leary to enter Canada because he was a "prohibited person" on account of his drug conviction.[17] By keeping Leary out of the country, state officials hoped that LSD would not receive more coverage than was necessary. By doing so, they put a face on the invasion and demonstrated that this new cultural phenomenon was led by an immoral and despicable leader who encouraged people to use a drug that had, according to its opponents, very dangerous mental and health effects. This strategy has some similarities with the narratives of the "other," depicted as a "social danger" and developed by the Ontario liquor board or city officials and concerned citizens living in Windsor about sex tourism analyzed in the chapters by Dan Malleck and Holly Karibo in this book. By preventing Leary from addressing the conference, officials hoped to be able to contain the spread of drug use. The call to experiment with a drug that promised consciousness-raising abilities was questionable since reports from physicians stated that the drug led to a loss of control, irresponsibility, and even criminal acts. When news reports about deaths attributed to LSD use surfaced, it confirmed the worst fears about this drug.

Almost a month after the end of the conference, Perception '67 was back in the media because of a deadly incident that played into the fears surrounding LSD use. In March 1967, newspapers headlined stories on the death of John Stern, a twenty-year-old music student. The *Globe and Mail* headline was specific on the cause of the death: "Sampled LSD, youth plunges from viaduc [sic]."[18] The conservative daily *Toronto Telegram* reported that the victim's father was categorical when asked about the cause: his son took LSD and it led him to commit suicide. Furthermore, the father blamed the disciples of LSD and "every publication that in any way glorifies this drug as a magic gift that can broaden and enlighten anyone." The *Toronto Telegram* reminded its readers that the student attended Perception '67 and one of the speakers, Dr. Richard Alpert, encouraged individuals to take LSD. The newspaper contacted Alpert and asked him if he felt responsible for the tragic event. Alpert declined to accept any responsibility because he argued that it was "extremely difficult to pin such a death exclusively to LSD." The father hoped his son's death would awaken politicians and they should ban LSD, except for medical use.[19]

The father's call for state regulation received favorable support from the police force. According to police officials, they were unable to stop young people from using LSD at the time because their hands were tied. The Canadian legislation had classified the drug as a prohibited substance. This meant that LSD could be used for scientific research, but no penalties were applied to its possession, as was the case for marijuana, cocaine, and other drugs classified under the Food and Drugs Act and the Narcotic Control Act. Consequently, police officers could not charge anyone in possession of LSD. If elected officials contemplated a crackdown on LSD users, the law had to be amended and LSD should be classified as a narcotic.[20]

LSD stories did not disappear from the media radar screen. On the contrary, they resurfaced often to highlight the health dangers, including death, resulting from its use, and crimes committed under the drug influence. For instance, American and Canadian studies were printed in the *Globe and Mail*. In October 1967, the Toronto newspaper printed a story about a young New York couple who went to a basement apartment in their quest for LSD. Their adventure turned tragic because they were murdered. The police took the time to specify that the accused raped the young girl several times before her death.[21] In January 1968, Dr. Joshua Brody, a Toronto psychiatrist, warned parents about LSD and marijuana. Their use was likely to become "more common among normal children from normal homes." What could "normal" parents from "normal" homes do to prevent this? According to the psychiatrist, parents should keep their children away from these drugs as they did "from other dangerous things" by spending, for instance, more time with their kids. In his presentation, he encouraged parents to do that because both drugs were dangerous and created "mental confusion" and "a panic state."[22] In February and May, the newspaper published the story of a teenager accused of killing Carl Theodore Lacourse, a LSD trafficker. The brother of the accused stole LSD capsules from Lacourse in February 1968. Lacourse showed up at the accused's apartment and asked for his money. According to the accused, he got scared and his gun went off.[23] A couple of months later, there was a brief story about an American man who was sent to jail for six years. Although under the influence of LSD, he was acquitted of murder but found guilty of manslaughter of a prostitute. For opponents of drug use for recreational purpose, these stories supported their concerns.[24]

Reports about dangerous health effects, crimes committed under the influence of the drug, and deaths gave ammunition to opponents of LSD. Calls for government action caused the Swiss-based Sandoz Pharmaceutical Company, the producer of LSD, to rethink their marketing of the drug. Faced with growing criticisms, the company temporarily suspended distribution in 1963, hoping to help unmask underground suppliers.[25] However, company officials remained nervous because the United Nations Economic and Social Council that monitored drug production came under pressure from governments to act on the LSD issue. Confronted with the fact that LSD was now used for recreational purposes, the United Nations

Economic and Social Council strongly encouraged countries to regulate the drug in such a way that LSD would be restricted to research and medical purposes.[26] This appeal for action by the United Nations could only mean state interference and possible regulation of an economic sector dominated by the private sector.

The LSD issue divided the medical community. While many health experts warned against the physical and mental dangers of nonmedical use of LSD, others knew that their scientific work with LSD was under siege. Hoffer and Osmond, who pioneered scientific research with LSD, denounced individuals who used LSD for recreational purposes, in particular scientists such as Leary who promoted this practice. They feared that Leary's action was undermining their work and science in general. In 1966, Osmond contacted Leary and told him that "as a good member of my profession [I] *strongly* oppose you." He was particularly upset by "Leary's self-identification as a medical expert on psychedelics."[27]

Parents, law enforcement officers, health experts, scientists, and media drew the boundaries of illegitimate LSD use: it was unacceptable when taken without any medical supervision. Since death was equated with nonmedical use, these social agents felt that they should intervene. As for parents, they knew what was best for their kids and LSD certainly was not good for them. For police officers, LSD use for recreational purposes led to disorder. They claimed that existing laws hindered their work, since these did not identify LSD as a dangerous substance and consequently police could not arrest young people in possession of the drug. Scientists were divided over the issue. Although some were careful not to link the LSD experience with death, others pleaded in favor of keeping its use to capable and knowledgeable scientific hands. The media for their part were eager to report on any aspect of the new social practice of LSD use for recreational purposes, and the death of the young Torontonian provided an opportunity to voice the concerns and fears expressed by various social agents. Given that LSD use had made a remarkable entry into the public domain, and that this entry was tainted by tragedy, the debate caught the attention of politicians.

What to Do? The Ontario Government Intervenes

Since borders were porous, it was crucial to prevent the new cultural phenomenon of nonmedical use of LSD from spreading. Government had to assert its sovereignty and protect its citizens. Repression became the order of the day. Because of the nature of the political system in Canada, the coordination of provincial and federal responses was a challenge. Since health is the responsibility of provincial governments, but drug regulation comes under the authority of the federal government, it is not surprising that governments' response to the LSD phenomenon triggered debates both in the provinces and at the federal level. Politicians struggled with questions such as how to stop the invasion, which approach should be considered, and how the provinces could coordinate their responses with the action undertaken by the federal government.

The case of Ontario is fascinating because its medical experts chose health-oriented policy and education over repression, contrary to other provinces such as Alberta and British Columbia. In an attempt to assert its sovereignty, the province of Alberta adopted repression as an approach to dealing with LSD use for recreational purposes. In 1967, the government, led by Ernest Manning, leader of the Social Credit Party, passed a law that made the production, possession, and distribution of hallucinogenic drugs (including LSD) illegal. The penalties included a prison sentence.[28] The British Columbia government, led by the conservative Social Credit leader W. A. C. Bennett, also believed that criminal law remained the best device to discourage young people from using drugs that were not prescribed by physicians. Therefore, in March 1967, the Legislative Assembly of British Columbia passed the Act Respecting Proscribed Substances that outlawed the use of LSD and stipulated that anyone found guilty under this law could face, on summary conviction, a fine of up to two thousand dollars and/or six months in jail.[29] Another law targeting LSD, the Act to Amend the Health Act, stipulated that anyone in possession or aware of the presence of this substance should inform the police or a health professional or face a maximum fine of two thousand dollars and/or six-months in jail.[30] However, the actions of the government of British Columbia were declared unconstitutional by the British Columbia Court of Appeal because the province did not have the power to legislate in the field of criminal law, which is the responsibility of the federal government.[31]

Following news reports about the death of the young man in Toronto, as mentioned in the first section of this chapter, Ontario provincial politicians were quick to condemn LSD users, and its personal pleasure proponents, and pleaded for action. Several elected officials who intervened during the parliamentary debate insisted on the dangerous health and mental effects of LSD use. These statements were not very reassuring for worried parents and other concerned citizens.[32]

In the debate generated by the media coverage of the death of a young

Torontonian, the Ontario government was limited in its public policy options. It could not make the possession of LSD a criminal offence as the provincial governments of British Columbia and Alberta did in 1967, since the criminal code was under federal jurisdiction. For its part, the Alcoholism and Drug Addiction Research Foundation of Ontario (ARF), which advised the Ontario government on drug issues, viewed drug use as a health issue, as did several American health organizations.

Founded in 1949, the ARF was well known for its research on alcohol and rehabilitation programs. The dissemination of its research projects and the creation of educational programs in 1953 aimed at youth and parents led to the implementation of the programs by several school boards in Ontario and other provinces in Canada. In 1961, the Ontario government included other drugs as part of the ARF's mandate.[33] Used by psychiatrists and other health experts since 1949 in the United States, LSD had shown promising results in treating autism, helping cancer patients coping with the prospect of their own death, and aiding heavy alcohol users cope with their addiction.[34] Thus the ARF counseled that any actions on the part of the Ontario government should take into consideration the benefits of the drug and consider any health consequences of drug abuse. Consequently, health dangers associated with illicit drug use and the addictive properties of some drugs demonstrated that health public policies should be implemented. In the case of LSD, the ARF insisted that there was much still unknown, such as the number and profile of users and the short- and long-terms health risks and impact.

In late 1960s, the ARF commissioned studies on drug use by young people in Ontario, especially in large urban centers. The first study, published in 1969, was based on the results of questionnaires distributed to some Toronto high school students in 1968. Students completed a questionnaire on their use of a variety of drugs such as alcohol, cigarettes, tranquilizers, heroin, marijuana, etc. However, they had to secure the permission of their parents in order to participate. The results demonstrated that alcohol and cigarettes were used by a greater number of participants than marijuana and other hard drugs. Use of LSD was reported by 1.1 percent of students in grade 7, 3.9 percent in grade 9, 2.1 percent in grade 11, and 3.8 percent in grade 13.[35] A 1970 study conducted in Metropolitan Toronto schools using a similar methodology indicated an increase in the number of students who tried LSD. The percentage for all students in all grades was 8.5.[36] In 1972 and 1974, the percentages were 7.1 and 4.1, respectively.[37] By reporting low LSD use among young people, the ARF challenged the narrative being constructed on the dangers of LSD, and that repression was the best course of action. Furthermore, it decided to launch a frontal attack against those who argued that there was a serious drug problem in the province. Based on its studies, the drug problem was not LSD but alcohol and smoking cigarettes, which were widely used and described as "social drugs."

Conducting research and publishing results were part of the Ontario response to the LSD issue. The ARF also invested resources in educating people. In the case of young people, the Ontario organization produced documents for school boards. Educating young people did not mean that warnings would not be incorporated in the educational material. One of a series of documents entitled *Facts about . . .* produced by the ARF focused on LSD. The document described the substance, its short-term effects, and its hazards such as anxiety and convulsions. However, it listed what was still unknown about the substance such as "the proportion of 'bad trips' among users," effects on the brain, on unborn children, blood cells, and treatment of alcoholism. The last section of the document dealt with the law. It pointed out that the Canadian federal government had criminalized the possession and trafficking of LSD and warned its readers about the legal consequences if arrested.[38] With this educational approach, the ARF strongly believed that its solution of providing more time for alcohol and drug education in the Ontario classrooms was a very promising prevention strategy.

Measuring the Limits of Provincial Action: The Federal State Dives In

Although the Ontario government opted for a health-oriented approach in its dealing with LSD, other provinces decided on repression. For their part, social actors such as individuals, scientists, police forces, and organizations that believed that LSD use for nonmedical purpose was a danger and should not become a socially accepted phenomenon targeted another level: the federal government.

In 1962, the federal government restricted LSD use to research only, as did the American government, but left a loophole by not creating penalties for possession and trafficking. However, with the growing popularity of LSD in the United States and Canada, the Canadian federal government came under pressure to take further action.[39] In 1967, parliamentarians debated a bill that dealt with this loophole. Hearings allowed opponents and proponents of LSD use to express their opinions and convictions; these included members of the scientific community, the Department of

National Health and Welfare, law enforcement representatives, and politicians who opposed drugs. This debate gave opponents of LSD an opportunity to repeat arguments against drugs such as the risks to physical and mental health and the kind of society that would emerge if LSD use for recreational purposes were allowed to continue. In other words, did a society need drugs in order to function? Furthermore, what message would Canada send to its citizens and the international community if the use of LSD for nonmedical purposes remained unregulated by the state? Of course, opponents failed to acknowledge that drugs were part of human life. The use of morning coffee or sleeping pills and other drugs prescribed by physicians, or of chemicals in dealing with various illnesses, health-related matters, or habits illustrated how deeply embedded drugs were in daily life in Canada and elsewhere.

Others, including the industry and physicians who were using LSD for treating alcoholism, did not want the government to intervene and regulate the use of LSD. They perceived criminalization or an outright ban as the worst-case scenario. Acknowledging that they were unable to prevent the phenomenon of LSD use for recreational purposes and, in the case of the industry, unable to prevent the substance from reaching beyond the scientific community, their objective was to prevent a ban by providing suggestions to the federal government on public policy.

During the hearings, witnesses and parliamentarians referred to the United States and how it handled this issue. Restrictions imposed by American legislators on LSD use for research were denounced by several witnesses. By referring to a variety of American sources such as research papers, studies, and laws, they demonstrated that their views were part of a larger social problem resonating south of the Canadian border, and that their opinions were not the expression of a narrow point of view. On the contrary, American references conferred legitimacy on the views expressed during the hearings.

Two American proponents of LSD use took part in the hearings. They urged Canadian parliamentarians to reconsider the repressive approach of the drug legislation under consideration. Dr. Stanley Krippner, then a senior research associate for the Department of Psychiatry at the Maimonides Medical Center in New York, warned Canadian legislators against the criminal approach. Prohibition did not work in the United States as shown by the alcohol prohibition in the 1920s. Furthermore, Prohibition would encourage rather than discourage young people from using the substance, by making it more attractive to those who were eager to challenge government and its drug legislation. Finally, the American researcher reminded

Canadian parliamentarians that it was relatively easy to produce LSD. For his part, Dr. John H. Perry-Hooker from the Medfield State Hospital in Harding, Massachusetts, cautioned legislators not to follow the route taken by the state of Massachusetts. With its legislation, Massachusetts had made it very difficult for researchers and scientists to pursue research with LSD. Furthermore, the state law made it impossible for him to prescribe LSD to patients who would benefit from it. For Perry-Hooker, the best form of regulation was to leave scientists in charge and not the state, because physicians would then prescribe LSD only to patients who required it for treatment.[40]

In 1969, the federal government in Canada concluded the LSD debate by amending the Food and Drugs Act. The amendments meant that LSD had become a restricted drug and that its possession and trafficking became criminal offences. The penalties for possession were a maximum fine of a thousand dollars and/or six months in jail. There was no minimum.[41] However, the penalty was not as severe as it was for marijuana and other narcotics. This course of action was similar to those undertaken by other national governments. In Britain, possession of LSD became a criminal offence in 1966, and two years later, the possession of this substance became illegal in the United States.

Conclusion

The debate on LSD use was an opportunity for several social agents to be heard and to promote their solution. For opponents, federal and provincial governments had an obligation to regulate a practice labeled as unacceptable since it put people's lives at risk. The call for intervention also involved territorial sovereignty. Canada had to assert its sovereignty and deal with the issue. However, there was disagreement over what the government should do. Newspapers helped set what constituted legitimate and illegitimate uses of LSD by reporting stories, but also by letting parents, medical experts, law enforcement officers, and others express their views on this issue. Although the voices of users often were not heard, proponents and opponents gave meaning to users' actions. LSD use was to be considered illegitimate unless taken under medical supervision, and any other use should not be allowed, since it constituted a danger to its users.

Before repression and criminalization of the nonmedical use of LSD emerged as solutions, those affected by this choice of public policy challenged it. Researchers did so because their scientific work was about to be terminated. The industry was under pressure because its economic viability was at stake. However, these groups lost the war. LSD was outlawed by the Canadian government and the international community, in 1969 and 1971 respectively.

Due to the federal nature of the Canadian state, it was the federal government that had the power to make the possession of LSD a criminal offense. Although the provinces of Alberta and British Columbia chose repression, the Ontario government rejected repressive policies. It adopted the ARF advice that education and treatment were better solutions. When the federal government intervened, it asserted its sovereignty by taking into consideration domestic pressures and policies implemented by provincial governments and by other countries. Furthermore, as a member of the international community and a country supporting the creation of an international regulatory mechanism for drug production to deal with a global drug problem requiring coordination among states, Canada aligned its domestic drug policy with the action taken by the international community.

Did borders matter in this drug issue? In their chapter of this book, Andrae Marak and Laura Tuennerman argue that borders do matter. Governments on both sides of the American-Mexican border targeted behaviors defined as vice. But the means and the narrative developed in battling vice were different. In our case, the perceived LSD invasion faded away at the end. The opponents of the nonmedical use of LSD gave credit to governments' regulatory power in resolving the issue. The proponents of the use of LSD and others who were critical of government drug regulations claimed that changes in drug habits explained the decline in the nonmedical use of LSD. It could be argued that borders mattered since a country cannot intervene in the internal affairs of another sovereign state. Only international treaties and conventions circumscribed state sovereignty. Once a state has willingly signed a treaty or a convention on drugs, it has obligations. Failing to meet them could lead to sanctions. The challenge is to enroll more countries in the international movement of drug regulation, but the lack of enforcement mechanisms aimed at delinquent states handicaps the efforts of the international community. However, we should not forget that government action on drugs is very symbolic, because it does not alter the relationship that individuals have with drugs and demonstrates the limits of a government's power in regulating the human body. What a government's drug policy does is to shift people's interest toward new drugs until they are regulated by the state. Nevertheless, government action in the domestic and international spheres stems from the domestic pressure applied by individuals and groups who have strong views on drugs and push governments to impose their views on their society and the international community. They believe that they have the authority to do so, and that they can draw the line between the legitimate and illegitimate use of drugs.

Afterword

Crime on and across Borders

Josiah McC. Heyman and Howard Campbell

This book proposes a critical rethinking of the relationship between societies, states, and crime. A previous work, *States and Illegal Practices*, breaks with the assumption that legality and illegality are opposites by definition and explores the complex interpenetrations of actual laws, governments, and illegal activities and actors.[1] *Illicit Flows and Criminal Things* brings this perspective to bear on transnational flows and border crossing/controlling processes, and it introduces an important distinction, much used in this book, between classifying goods and practices as legal or illegal (by law) versus licit or illicit (by socially accorded acceptance or rejection).[2] More generally, anthropologists, geographers, and historians have recently studied borders in ways that step aside from the assumption that national territories and their boundaries are clear, definitive, natural, and atemporal.[3]

To these developments, the present work adds rich case studies, deepens our understanding of key points (e.g., licit/illicit), and comes back around to influence those like ourselves who work on contemporary borders. For us, the energy-consuming attraction (and importance) of immediate public policy debates and the massive presence of state apparatuses and sophisticated criminal organizations makes it easy to slip into a certain "inherency of the present," thereby missing much of the fluidity and constructedness of laws, illegal practices, borders, and flows. What we offer, then, are reflections on the present study of borders and illegalities that draw inspiration from the fine work in this book.

Several chapters (Rensink, Díaz, and Marak and Tuennerman) address phenomena that combine two fundamentally different ways that people have of relating to "crime," or what might today be labeled as crime. Teasing this out is helpful in understanding the trajectory toward the criminal and law enforcement organizations of the present. At least some of the people in some circumstances in those chapters are acting on cultural frameworks and models of social relations that give little importance to territorialized nation-states, as opposed to nonstate relations of mutual recognition and reciprocity. This is most evident in the cases of the indigenous peoples onto whom the nations of Canada, Mexico, and the United States were imposed. Furthermore, some activities that might be classified as crime in terms of formal state law (e.g., the rustling described by Rensink) are organized and understood quite differently, through a continuum across positive, balanced, and negative reciprocity. Reciprocity involves a series of giftlike exchanges, conducted over time (that is, not immediate barter), and carried out with a spirit of mutual generosity and obligation. Negative reciprocity is particularly relevant, as it involves mutual theft operating over time as a patterned form of social relationship.[4]

None of these case studies ought to be viewed as examples of premodern isolates. Rather, each one of them depicts an instance of the intersection between the penetrating capitalist economy, the administrative (including legal) framework of the modern nation-state, and the alternative ways of living and relating just described. Thomas Gallant has explored the complex web of violence, predation, expropriation, and theft that appeared across the world during these periods of transformation when the world market expanded and the nation-state imposed its rule.[5] Often, in these chapters, state law arrives as an imposition, challenging existing practices of exchange and legitimacy, and serving, in part, as a means of primitive accumulation, seizing resources and power from previously resident peoples, while reworking local knowledge in a related fashion. New definitions of what is legal or illegal are forcibly inserted, and key debates (open and hidden) take place over what is licit and what is illicit. These conflictive transformations, of course, are far denser and more complex than this brief distillation indicates.[6]

As scholars of the present, we are particularly interested in this moment of transformative struggle because key patterns emerging at that time are now the fundamental lines of organization of contemporary law and illegality. Let us consider for a moment the changes in smuggling described by Díaz. Initially, small-scale smugglers, based in Norteño (northern Mexican) and Tejano (Latino Texan) society, carried alcohol along remote routes on horseback. Interestingly, they seem to have shied from violence.

An intensive police response, in some cases brutally violent, largely drove those smugglers out of business. They were replaced by higher-volume smugglers, using cars and trucks on main roads, and wielding deadly force.

We suggest that over the course of the twentieth and early twenty-first century, this dynamic has taken place repeatedly — admittedly, with many variations — a dialectic of growth and sophistication between criminal organizations in high-value markets and government law enforcement agencies in high-value budgetary arenas. The dynamic has likewise taken place across various political and social borders, as illustrated by the chapters in this book describing contests of illegal trade and police bureaucracy at the US-Canada border as well as the US-Mexico border. If the Mexican border seems to encompass all the notorious instances of "wild illegality" in North America today, this is not because there is some essence to this border, for indeed there have in the past been such moments at the Canadian border also, as well as at other social boundaries in each nation's interior. For reasons that still need to be explored, a deep intensification of this tragic illegality/policing dialectic, a topic of considerable historical and contemporary interest, has occurred at the US-Mexico border. We then focus on it, partly because of its compelling nature and partly due to our own expertise,[7] but we take the US-Canada examples as object lessons that such dynamics can and do occur elsewhere.

Examining, then, the contemporary endpoint of these escalatory processes (if indeed they have ended), we encounter both state agencies and criminal organizations with commodity and wage forms of exchange, huge workforces, sophisticated multilevel managements, diverse specialists, vast incomes and resources, advanced technologies, and enormous capacities for violent force. Today's US antidrug budget has reached an estimated $20 billion, two-thirds of the estimated $30-billion profits reaped by Mexican cartels alone.[8] The vast law enforcement infrastructure has not eliminated the illegal drug system, but in the process it has produced a novel, expensive, and coercive sociopolitical architecture of apparently opposed but mutually reinforcing giant organizations.

The dialectical relationship between the US state and US-Latin American organized crime organizations is vividly exemplified by the expansion of Mexican drug cartels in tandem with the growth of US antidrug enforcement efforts and the spread of neoliberal economic policies from the United States to the rest of the Western hemisphere. The DEA's success in closing Florida and other east coast transshipment ports for cocaine in the 1980s squeezed the existing balloon of drug supply and rechanneled it from Colombia to Mexico. Furthermore, Colombian government cooperation with US law enforcement (via Plan Colombia) led to the dismantling of the Medellín and Cali cartels. In the 1990s Mexican drug cartels grew dramatically and eventually surpassed in size and power their Colombian suppliers who, weakened by the joint US-Colombian government campaign, divided into dozens of small, yet efficient, minicartels.

The emergent Mexican megacartels exploited the new trade, communication, and transportation opportunities presented by the North American Free Trade Agreement (NAFTA) of 1994 to stay ahead of their US law enforcement adversaries and other global cartel rivals. NAFTA tripled the volume in the land border trade between the United States and Mexico, giving an advantage to Mexican over Colombian cartels. Most of the illegal drugs smuggled across the border to the United States and arms smuggled to Mexico move within this great mass of trade. Cartel members coordinate their efforts with the most up-to-date mobile phones and other forms of electronic and cyber-communication (and cyber-money laundering). Skillfully hidden among the tens of thousands of eighteen-wheel trucks transporting auto parts and electronics from Ciudad Juárez, Mexico, into the United States were hundreds of tons of clandestine cartel cocaine, marijuana, methamphetamine, and heroin. Along the transportation corridor, spotters with cell phones instantly communicated the passage of the drugs from their source in Mexico to markets in the United States. Submarine technology for shipping cocaine was introduced as a response to greater DEA surveillance of the skies over the ocean. Each innovation by US antidrug warriors and/or immigration law enforcers, whether it be placing more agents on the border or in other strategic locations, new scanning devices, more checkpoints, border walls, or sting operations, and other large-scale investigations, has been quickly countered by cartel strategists.

The emergence of a global economy made it more profitable and easier for Mexican drug trafficking organizations to distribute drugs in the United States. Increased revenues and the relatively low price the Mexican cartels paid for cocaine and other drugs from producers meant that the cartels could survive the confiscation of large volumes of drugs and the arrests of hundreds or thousands of low-level smugglers by US law enforcement. The drugs and smugglers were easily replaced. United States law enforcement success only served as a prod for the Mexican cartels to further innovate. Paradoxically, the rise of US neoliberalism and its spread to Latin America — though strengthening US economic and political power over many Latin American states — has actually facilitated the growth of the transnational narcotics trade.

Josiah Heyman and Peter Andreas propose an escalatory cycle in which the ability of covert actors to defeat government control actually leads to a further buildup of the government apparatus, in an effort to demonstrate (especially in a mass-media shaped symbolic sphere) the value and seriousness of the government response.[9] It entails throwing good money after bad. However, the issue that both authors examine is undocumented migration at the US-Mexico border, where the criminal networks have remained lower in scale, though quite effective, as contrasted with the drug case. Larger and more sophisticated migrant smuggling organizations, somewhat akin to drug cartels, or in fact run by them, occur where migrants pay high fees to cross borders,[10] a contemporary phenomenon that perhaps emerges out of the processes described in Romero's chapter. Obviously, then, there is much more specification that is needed in terms of why and when the large government agency–large criminal enterprise dialectic occurs.

It is also the case that not all illegal practices have an escalatory dynamic. Some issues and concomitant organizations seem to wither away, as described in a number of chapters in this book (e.g., Evans, Karibo, Mallek). Clearly, wider contexts shape some instances of decline — such as the relegalization of alcohol in the United States — and there are also peculiar comings and goings of local manifestations of issues that on a larger scale have by no means disappeared, such as commercial sex. Again, there is much to be said about why and when the escalatory cycle weakens and disappears (a relevant literature explores the life cycle of controversial issues, including if and how issues cross international borders).[11] Still, crime and law enforcement today often look vastly different in both size and kind when compared to the radically different "negative reciprocity" model of social relations and the fragmentary, modern forms of crime and law enforcement found at the time of world market and nation-state penetration. And borders have much to do with this dynamic.

The historical change in scale extends to other domains. An important feature of these chapters is the presence of the mass media, initially newspapers and other mass circulation print. Almost every chapter provides examples, but the role of the media in hyping fear and escalating responses to real and perceived illegalities stands out in the chapters by Carey, Díaz, Karibo, Martel, and Rensink. Obviously, then, this is not new. But we suggest that it has grown enormously in scale over time. Today, we live in sociocultural environments that are quite saturated in information bites (in the sense of being small, consumable, and thoroughly nonnutritious, at least as far as gaining sophisticated understanding). The visceral newspaper reporting of the past has amplified into the visual imagery of the present, memorable and manipulable all at once. Entirely in keeping with the chapters in this book, an important line of contemporary analysis focuses on the powerful dynamic between mass media depictions of crime and sociopolitical arrangements such as race and class, as in the classic study, *Policing the Crisis*.[12] The particular content of such representations will be taken up later; the point here is simply that historians have detected trends that have grown in importance.

The example above of NAFTA suggests that we include another "growth-of-scale" context: that of domestic and global trade, legal and illegal. There was a particularly intensive period of cross-border trade and investment in the late nineteenth and early twentieth centuries, a period that followed when most of the growth occurred within national territories (often protected by restrictive commercial border controls), and then another wave of growth in global flows after 1965. The particular stories told in this book about border crossing and illegality roughly reflect this chronology (for example, the chapter on contraband twine by Evans reflects the emergence of increasingly protected national markets). As we move into the late twentieth and early twenty-first centuries, there are many legal flows of capital, goods, and (some) people through borders, but a few goods and people that are markedly illegal and forcefully interdicted. The dilemma faced by law enforcement agencies (some of which themselves have begun to globalize) is how to "sort" flows across borders, to facilitate some flows, interdict others, and both maintain and remove boundaries simultaneously.[13] While still incompletely successful, the scale at which this border management is done in the present is vastly greater than in the past.

One theme that is implicit in this book, but is not brought far enough to the front, is that many of these illegal activities and flows, including (perhaps especially) the transnational ones, are constitutive and transformative of major political and social formations.[14] Their apparent deviance may make them seem the opposite of the obvious constitutive role of the formal and accepted (to wit, "constitutions"). A brief detour, however, into the recent history of Mexican drug cartels shows how they are shaping both Mexican and US political-administrative dynamics.

The oldest and most "traditional" Mexican cartels — the Sinaloa Cartel, Cartel de Juárez, and Gulf Cartel — are rooted in specific regional cultures. In the past, they also claimed to abide by a kind of unwritten "gentleman's agreement" or "code of honor" in terms of interactions with other cartel members, duties, and customs. The newest and most dynamic cartels, the Zetas and La Familia Michoacana (or simply La Familia), however, have forged new organizational structures, strategies, and tactics. La Familia introduced the tactic of decapitation to the Mexican drug war and unveiled other innovations such as the propagation of a messianic religious ideology complete with its own crude bible, use of homemade military uniforms, and a kind of populist takeover of whole regions of the state of Michoacán. In a sense, La Familia created its own mini-narco-state within Mexican national territory.

The Zetas, formed by highly trained deserters from the Mexican military, forged an innovative, para-military-style, small criminal army. The Zetas, eschewing the old "rules" of traditional drug trafficking organizations, conduct themselves like a military platoon engaged in field operations. Their brutal tactics — involving employment of the most modern weaponry and technology, terrorizing forms of torture often videotaped and posted on YouTube, choreographed massacres and public display of bodies, impersonation of the Mexican military, and the public placement of quasi-political manifestos — have set the tone for a new kind of intensified narco-warfare and narco-propagandistic ideological combat. They have also branched out from the traditional drug smuggling racket to engage in carefully orchestrated campaigns of robbery, kidnapping, and extortion. The Zetas have spread into areas of Mexico that formerly were not plagued by the worst excesses of drug crime and violence, such as Aguascalientes, Zacatecas, Oaxaca, Chiapas, Veracruz, the Yucatán Peninsula, and elsewhere. The tentacles of the Zeta organization are so widespread as to cross the borders of Mexico into the heartland as well as the east and west coasts of the United States. This is also true of the other major Mexican cartels, which are truly transnational, Pan-American organizations and connected to local drug-trafficking gangs on the streets of US cities. Consequently, what would appear to be strictly parochial skirmishes between contending drug cartels in Mexico, in fact affect the flow, quantity, and price of drugs that cross the US border to American consumers.

These emerging dynamics of Mexican cartels and the ongoing drug war further complicate the already difficult task of US antidrug law enforcement officials. The Mexican state's policies may have paradoxical effects on the functioning of the transnational drug business. Current president Calderon's military war on the cartels backfired to produce more violence and instability, which facilitated the growth and evolution of groups like the Zetas and La Familia. Moreover the cartels, as noted, recruit heavily from military deserters. Bad government (especially the corrupt practices of police and military officials) generate sympathy for cartels. Bad economic policies combined with tougher US immigration polices push unemployed youth into cartels. Finally, the general corruption of the Mexican government is such that in some places cartels and government are interwoven, not separate entities.

In this context, nonstate actors (cartels) are starting to determine the course of important current events in Mexico; for instance, the drug war in Nuevo Laredo/Laredo ended not because the government stopped it but because the Gulf Cartel/Zetas were defeating the Sinaloa Cartel so it retreated. Likewise, at present, the Mexican government does not control Ciudad Juárez. The expansion of Mexican drug trafficking organizations — affiliated with American-based drug gangs — into all corners of the United States has a profound impact on local drug consumption patterns and neighborhood life. United States law enforcement has responded by widening and deepening its efforts to imprison traffickers and police borders and smuggling routes, which further expands federal bureaucracies.

These trends show the power of seemingly isolated events and individuals within Mexico to affect patterns in transnational crime that profoundly affect US society.

In our argument about the mutual causality between government agencies and criminal enterprises, we posit a tendency toward "massification," though we admit much complexity and many countertrends. Yet the huge entities and processes that have emerged are not made up of large numbers of uniform workers or managers, on either the state or the criminal organization sides. These organizations have a complex division of labor, with many roles and inequalities of power, reward, and prestige among the people who hold those roles. The various positions in these organizations are held broadly by people from different social positions, women and men, nationalities, races, class origins, and so forth. And even these social patterns are altered and inflected by individual qualities, such as brilliant skills and drive (as illustrated in Carey's history of La Chata). It is perhaps best to think of the contemporary situation as involving both formal organizations and also networks and subcontractors, linking together diverse powers, roles, knowledges, stances, and actors across multiple settings, but coordinated together for collective action in the dialectic struggle between legalized coercive power and illegalized coercive power.

The largest contemporary Mexican drug cartels compare in size to small US corporations and are equally complex. One or several capos, often related by blood and/or regional ties, direct cartel operations. Below them cadres of higher-level operatives, including negotiators, liaisons/diplomats, money-launderers, business fronts, accountants, lawyers, intelligence agents, and others perform the white-collar work of the drug trafficking organizations.[15] Lieutenants take charge of logistical operations. Squadrons of farmers, processors of drug crops, truck drivers, warehousemen, guards, car thieves, arms traffickers, hit men, and a wide variety of smugglers do the dirty/dangerous "blue-collar" work for cartels. Today cartels farm out much of the blue-collar work (which is in fact the majority of the activity) to poorly paid members of gangs or cells, often on a job-by-job basis, that are only loosely connected to a cartel per se. Smugglers and hit men, though relatively poorly paid, often die or are arrested (and face long prison terms) during the course of their work. They may be murdered for relatively minor infractions of unwritten cartel rules or simply because they are suspected of being disloyal. The lower-level proletarians in the drug trade are some of the most exploited and "disposable" workers in contemporary capitalist societies.

Diversity within cartels not only extends to functional roles within the drug business but also to the ethnic, gender, and national origins of cartel members and hired employees. The increasing participation of women in international drug trafficking has been documented by several authors. Women's greater role in the drug business is a result of a number of factors, including economic necessity and family ties and pressures, as well as conscious decisions to use women in specific smuggling roles because it is felt that they are more trusted by law enforcement officials and the general public and hence can more readily carry drugs and cross borders undetected. Likewise, older people, sometimes Anglo-Saxons (who are less likely to be racially profiled), are chosen to smuggle drug loads because of their supposed trustworthiness and lesser likelihood of engaging in criminal activity.

Cartels located on the border have very tight working relationships with Mexican American gangs that originated in El Paso, San Diego, Laredo, and elsewhere. Such gangs may cross the border and be involved in cartel operations in both Mexico and the United States. Farther away from the border, Mexican cartel members sell their wares to brokers from all the different ethnic groups represented in the United States (this also occurs, but to a lesser extent, in US border cities). In any case, the bottom line for cartel strategists is profit. Ethnicity, gender, age, and nationality are secondary issues or resources to be mobilized in the pursuit of money. Yet representations of people involved in the drug business work in almost the opposite way: they expose various ideologies about kinds of people through the rhetoric of illegal drugs (vulnerable female victims, men as leaders, scary women who cross into the world of men, among others, as discussed by Carey). A related, but poorly understood, issue is the motive of people involved in the drug business.[16] There is a wide and rich range of motivations and life projects among people involved in the world of drug trafficking. Yet again, the representation of motives tells us more about the representor than the representee. People who argue against Prohibition often use a clear-minded, rational economic motivation model; those who argue for it use a reductionist, victim, or deviant morality model. To make progress against these simplifications, it is crucial that we think at both levels — the complex diversity of actual individuals and organizations, and the rhetorical role of emotionally charged images of and discourses about them.

Why do these phenomena seem to concentrate at political borders (and related social, culture, and linguistic borders)?[17] The answers can be roughly categorized into border practices and border representations of illegality. To take the first set of phenomena, political borders — which are also legal and administrative boundaries — are the interface of different laws and regulations.[18] As a practice, then, there are many cases where market profits can be realized by moving goods, people, and activities from one zone (where, say, the good is legal) to another zone where it is prohibited, limited, or taxed (e.g., chapters by Carey, Díaz, Evans, Karibo, Mallek, and Romero). It is not only relevant to cases in which there are literally different legal treatments of particular goods and activities, but also geographic differences that allow particular illegalities to have bases where they are tolerated and thus can thrive (for example, as platforms for either bringing consumers in or for smuggling goods and people outward). Such spaces of tolerance are often internal to nation-states, and even in such cases still have borders, and they are often critical to understanding international political borders. What remains to be understood, however, is why geographies of toleration (and, conversely, prosecution) emerge and decline historically, in systematic terms. At the level of representation, tolerant spaces are often "explained" by some combination of moral stigma and corruption, but this is usually more of interest for the analysis of discourse than a realistic account of the actual politics of regulation.

But the logic of border crossing goes beyond literal differences in laws, economics, and administration. International borders are often important interfaces between large social formations with different cultural practices and economic standards of living (wage levels, etc.). Obviously, this can be overstated. There are many cross-cutting ties and cultural flows between nation-states, so borders are hardly absolute divisions. Nevertheless, what it creates in practice are movements to obtain the economic and cultural values to be found on the "other side of the border," such as cheap services and exotic tourism. There is a rich body of ideas to be researched, in the past and present, about what people are after when they cross borders.

Such distinctions also create a ground for representing the other nation as somehow different in kind, as stricter or easier, more indulgent or more moderate, and so forth. This comes out in the ways that Canadians viewed the desirability and perils of US residents crossing the border for various forms of tourism (alcohol, commercial sex [Karibo, Mallek]) and even the potential crossing of social practices, like LSD (Martel). It is also implicit in the way Mexico is represented from the United States' perspective and vice versa (Carey, Díaz).

If we examine borders, again, as actual places where extralegal activities occur, we note two different phenomena: flows of people as border crossers *to* the source of experiences, activities, services, or goods (e.g., the several chapters on US alcohol and sex tourism to Canada and Mexico), and flows of regulated or illegal goods and unauthorized people crossing boundaries *to* the market/society on the other side (e.g., other chapters on alcohol, drug, commercial goods, and migrant smuggling). The former (in-coming movement) may or may not be illegalized; it may be regarded as a morally reprehensible form of tourism by some people in the sending society, or just as a normal form of consumption. The boundary-crossing movement of prohibited items is in most cases illegal, precisely because the rules of the new space should apply on entry, although enforcement efforts may vary considerably.

However, the causes of these flows often emerge from the tendencies of whole societies (or sectors thereof). The markets for prohibited drugs in northern Mexican and southwestern US border cities are not trivial, but certainly they do not account for the overall vast drug market and the organizations that serve it. Drug production, transportation and logistics, wholesaling and marketing, and consumption are all continental-scale phenomena. They have deep roots in the social structure, economy, politics, and culture of the interiors of Canada, the United States, and Mexico. Thus to represent them as a border phenomenon, and to concentrate law enforcement against them substantially along borders, distinctly works to hide the functioning of interior people, markets, and institutions in this vast and complex trade. A similar erasure comes from blaming (demonizing, criminalizing, pitying) another nation. It helps reduce the awareness of self-contradictions in the societies away from the border. A number of the chapters in this book point to precisely this phenomenon, which we might call "hiding behind borders."

Political borders are profoundly important representations of the contemporary nation-state and related entities (such as Europe's controlled immigration and movement region, colloquially called Schengenland).

While nations actually are composed of an immense web of social relations and political-legal systems spread across the national geography, as well as vast transnational relations and flows, it is common and easy to reduce them to containers bounded by lines on a map,[19] and absolutely differentiated from the society on the other side of the border. Such understandings partake of some of the most powerful themes in human symbolic thinking, which is the role of external boundaries of all types (bodies, homes, kin, and other social units, etc.) in maintaining safety, purity, and order, and importantly, the danger posed by all types of movement and flow that cross such boundaries.[20]

Because of these symbolic dynamics, borders are often focal points for fears and anxieties (though sometimes also symbols of change and positive futures, and also exoticism, pleasure, etc.). The US-Mexico border (and to a much lower extent, the US-Canada border) is a magnet for moral panics, cycling almost constantly in the media and politics between immigration, drugs, and terrorism. Conversely, border enforcement is readily represented as a "barrier to all bads." An ideal border seals off and protects the self, the family, the community, the economy, and the polity from dangers (and even just changes) often understood as mainly external.[21] It is easy, then, to see how illegitimacy, crime, and law enforcement are often conceptually connected to borders and external flows, producing (via the sphere of politics) not only discourses but also real material practices, such as border walls. This book constantly illustrates this political dynamic of border law enforcement (a clear example being Díaz). Even more important, it illustrates the difficulty in analyzing the realities of borders, where there really are numerous illegal practices and flows, but also immense distortions, exaggerations, simplifications, and hiding of other locations and issues due to the role of border discourses.

Finally, borders are used in the process of representation as tropes for internal subpopulations, social cleavages, and so forth. For example, Mexico is commonly used in the United States as shorthand for US drug and migration consumption, and within that, the border is particularly used as a way of marking people as outsiders (e.g., immigrants as border crossing outsiders). Several chapters offer interesting case material on borders and national symbolism to interpret and police complicated and conflictive gender and sexual relations (e.g., Carey, Karibo, and Marak and Tuennerman). One of the challenges of this book is that we refer to more than one phenomenon by "border," including boundaries of political-legal jurisdictions and wider sorts of social divisions and edges, some but not all with distinctive geographic manifestations.[22] The point is not to designate only one use of border as correct. Rather, it is to urge us to be clear which usages we are using, and also to ask interesting questions about how the jurisdictional borders interact with the social borders in both practice and representation

Drugs vary considerably in how they are treated in law: tobacco, a powerfully addictive and dangerous drug, is legal (though regulated and taxed), while marijuana is a mainstay of the North American illegal drug system. This example, like many others, points to our final theme, the social construction of legality and illegality. Although criminological theories differ, broadly we accept the idea that what is legal and what is illegal is substantially social constructed.[23] That is, social processes, often involving considerable inequalities of power, culturally produce particular groups, activities, and goods as illegal and (importantly) particularly prone to deviance. It is hard not to take a social constructionist position (at least in part) when we consider some of the cases in this book, where criminality is defined and treated so differently across borders and over time, and where powerful figures in governments portray some actors as dangerous deviants and others as innocent victims. Likewise, an idea that cuts across this book is the distinction from Van Schendel and Abraham (see above) between licit/illicit and legal/illegal. Obviously, both are socially constructed, so what defines the legal/illegal pair is some specific people and social sectors with access to the making of formal state law, while the licit/illicit pairing refers to a much wider range of judgments of legitimacy made in various different social milieux.

The social construction of crime has limits, however. While theories of social construction tell us something about the contested ontological nature of crime (it is not just obvious, universal, and inherent) and point us toward the way crime as a label is constituted and applied, they lack a more substantive theory of just what, how, and why particular constructions emerge. Why are labor migrants, heavily from Mexico and Central America, who cross borders construed as criminals?[24] Why are mobile elites from many parts of the world, including those countries, rarely viewed or sought as criminals, even when they violate immigration laws?[25] To understand what is treated as border transgression and what is not, we need to connect particular sequences of construction to wider developments, such as class inequalities and privileges, global cultural and economic flows, stratified labor markets and systems of exploitation, racist and nationalist ideologies, and so forth. Obviously, that vast connective effort must wait for another occasion, but it illustrates where scholars will go in the future, contextualizing "crime" in major power processes.[26]

Borders are thus particularly crucial to exploring that which is hidden in the social construction of law and crime. On the one hand, borders are powerful ways to construe dangerous others — those "threats" coming from across the "line." On the other hand, borders are effective means to hide operations that might be exposed to legal prosecution and public opprobrium, were they conducted in a domestic space. For example, while the public of North America debates legalizing drugs and witnesses, through the media, heavily constructed images and narratives of drug violence in Mexico, international financial fraud far eclipsed even the largest drug cartels. Recent reporting by the McClatchy press chain finds that Goldman Sachs in the 2000s used the Cayman Islands to market in deceptive ways packages of US-based mortgage-based securities with deep problems (many including fraud in their origination) to customers outside the United States, often in Europe, for billions of dollars.[27] Tax avoidance, unaccountable finance, pollution havens, and so forth: all of these are arguably crimes made possible by legal borders and transnational flows across them.[28] Our public representation of certain crimes in moral panic terms as scary global issues (drug cartels, sex trafficking) distracts us from other, equally frightening global issues, especially elite crime.[29] Borders thus do their complex work throughout the whole space of society.

Notes

Introduction

1. H. Richard Friman notes that narratives that focus on the unprecedented rise of criminal networks and the never-before-seen levels of transnational criminal activities are often based on methodologically shaky grounds and can also be inflated due to the "public relations considerations" of otherwise reliable international organizations. See H. Richard Friman, "Crime and Globalization," in *Crime and the Global Political Economy*, ed. Friman (Boulder, CO: Lynne Rienner, 2009), 2–5.

2. Frances Berdan, "Living on the Edge in an Ancient Imperial World: Aztec Crime and Deviance," *Global Crime* 9, no. 1–2 (February–May 2008): 28; Sophie D. Coe and Michael D. Coe, *The True History of Chocolate* (New York: Thames and Hudson, 2007), 101.

3. John Mayo, "Consuls and Silver Contraband on Mexico's West Coast in the Era of Santa Anna," *Journal of Latin American Studies* 19, no. 2 (November 1987): 390.

4. Gilman M. Ostrander, "The Colonial Molasses Trade," *Agricultural History* 30, no. 2 (April 1956): 77–84.

5. Petrus van Duyne notes that it is so obviously the case that laws are the "great creator of forbidden fruits" that there is no need for scholars to dwell on the matter. See van Duyne, "Medieval Thinking and Organized Crime Economy," in *Transnational Organized Crime: Myth, Power, and Profit*, ed. Emilio C. Viano, José Magallanes, and Laurent Bridel (Durham, NC: Carolina Academic Press, 2003), 12.

6. Peter Andreas, *Border Games: Policing the U.S.-Mexico Divide* (Ithaca: Cornell University Press, 2000), 30; David Phillipson, *Smuggling: A History, 1700–1970* (Newton Abbot, UK: David and Charles, 1973); Pablo Pérez-Mallaína Bueno, *La metrópoli insular: rivalidad comercial canario-sevillana, 1650–1708*, Colección "Alisios," no. 9. (Las Palmas de Gran Canaria: Ediciones del Cabildo Insular de Gran Canaria, 1993); Kris E. Lane, *Pillaging the Empire: Piracy in the Americas, 1500–1750*, Latin American Realities (Armonk, NY: M. E. Sharpe, 1998); Roy Moxham, *Tea: Addiction, Exploi-*

tation, and Empire (New York: Carroll and Graf, 2003); Edwaurd Butts, *Outlaws of the Lakes: Bootlegging and Smuggling from Colonial Times to Prohibition* (Holt, MI: Thunder Bay Press, 2004); Eric Tagliacozzo, *Secret Trades, Porous Borders: Smuggling and States along a Southeast Asian Frontier, 1865–1915* (New Haven: Yale University Press, 2005).

7. Paul Gootenberg, *Andean Cocaine: The Making of a Global Drug* (Chapel Hill: University of North Carolina Press, 2008), 7.

8. *Continental Crossroads: Remapping U.S.-Mexico Borderlands History*, ed. Samuel Truett and Elliot Young (Durham, NC: Duke University Press, 2004), ix. Alejandro Lugo points out that not all people can cross borders, usually on account of their race, class, and/or ethnicity. See Alejandro Lugo, *Fragmented Lives, Assembled Parts: Culture, Capitalism, and Conquest at the U.S.-Mexico Border* (Austin: University of Texas Press, 2008), 117. We borrow the concept of "borderlanders" from Willem van Schendel, "Spaces of Engagement: How Borderlands, Illegal Flows, and Territorial States Interlock," in *Illicit Flows and Criminal Things: States, Borders, and the Other Side of Globalization*, ed. van Schendel and Itty Abraham (Bloomington: Indian University Press, 2005), 55; and from Oscar J. Martínez, "Border Interaction: New Approaches to Border Analysis," in *Global Boundaries*, ed. Clive H. Schofield (London: Routledge Press, 1994), 1–15; and Martínez, *Border People: Life and Society in U.S.-Mexico Borderlands* (Tucson: University of Arizona Press, 1994).

9. Sam Truett and Elliot Young, "Introduction: Making Transnational History: Nations, Regions, and Borderlands," in *Continental Crossroads*, ed. Truett and Young, 6; Roger Rouse, "Mexican Migration and the Social Spaces of Postmodernism," in *Between Two Worlds: Mexican Immigrants in the United States*, ed. David Gutiérrez (Wilmington, DE: Scholarly Resources, 1996), 247–65; Michiel Baud and Willem Van Schendel, "Toward a Comparative History of Borderlands," *Journal of World History* 8, no. 2 (fall 1997): 211–42. For a contemporary study of the impact of drugs on borderlanders and on a particular border site, see Howard Campbell's *Drug War Zone: Frontline Dispatches from the Streets of El Paso and Ciudad Juárez* (Austin: University of Texas, 2009).

10. Karl Jacoby, "Between North and South: The Alternative Borderlands of William H. Ellis and the African American Colony of 1895," in *Continental Crossroads*, ed. Truett and Young, 230; Kimberly L. Thachuk, "An Introduction to Transnational Threats," in *Transnational Threats: Smuggling and Trafficking in Arms, Drugs, and Human Life* (Westport, CN: Praeger Security International, 2007), 3–20. These entrepreneurs should also include what Peter Andreas and Ethan Nadelmann call "transnational moral entrepreneurs" who generally work to convince foreign elites to adopt the moral codes of one society as if they were universal truths. See Peter Andreas and Ethan Nadelmann, *Policing the Globe: Criminalization and Crime Control in International Relations* (Oxford: Oxford University Press, 2006).

11. Tom Miller, *On the Border: Portraits of America's Southwest Frontier* (New York: Harper and Row, 1981), 108–9 and Peter Andreas, *Border Games*, 30–31. Cormac McCarthy provides a vivid illustration of a clandestine wax camp in *All the Pretty Horses* (New York: Alfred A. Knopf, 1992), 65, 73, and 75. We want to thank Sterling Evans for suggesting candelilla as a viable topic and directing us to these references.

12. Josiah McC. Heyman, "U.S. Ports of Entry on the Mexican Border," in *On the Border: Society and Culture between the United States and Mexico*, ed. Andrew

Grant Wood (Lanham, MD: SR Books, 2004), 222. Peter Andreas notes the symbiotic relationship between smugglers and states, arguing that it is the perception that smuggling (of goods or people) is a "growing threat that is most critical for sustaining and expanding law enforcement." See Peter Andreas, "Smuggling Wars: Law Enforcement and Law Evasion in a Changing World," in *Transnational Crime in the Americas*, ed. Tom Farer (New York: Routledge, 1999), 94. Moisés Naím similarly argues that the focus on sending countries is "politically profitable" and the tools such as "helicopters, gunboats, heavily armed agents, judges, and generals" are more "telegenic" than focusing on demand. See Moisés Naím, *Illicit: How Smugglers, Traffickers, and Copycats are Hijacking the Global Economy* (New York: Bantam, 2005), 234–35.

13. Samuel Truett and Elliot Young, "Conclusion: Borderlands Unbound," in *Continental Crossroads*, ed. Truett and Young, 327; Jane Bayes and Mary Hawkesworth, "Introduction," in *Women, Democracy, and Globalization in North America: A Comparative Study*, ed. Jane Bayes, Patricia Begné, Laura Gonzalez, Lois Harder, Mary Hawkesworth, and Laura Macdonald (New York: Palgrave Macmillan, 2006), 3–28.

14. About the impact of the resettlement of refugees on exurban communities, see Warren St. John, *Outcasts United: A Refugee Soccer Team, An American Town* (New York: Spiegal and Grau, 2009).

15. Peter Andreas, "Smuggling Wars," 86.

16. Itty Abraham and Willem van Schendel, "Introduction: The Making of Illicitness," in *Illicit Flows and Criminal Things*, ed. van Schendel and Abraham, 4–25; David Kyle and Christina A. Siracusa, "Seeing the State Like a Migrant: Why So Many Non-Criminals Break Immigration Laws," in *Illicit Flows and Criminal Things*, ed. van Schendel and Abraham, 153.

17. Gootenberg notes that which drugs nation-states decide to regulate and ban are largely historical accidents. See, for example, Gootenberg, *Andean Cocaine*, 122, and Paul Gootenberg, "Talking Like a State: Drugs, Borders, and the Language of Control," in *Illicit Flows and Criminal Things*, ed. van Schendel and Abraham, 105–8.

18. Naím, *Illicit*, 239–42.

19. Andreas and Nadelmann, *Policing the Globe*, vi–viii.

20. Tyler Stovall, "Civil Rights Meets Decolonization: Transnational Visions of the Struggle for Racial Equality in France and America," *World History Bulletin* 26, no. 1 (spring 2010): 27.

21. Oscar J. Martínez, *Troublesome Border*, Profmex monograph series (Tucson: University of Arizona Press, 1988), and Martínez, *Border People: Life and Society in the U.S.-Mexico Borderlands* (Tucson: University of Arizona Press, 1994).

22. For example, see "Agent against Prohibition," in Howard Campbell's *Drug War Zone*, 259–64.

23. Andreas, *Border Games*, 9.

24. James R. Sheffield, Ambassador, to Aáron Saenz, Srio de Relaciones Exteriores, 7 February 1927, 2.015.4(1-4)-1, Caja 3, Bebidas Embriagantes (Cantinas), AGN — Dirreción General de Gobierno — Ramo Gobernación; and Pitman B. Potter, "The Positions of Canada and the United States in the Matter of Trade in Alcoholic Beverages," *American Journal of International Law* 24, no. 1 (January 1930): 131.

25. Naím, *Illicit*, 67; Thachuk, "An Introduction to Transnational Threats," 3–20.

26. Van Schendel, "Spaces of Engagement," in *Illicit Flows and Criminal Things*, ed. van Schendel and Abraham, 47–49.

27. Ibid.

28. Naím, *Illicit*; van Schendel and Abraham, eds., *Illicit Flows and Criminal Things*; and Tom Farer, ed., *Transnational Crime in the Americas*.

29. Colin Gordon, "Governmental Rationality: An Introduction," in *The Foucault Effect: Studies in Governmentality*, ed. Graham Burchell, Colin Gordon, and Peter Miller (Chicago: University of Chicago, 1991), 4–5.

30. Michael Kenney, *From Pablo to Osama: Trafficking and Terrorist Networks, Government Bureaucracies, and Competitive Adaptation* (University Park: Pennsylvania State University Press, 2007).

31. Van Schendel and Abraham, "Introduction: The Making of Illicitness," in *Illicit Flows and Criminal Things*, ed. van Schendel and Abraham, 23.

32. Ibid., 14.

33. Jeremy Adelman and Stephen Aron, "From Borderlands to Borders: Empires, Nation-States, and the Peoples in Between in North American History," *American Historical Review* 104, no. 3 (June 1999): 816.

34. For examples of serious historical investigations into smuggling along the US-Mexico border, see James A. Sandos, "Northern Separatism during the Mexican Revolution: An Inquiry into the Role of Drug Trafficking, 1919–1920," *Americas* 41 (1984): 208; Robert Buffington, "Prohibition in the Borderlands: National Government-Border Community Relations," *Pacific Historical Review* 63, no. 1 (1994): 19–38; and Gabriela Recio, "Drugs and Alcohol: U.S. Prohibition and the Origins of the Drug Trade in Mexico, 1910–1930," *Journal of Latin American Studies* 34, no. 1 (2002): 21–42.

35. For two examples, see Adelman and Aron, "From Borderlands to Borders," 816; and Samuel Truett, *Fugitive Landscapes: The Forgotten History of the U.S.-Mexico Borderlands* (New Haven: Yale University Press, 2006), 9.

36. Friman has argued that powerful states are often not "willing to fully engage in crime control" when doing so conflicts with other more important interests. Accordingly, we might also expect this same dynamic from local, state, and provincial governments. See Friman, "Crime and Globalization," 10. His argument is further fleshed out in, H. Richard Friman, "Externalizing the Costs of Prohibition," *Crime and the Global Political Economy*, ed. Friman: 49–65.

37. Friman, "Crime and Globalization," 15.

38. On the US-Mexico border as a locus of inequality, see Howard Campbell and Josiah McC. Heyman, "The Study of Borderlands Consumption: Potentials and Precautions," *Land of Necessity: Consumer Culture in the United States–Mexico Borderlands*, ed. Alexis McCrossen (Durham, NC: Duke University Press, 2009): 325–32. On the social construction of indigenous otherness, see Carlos Salomon, "*Indigenismo* Across Borders," *Journal of the West* 48, no. 3 (summer 2009): 48–52; and Robert Perez, "Confined to the Margins: Smuggling Among Native Peoples of the Borderlands," *Land of Necessity: Consumer Culture in the United States–Mexico Borderlands*, ed. Alexis McCrossen (Durham, NC: Duke University Press, 2009): 248–73.

39. Josiah McC. Heyman, ed. *States and Illegal Practices* (Oxford: Berg 1999); *Life and Labor on the Border: Working People of Northeastern Sonora, Mexico 1886–1986* (Tucson: University of Arizona Press, 1991); "The Mexico–United States Border in Anthropology: A Critique and Reformulation," *Journal of Political Ecology* 1 (1994): 43–65; and Howard Campbell, "Drug Trafficking Stories: Everyday Forms of Narco-

Folklore on the U.S.-Mexico Border," *International Journal of Drug Policy* 16 (2005): 326–33; and Campbell "Female Drug Smugglers on the U.S.-Mexico Border," in *Drug War Zone*.

40. Citation in William Kates, "Mohawks, Feds Have Different View of Smuggling Case," *Associated Press*, November 6, 1998. See also Estanislao Oziewicz, "Border Pipeline," *Globe and Mail*, December 11, 1998, A7; Doug George-Kanentiio, "Mohawks Shun Illegal Acts, Rebels Are Not Members of Mohawk Nation," *Post Standard*, July 26, 1998; Doug George-Kanentiio, "Recent Arrests Will Not End Smuggling Among Mohawks," *Cornwall Standard Freeholder*, December 19, 2006, 6; *Frozen River*, written and directed by Courtney Hunt, 2008.

41. Eric Breton, Lucie Richard, France Gagnon, Marie Jacques, and Pierre Bergeron, "Fighting a Tobacco-Tax Rollback: A Political Analysis of the 1994 Cigarette Contraband Crisis," *Journal of Public Health Policy* 27, no. 1 (2006): 77–99.

42. The median cost to get smuggled across the US-Mexico border by a *coyote* has increased from $400 to $1,600 over the course of the last decade and a half. In addition, increased border enforcement does not reduce undocumented migration (though economic recessions do); instead, the increased cost of getting across the border incentivizes longer stays in the United States. See, Jezmin Fuentes, Henry L'Esperance, Raúl Pérez, and Caitlin White, "Impacts of U.S. Immigration Policies on Migrant Behavior," in *Impacts of Border Enforcement on Mexican Immigration*, ed. Wayne A. Cornelius and Jessa M. Lewis (La Jolla, CA: Center for Comparative Immigration Studies, University of California, San Diego, 2007), 53–73; Douglas Massey, Jorge Durand, and Nolan J. Malone, *Beyond Smoke and Mirrors* (New York: Russell Sage Foundation, 2002).

Chapter 1. Chinese Immigrant Smuggling to the United States via Mexico and Cuba, 1882–1916

1. An earlier version of this chapter was first published in the *Amerasia Journal* 30, no. 3 (2004–5): 1–16.

2. Today such smuggling guides are known as "coyotes." Unbeknownst to most people the first "coyotes" of Mexico smuggled Chinese immigrants into the United States during the late nineteenth and early twentieth centuries.

3. Harry H. Weddle Inspector in Charge San Diego to Inspector in Charge Immigration Service Los Angeles, San Diego, 11 January 1912, 1–11; included in Francisco Rios(?), *Chinese Exclusion Act Case File no. 1000/1*, National Archives, Laguna Niguel.

4. Most of the existing literature on undocumented immigration to the United States from Mexico focuses on the topic of contemporary immigrant smuggling. For example, see, Peter Andreas, *Border Games: Policing the United States–Mexico Divide* (Ithaca: Cornell University Press, 2009). Unbeknownst to most people, undocumented immigrant smuggling from Mexico to the United States began in the late 19th century and was "invented" by the Chinese. This chapter builds on the historical literature on Chinese immigrant smuggling pioneered by Alan Perkins and Erika Lee. For more on this topic, see Clifford Alan Perkins, *Border Patrol: With the U.S. Immigration Service on the Mexican Boundary, 1910–1954* (El Paso: Texas Western Press, University of

Texas at El Paso, 1978); Erika Lee, *At America's Gates: Chinese Immigration during the Exclusion Era, 1882–1943* (Chapel Hill: University of North Carolina Press, 2003).

5. For more on the Chinese transnational commercial orbit and Chinese immigration to Mexico, see Robert Chao Romero, *The Chinese in Mexico, 1882–1940* (Tucson: University of Arizona Press, 2010).

6. Perkins, *Border Patrol*, 49. The Chinese Exclusion Act of May 6, 1882, barred the immigration of Chinese laborers to the United States for a period of ten years. According to certain exceptions built into the federal legislation, merchants, students, and teachers were allowed to enter the United States in small numbers on governmental issuance of special "Section Six" identification certificates. Congress expanded the restrictions of the Chinese Exclusion Act through the Scott Act of 1888 and the Geary Act of 1892, and in 1904, the federal legislature permanently barred Chinese immigration through the indefinite extension of the Chinese exclusion laws. Bill Ong Hing, *Making and Remaking Asian America through Immigration Policy, 1850–1890* (Stanford: Stanford University Press, 1993), 24–26.

7. Hudgins to Carlisle, San Antonio, Texas, 18 July 1896, 2; Ralph Izard Special Inspector of Customs to Col. W. P. Hudgins, Laredo, Texas, 12 January 1895; both letters from Record Group 36, Customs Bureau Special Agents Reports and Correspondence ca. 1865–1915, box 276, Hudgins — 1894 Hull — December 1890, National Archives, Washington, DC; Perkins, *Border Patrol*, 12.

8. Perkins, *Border Patrol*, 12.

9. Hudgins to Carlisle, San Antonio, Texas, 18 July 1896, 2; Ralph Izard Special Inspector of Customs to Col. W. P. Hudgins, Laredo, Texas, 12 January 1895; Izard to Hudgins, Laredo, Texas, 26 September, 1896, enclosed in letter from Hudgins to Carlisle Secretary of the Treasury, San Antonio, Texas, 28 September 1896; 4 letters from Record Group 36, Customs Bureau Special Agents Reports and Correspondence ca. 1865–1915, box 276, Hudgins — 1894 Hull — December 1890, National Archives, Washington, DC.

10. Hudgins to Carlisle, San Antonio, Texas, 18 July 1896, 2; Izard to Hudgins, Laredo, Texas?, 26 September, 1896, enclosed in letter from Hudgins to Carlisle Secretary of the Treasury, San Antonio, Texas, 28 September 1896; 3 letters from Record Group 36, Customs Bureau Special Agents Reports and Correspondence ca. 1865–1915, box 276, Hudgins — 1894 Hull — December 1890, National Archives, Washington, DC.

11. Izard to Hudgins, Laredo, Texas?, 26 September, 1896, enclosed in letter from Hudgins to Carlisle Secretary of the Treasury, San Antonio, Texas, 28 September 1896; 2 letters from Record Group 36, Customs Bureau Special Agents Reports and Correspondence ca. 1865–1915, box 276, Hudgins — 1894 Hull — December 1890, National Archives, Washington, DC.

12. For more on this "from borderlands to borders" argument, see Jeremy Adelman and Stephen Aron, "From Borderlands to Borders: Empires, Nation-States, and the Peoples in Between in North American History," *American Historical Review* 104, no. 3 (June 1999): 814–41.

13. Perkins, *Border Patrol*, 11–13.

14. Ibid., 13.

15. Wicker to The Honorable Charles Foster Secretary of the Treasury, 24 May 1891; Wicker to Foster, 29 May 1891, Wicker to Foster, 6 June 1891; US Attorney Wm. Grant to Wicker, 6 June 1891, enclosed in previous letter; all letters from Re-

cord Group 36, Customs Bureau Special Agents Reports and Correspondence ca. 1865–1915, box 424, F. N. Wicker, National Archives, Washington, DC.

16. Stokes to Secretary of the Treasury, El Paso, Texas, 12 August 1897; Stokes to Collector of Customs San Francisco, El Paso, 12 August 1897; 2 letters from Record Group 36, Customs Bureau Special Agents Reports and Correspondence ca. 1865–1915, box 392 Stokes Szabad, National Archives, Washington, DC.

17. Stokes to Carlisle, 13 March 1896; H. E. Tippett Chinese Inspector to Honorable John G. Carlisle Secretary of the Treasury, Plattsburgh, NY, 12 March 1896; 2 letters from Record Group 36, Customs Bureau Special Agents Reports and Correspondence ca. 1865–1915, box 392 Stokes Szabad, National Archives, Washington, DC.

18. Datus E. Coon Chinese Inspector to Collector of Customs of San Francisco, San Diego, 2 August 1890, marked "Exhibit B"; Coon to Honorable William Windom Secretary of the Treasury, San Diego, 13 October 1890; "Prisoner for Prisoner," "The Alameda Jail Trouble," newspaper articles attached to October 13 letter and marked as "Exhibit A." 2 letters from Record Group 36, Customs Bureau Special Agents Reports and Correspondence ca. 1865–1915, D. E. Coon, National Archives, Washington, DC.

19. Richard Rule Special Inspector to Mr. W. P. Hudgins Special Agent in Charge, El Paso, 1 April 1897, enclosed with letter from Hudgins to Honorable L. J. Gage Secretary of the Treasury, 28 April 1897; letters from Record Group 36, Customs Bureau Special Agents Reports and Correspondence ca. 1865–1915, box 276 Hudgins — 1894 Hull — December 1890, National Archives, Washington, DC.

20. Ibid.

21. Hudgins to Honorable L. J. Gage Secretary of the Treasury, 28 April 1897; from Record Group 36, Customs Bureau Special Agents Reports and Correspondence ca. 1865–1915, box 276 Hudgins — 1894 Hull — December 1890, National Archives, Washington, DC.

22. Ibid.; Izard to Hudgins, 24 April 1897, enclosed in previous letter from 28 April 1897.

23. F. N. Wicker Special Inspector to O. L. Spaulding Assistant Secretary of the Treasury, 6 August 1891, box 424 F. N. Wicker; W. F. Norman Chinese Inspector to Honorable J. G. Carlisle Secretary of the Treasury, 25 July 1895; Norman to Hon. C. S. Hamlin Assistant Secretary of the Treasury, 24 July 1895; both from box 353 Noble Norton, W. F. Norman File; E. T. Stokes Special Agent to Mr. Chas. Davis Collector of Port at El Paso, Eagle Pass, Texas, 19 May 1897, from box 392 Stokes Szabad; Richard Rule Special Inspector Acting in Charge to Mr. George W. Whitehead Special Agent, El Paso, Texas, 15 March 1897, from box 374 Rodmans Ryan; all letters from Record Group 36, Customs Bureau Special Agents Reports and Correspondence ca. 1865–1915, National Archives, Washington, DC.

24. F. N. Wicker Special Inspector to O. L. Spaulding Assistant Secretary of the Treasury, 6 August 1891, box 424 F. N. Wicker; from Record Group 36, Customs Bureau Special Agents Reports and Correspondence ca. 1865–1915, National Archives, Washington, DC.

25. McEnery to C. S. Hamlin Assistant Secretary of the Treasury, New Orleans, 4 July 1894; McEnery to Honorable John G. Carlisle Secretary of the Treasury, New Orleans, 25 July 1894; from Record Group 36, Customs Bureau Special Agents Reports and Correspondence ca. 1865–1915, box 314 McDowell McFarland, National Archives, Washington, DC.

26. Special Agent McEnery to Hon. C. S. Hamlin, Ass't Sec. of Treasury, 3 May 1894; McEnery to Hamlin, New Orleans, 29 May 1894; from box 314 McDowell McFarland, J. A. McEnery file; Izard to Hudgins, New Orleans, 14 May 1894; "List of Chinamen naturalized at New Orleans La.," enclosed with 14 May 1894 letter from Izard to Hudgins; Acting Secretary of the Treasury Department to Mr. J. A. McEnery Special Agent, enclosed with above 14 May 1894 letter from Izard to Hudgins; Acting Secretary to Mr. W. P. Hudgins, 28 May 1894, enclosed with May 14 letter; from box 278 Hussey Izard, Ralph Izard file; all from Record Group 36, Customs Bureau Special Agents Reports and Correspondence ca. 1865–1915, National Archives, Washington, DC.

27. Richard Rule Special Inspector Acting in Charge to Mr. George W. Whitehead Special Agent, El Paso, Texas, 15 March 1897; from box 374 Rodmans Ryan; E. T. Stokes Special Agent Office of Special Agent Treasury Department to Honorable John G. Carlisle Secretary of the Treasury, Plattsburgh, NY, 2 January 1894; E. T. Stokes Special Agent to Hon. John G. Carlisle, Plattsburgh, 2 January 1894; sworn statement of Adelbert F. Miles before Wendell A. Anderson, Consul General of the United States of America at Montreal, 30 December 1893, enclosed with above letter of Stokes to Carlisle from 2 January 1894; from box 391 Stealey, O. O. Stebbins Stokes, Stokes file; all from Record Group 36, Customs Bureau Special Agents Reports and Correspondence ca. 1865–1915, National Archives, Washington, DC.

Chapter 2. Cree Contraband or Contraband Crees?

1. Willem van Schendel and Itty Abraham, "Introduction," in *Illicit Flows and Criminal Things: States, Borders, and the Other Side of Globalization* (Bloomington: Indiana University Press, 2005), 1–37.

2. See James C. Scott, *Seeing Like a State: How Certain Schemes to Improve the Human Condition Have Failed* (New Haven: Yale University Press, 1998), 1–3.

3. The term *Montanans* will be used generically to denote the general Euro-American population of Montana. They were a diverse group in economic, social, and cultural terms, hailing from distant and more recent European immigrant roots. However, they all shared a common self-perception that placed themselves and their interests at stark odds with Native Americans, be they of American or Canadian origin.

4. Elaine Carey and Andrae Marak, "Introduction," in this book.

5. Chippewa migration in this period followed similar trajectories, bringing them west and south, toward and across the 49th Parallel.

6. For a rough geographic chronology of Cree and Chippewa migrations, see the following sources: John C. Ewers, *Ethnological Report of the Chippewa Cree Tribe of the Rocky Boy Reservation, Montana, and the Little Shell Band of Indians*, Docket No. 221-B, Indian Claims Commission (New York: Garland, 1974), 19, 22–23, 50; Alexander Henry and David Thompson, *New Light on the Early History of the Greater Northwest* (New York: F. P. Harper, 1897), 53, 314, 408, 419, 540–87, 938; Alexander Mackenzie, *Journals and Letters of Alexander Mackenzie* (Cambridge: Hakluyt Society, 1970), 174, 179, 271, 275, 281; Gary Moulton, ed., *The Journals of the Lewis and Clark Expedition August 25, 1804–April 6, 1805* (Lincoln: University of Nebraska Press, 1987), 3:433; Floyd W. Sharrock and Susan R. Sharrock, *History of the Cree In-*

dian Territorial Expansion from the Hudson Bay Area to the Interior Saskatchewan and Missouri Plains, Docket 221b-191, Indian Claims Commission (New York: Garland, 1974), 12; and David Thompson, *David Thompson's Narrative, 1784–1812* (Toronto: Champlain Society, 1962), 48–49, 72, 107, 240.

7. Walter Denny, *Stories from the Old Ones: As Told to Walter A. Denny* (Missoula, MT: Rising Wolf, 1979), 29–33.

8. Walter Denny, "Story of the Bear Paws," Rocky Boy School Archive (RBSA), box Elder, MT. The later migration of Little Bear's band to Montana after the 1885 Northwest Rebellion adds to this tradition. One night, in a dream, a figure told Little Bear that the "land of the Big Knife" was the place for his people. Pointing south, the figure told Little Bear to look, and before his gaze stood the Bear Paw Mountains. For Crees, Montana was a land for which they were destined. See Interview with Four Souls, May 1975, in Catherine Isabel Littlejohn, "The Indian Oral Tradition: A Model for Teachers" (MA thesis, University of Saskatchewan, 1975), 91.

9. "British Indians over the Line," *Benton Weekly Record*, August 3, 1882.

10. One of the earliest accounts placing Crees in Montana came from Hudson Bay Company employee Peter Fidler in 1793. Much to the consternation of his employers, he reported of Cree intermediaries trading furs between Piegan, Snak, and Kootenay tribes near and south of the 49th Parallel and Anglo merchants in northern Saskatchewan. See J. G. Nelson, *The Last Refuge* (Montreal: Harvest House, 1973), 44. Lewis and Clark's Corps of Discovery likewise place Cree traders south of the 49th Parallel, trading along the present reaches of the Montana-North Dakota border, near the Missouri-Yellowstone confluence. They reported, "They are a wandering nation . . . are well disposed toward the whites, and treat their traders with respect. . . . They might, probably be induced to visit an establishment on the Missouri, at the Yellowstone river." See Gary Moulton, ed., *The Journals of the Lewis and Clark Expedition, August 25, 1804–April 6, 1805*, vol. 3 (Lincoln: University of Nebraska Press, 1987), 433. Both of these accounts place Crees well within US territory, and in the case of Lewis and Clark, even pronounce a positive view of them as potential trade allies. More nonchalant mention was made of Cree traders in the 1850s. See Edwin A. C. Hatch Diary, June 26, July 5, July 6, 1856, Montana State Historical Society (MSHS), Helena, MT, SC 810.

11. "The Overland Trail," MSHS, David Higler Papers, 1867–1935, SC 864.

12. In 1844, Commissioner of Indian Affairs, T. M. Crawford articulated a newly negative interpretation of Canadian Natives, Métis in this particular example, south of the line. He wrote that they "ought not be permitted to hunt within our boundaries, to the injury of our Indians and the citizens of the United States who are trading among them." See United States, Office of Indian Affairs, 1844 Annual Report of the Commissioner of Indian Affairs (Washington DC: T. Barnard, Printer, 1846), 7.

13. "Our Threatened Border," *Benton Record*, December 21, 1877.

14. Samuel Breck to Fort Assiniboine, August 15, 1881, Montana State University Archives (MSUA), Bozeman, MT, Fort Assiniboine Telegrams Received (FATR), 1881, Collection 2456. Emphasis added.

15. "3000 Strong!" *Benton Weekly Record*, August 25, 1881.

16. "The Indian News," *Benton Weekly Record*, August 25, 1881.

17. G. S. Turner to Fort Assiniboine, September 10, 1881. MSUA-FATR.

18. "Indians on the Marias," *Daily Independent* (Helena), September 30, 1881.

19. "A Little Indian News," *Benton Weekly Record*, October 13, 1881.

20. Gustavus Doane to Mary Hunter Doane, October 22, 1881, MSHS, Gustavus Doane Letters, SC 28. Lea Lawrence, a foreign correspondent from Chicago, reported that the camp may have been as large as 1,600 lodges, or 8,000 individuals. See a redacted version of the report in "Canadian Crees Trespassing on U.S. Territory in October 1881," *Winners of the West* 8, no. 10 (September 30, 1931).

21. "An Indian Rumpus," *Benton Weekly Record*, October 27, 1881.

22. "Recovered from the Crees," *Benton Weekly Record*, February 16, 1882.

23. "Montana Matters," *Daily Independent*, March 3, 1882.

24. "Another Indian Raid," *Benton Weekly Record*, March 2, 1882.

25. In April, Canadian authorities specifically identified the Sweet Grass Hills corridor as being a conduit for transnational Cree horse raiding and warned Fort Assiniboine officials of inbound groups. See Guido Ilges to Fort Assiniboine, April 19, 1883, National Archives of Canada (NAC), Indian Department Records, Black Series, RG 10, vol. 3740, reel C-10130, file 28748-2.

26. "Captured by Crees," *Daily Helena Independent*, March 8, 1882.

27. "No Further News," *Daily Helena Independent*, March 9, 1882; "The Expected Fight," *Daily Helena Independent*, March 10, 1882.

28. "Healy's Account," *Daily Helena Independent*, April 1, 1882.

29. Gustavus Doane to Mary Hunter Doane, March 26, 1882, MSHS, SC 28.

30. "The Assiniboine Expedition," *Benton Weekly Record*, March 30, 1882.

31. "Back Again," *Benton Weekly Record*, May 4, 1882.

32. "Indian Iniquities," *Benton Weekly Record*, May 4, 1882.

33. "More Cavalry Needed for Assiniboine," *Benton Weekly Record*, May 4, 1882.

34. Ibid.

35. Patrick Burke to Mr. Burke (father), June 21, 1882. MSHS, Patrick Francis "Frank" Burke Papers, Letters, 1881–1885, SC 304.

36. "More Cavalry Needed for Assiniboine."

37. Ibid.

38. "Big Bear and his Blanketed Band," *Daily Independent*, May 17, 1882. Emphasis added.

39. "Montana Matters," *Daily Helena Independent*, May 10, 1882.

40. See "Montana Matters," *Daily Independent*, May 30, 1882; "Recovery of Stolen Horses," *Benton Weekly Record*, June 1, 1882; "Montana Matters," *Daily Independent*, June 2, 1882; "The Blood War Party and Lively Crees," *Benton Weekly Record*, June 15, 1882; "Seventy Twin Brothers: The Remarkable Manner in Which a Band of Crees Were Fooled," *Daily Independent*, June 18, 1882; "War Among the Redskins," *Benton Weekly Record*, June 22, 1882; "Horse Stealing," *Benton Weekly Record*, June 22, 1882; "Montana Matters," *Daily Independent*, July 14, 1882; and "Festive Redskins," *Daily Independent*, July 19, 1882.

41. See Gustavus Doane to Mary Hunter Doane, July 10, 1882, MSHS, SC 28.

42. "Corralling the Crees," *The Daily Miner* (Butte), August 11, 1882.

43. "Chasing the Crees," *The Daily Miner*, August 16, 1882.

44. Augustus Jukes to Fred White, October 7, 1882, NAC, Indian Department Records, Black Series, RG 10, vol. 3744, reel C-10130, file 29506-2.

45. Hugh A. Dempsey, *Big Bear: The End of Freedom* (Lincoln: University of Nebraska Press, 1984), 108.

46. See "Montana Matters," *Daily Independent*, October 14, 1882; "Montana Matters," *Daily Independent*, October 17, 1882; "Marauding Crees," *Benton Weekly Record*, October 19, 1882.

47. "Big Bear's Surrender," *Benton Weekly Record*, December 28, 1882.

48. "Indian Marauders," *Daily Independent*, March 23, 1883.

49. See "Indian News," *Daily Independent*, March 24, 1883; "A Cree Raid," *Benton Weekly Record*, March 24, 1883; "An Indian Raid: Cree Cattle Thieves Whipped by Whites and Piegans — Troops in Pursuit," *Daily Miner*, March 27, 1883; "The Indian Raiders," *Daily Independent*, March 27, 1883; "The Cussed Cree: Raid of British Redskins into the Marias Country," *Daily Miner*, March 30, 1883; and "Montana Matters," *Daily Independent*, April 5, 1883.

50. "Crees on the Warpath," *Washington Post*, March 24, 1883. The *Washington Post* wrote again on the matter in April, offering details of US Army attempts to drive Crees north of the border and prevent their reentry. They concluded their report of the skirmishes by stating, "British Indians have been annoying settlers considerably of late stealing stock. It is expected that there will be lively work on the border if they cross again." See "Raiding Across the Border: Thieving Canadian Crees Pursued by Troops and Their Chief Killed," *Washington Post*, April 24, 1883. The *Chicago Daily Tribune* picked up on the story in early May and told of the capture of some 90 Crees near the Bear Paw Mountains and their return to the border. "Canadian Crees Captured," *Chicago Daily Tribune*, May 3, 1883, and "Capture of Canadian Crees," *Chicago Daily Tribune*, May 8, 1883. The *Washington Post* made further observations of the looming threat along both US borders — one with Apaches in the South, and the other with Crees in the north. See "The Restless Apaches," *Washington Post*, May 16, 1883.

51. "Big Bear's Surrender," and "A Cree Raid."

52. See "Important Indian News," *Benton Weekly Record*, April 14, 1883; "The Crees Again," *Daily Independent*, April 15, 1883; "Capture of Crees," *Daily Independent*, April 17, 1883; "The Cree Raiders," *Daily Independent*, April 27, 1883; "Captured Crees," *Daily Miner*, April 19, 1883; "More Cree Devilment," *Benton Weekly Record*, April 21, 1883; "Driven over the Border," *Helena Independent*, April 24, 1883; "Capture of Some of the Cree Marauders," *Benton Weekly Record*, April 28, 1883; "Another Rumpus," *Benton Weekly Record*, May 5, 1883; "Crees vs. Piegans," *Benton Weekly Record*, May 9, 1883; "Another Cree Raid: A Large Band of Horses Stolen on the Marias by Northern Indians," *Daily Independent*, May 11, 1883; "Territorial News," *Butte Daily Miner*, May 11, 1883; "Cree Indians after Scalps," *Butte Daily Miner*, May 12, 1883; "Another Raid," *Benton Weekly Record*, May 12, 1883.

53. "Heap Hungry: The Piegan Indians Leave the Agency and Raise the Dickens," *Daily Independent*, May 6, 1883.

54. "Montana Matters," *Daily Independent*, March 29, 1883.

55. "Crees Preparing for War," *Daily Independent*, May 13, 1883; and *Butte Daily Miner*, May 15, 1883.

56. See Dempsey, *Big Bear*, 111–112.

57. "Arrest of Louis Riel," *Benton Weekly Record*, May 19, 1883; *Daily Independent*, December 19, 1882; and "The Herald and Louis Riel," *Benton Weekly Record*, September 1, 1883.

58. "Montana Matters," *Daily Independent*, May 25, 1883.

59. "Captured Reds," *Benton Weekly Record*, May 26, 1883.

60. "Rumor that Ilges Has Been Defeated," *Daily Independent*, July 7, 1883; *Daily Independent*, July 26, 1883.
61. "Montana Matters," *Daily Independent*, August 25, 1883.
62. Patrick Burke to Mrs. Burke (mother), November 4, 1883. MSHS, SC 304.
63. See "The Eccentric Red Men," *Daily Independent*, May 24, 1884; "Hostile Crees," *Daily Independent*, June 8, 1884.
64. "Riel Rebellion," *The Daily Miner*, March 31, 1885.
65. Josiah Heyman and Howard Campbell, Afterword of this book.
66. Interview with Four Souls, May 1975, in Catherine Isabel Littlejohn, "The Indian Oral Tradition," 85.
67. Consider the robust forum hosted by the American Historical Review on the evolutionary nature of borderlands and bordered-lands. See *American Historical Review* 104 (June 1999).

Chapter 3. Contraband Twine

1. See Stephen T. Moore, "Refugees from Volstead: Cross-Boundary Tourism in the Northwest during Prohibition," in *The Borderlands of the American and Canadian Wests: Essays on Regional History of the 49th Parallel*, ed. Sterling Evans (Lincoln: University of Nebraska Press, 2006), 247–261; Moore, "Defining the 'Undefended': Canadians, Americans, and the Multiple Meanings of Border during Prohibition," *American Review of Canadian Studies* 34 (spring 2004): 3–36; Robert A. Campbell, *"Sit Down and Drink Your Beer": Regulating Vancouver's Beer Parlours, 1925–1954* (Toronto: University of Toronto Press, 2001); Pitman B. Potter, "The Positions of Canada and the United States in the Matter of Trade in Alcoholic Beverages," *American Journal of International Law* 24 (January 1931): 131–33; Edwin D. Dickinson, "Treaties for the Prevention of Smuggling," *American Journal of International Law* 20 (April 1926): 340–46; and Dan Malleck, "Crossing the Line: Transnational Drinking and the Biopolitics of Liquor Regulation in Ontario, 1927–1944," chapter 7 of this volume. On the whiskey runners in the nineteenth-century borderlands, see Paul F. Sharp, *Whoop-Up Country: The Canadian American West, 1865–1885* (Minneapolis: University of Minnesota Press, 1955).
2. Dickinson, "Treaties for the Prevention of Smuggling," 345.
3. Moisés Naím, *Illicit: How Smugglers, Traffickers, and Copycats Are Hijacking the Global Economy* (New York: Doubleday, 2005), 2.
4. John Lea, *Crime and Modernity: Continuities in Left Realist Criminology* (London: Sage Publications, 2002), 10.
5. Elaine Carey and Andrae Marak, Introduction to this book.
6. I have more thoroughly examined the history of binders, twine, and their transregional connections in Sterling Evans, *Bound in Twine: The History and Ecology of the Henequen-Wheat Complex for Mexico and the American and Canadian Plains, 1880–1950* (College Station: Texas A&M University Press, 2007). Specifically on the history of binders, see *Bound in Twine*, chapter 1; Thomas D. Isern, *Bull Threshers and Bindlestiffs: Harvesting and Threshing on the North American Plains* (Lawrence: University Press of Kansas, 1990); Graeme Quick and Wesley Buchele, *The Grain Harvesters* (St.

Joseph, MI: American Society of Agricultural Engineers, 1978); Paul C. Johnson, *Farm Inventions in the Making of America* (Des Moines: Wallace-Homestead, 1976); Cyrus Hall McCormick, *A Century of the Reaper* (Boston: Houghton-Miflin, 1931); and Herbert N. Casson, *The Romance of the Reaper* (New York: Doubleday, 1908).

7. The inventor of the knotting device was John F. Appleby of Wisconsin. See F. B. Swingle, "The Invention of the Twine Binder," *Wisconsin Magazine of History* 10, no. 1 (September 1926): 35–41; Evans, *Bound in Twine*, 4–6; and Quick and Buchele, *The Grain Harvesters*, 78–79.

8. Merrill Denison, *Harvest Triumphant: The Story of Massey-Harris* (Toronto: McClelland and Stewart, 1948), 77; Grant MacEwan, *Between the Red and Rockies* (Toronto: University of Toronto Press, 1952), 206.

9. Johnson, *Farm Inventions in the Making of America*, 50.

10. United States Department of Agriculture, *Wheat: Acreage Yield Production by States, 1866–1943*, Statistical Bulletin No. 158, February 1955 (Washington: U.S. Department of Agriculture, Agricultural Marketing Service, 1955), 1–20. Gerald Friesen, *The Canadian Prairies: A History* (Toronto: University of Toronto Press, 1987), 329.

11. "Canada Must Be Ready to Feed the Empire," *Edmonton Bulletin*, March 9, 1915, 2. For more on how Canadian prairie farmers took advantage of the international wheat market during and after World War I, see John Herd Thompson, *The Harvests of War: The Prairie West, 1914–1918* (Toronto: McClelland and Stewart, 1978).

12. *Toronto World*, February 3, 1916, 1.

13. For details, see Tony Ward, "Farming Technology and Crop Area on Early Prairie Farms," *Prairie Forum* 20 (spring 1995): 24; and William T. Hutchison, *Cyrus Hall McCormick: Harvest, 1856–1884* (New York: Appleton-Century, 1935), 647–65.

14. Quotation is from MacEwan, *Between the Red and the Rockies*, 207. Sales information is from Denison, *Harvest Triumphant*, 84.

15. Canada, *House of Commons Debates*, 12th Parliament (George V), 5th Sess., 1915, 1649–1650.

16. IH Department Managers Conference, minutes, August 1, 1923, file 01605, International Harvester / Navistar Archives; Norman G. Owen, *Prosperity without Progress: Manila Hemp and the Material Life in the Colonial Philippines* (Berkeley: University of California Press, 1984), 48; Canadian Department of Statistics as cited in *Canadian Farm Implements*, ed. E. H. Evans, September 15, 1945, R-266, file IV-8, Saskatchewan Archives Board-Regina.

17. Evans, *Bound in Twine*, 21–22.

18. *Harvester World* 1 (March 1910): 29; Lyster Dewey, "Fibers Used for Binder Twine," *Yearbook of the Department of Agriculture, 1911* (Washington: Government Printing Office, 1912), 200.

19. See Evans, *Bound in Twine*. For more on the theory of commodity dependencies, see Allen Wells, "Reports of Its Demise Are Not Exaggerated: The Life and Times of Yucatecan Henequen," in *From Silver to Cocaine: Latin American Commodity Chains and the Building of the World Economy, 1500–2000*, ed. Steven Topik et al. (Durham, NC: Duke University Press, 2006), 300–320; and Sterling Evans, "Dependent Harvests: Grain Production on the American and Canadian Plains and the Double Dependency with Mexico in the Early Twentieth Century," *Agricultural History* 80, no. 1 (winter 2006): 35–63.

20. Gilbert Joseph, "Revolution from Without: The Mexican Revolution in Yucatán, 1915–1924" (Ph.D. diss., Yale University, 1978), 101.

21. From Brantford letterhead and brochures in RG 30, series V-A-9-h, Vol. 9263, file 10436, Library and Archives of Canada, Ottawa (hereafter, LAC).

22. Evans, *Bound in Twine*, 20; Allen Wells, "Henequen and Yucatán: An Analysis in Regional Economic Development, 1876–1915" (Ph.D. diss., State University of New York—Stony Brook, 1979), 39, 57.

23. *Regina Leader*, June 27, 1892, 2; *Regina Leader*, May 2, 1892, 4; Ward, "Farming Technology," 24; "Patrons of Industry Petition for Removal of Duty on Coal Oil and Binder Twine," Feb. 13, 1892 in RG 17, vol. 717, file 82338, LAC. The UFA resolution is in MG 26-J1, microfilm reel C-2294, vol. 141, MacKenzie King Papers, LAC. Interestingly, as part of the story here, the Patrons of Industry went on to establish their own twine for farmers in Canada, but since it was imported from a factory in St. Paul, MN, it was two and half cents per pound more expensive than Canadian brand-name twines. For more on the Patrons' twine, see *The Commercial* (Winnipeg), August 20, 1894, 1.

24. R. D. McGibbon, "Binder Twine Duty," *Montreal Daily Witness*, January 15, 1898, 5.

25. George Clark, Department of Agriculture, Seed Branch, to J. H. Grisdale, Deputy Minister, Department of Agriculture, Feb. 17, 1925, RG 17, vol. 3088, file 47-2, part 1, LAC; Grisdale to Senator Benard, June 23, 1923, RG 17, vol. 3223, file 160-3, LAC.

26. Quoted in Joseph, "Revolution from Without," 101. For more details on the history of the penitentiary twine mills, see Evans, *Bound in Twine*, chapter 5.

27. International Harvester Co., *The Story of Twine* (1937 pamphlet), International Harvester Company Records, file 92148, IHCA / Navistar. For more on the South Dakota episode, see Sterling Evans, "Entwined in Conflict: The History of the South Dakota State Prison Twine Factory and the Controversy of 1919–1921," *South Dakota History* 80, no. 1 (winter 2006): 35–63.

28. Louis N. Robinson, *Should Prisoners Work? A Study of the Prison Labor Problem in the United States* (Chicago: John C. Winston, 1931), 54.

29. *The Winnipeg Commercial*, August 27, 1894, 1.

30. For more on the Philippine "threat," see Norman G. Owen, "Winding Down the War in Albay, 1900–1903," *Pacific Historical Review* 48, no. 4 (November 1979): 575–78.

31. *Calgary Albertan*, August 12, 1912, 1; *Grain Growers Guide*, June 4, 1913, 11.

32. Joseph H. Shubert to Bennett, Aug. 3, 1931, and C. H. Gavreau to Bennett, Aug. 3, 1931, in Collected Papers of Richard Bedford Bennett, MG26-K, M-1450, LAC.

33. Telegram, Council of R.M. of Grass Lake to Minister of Agriculture, July 11, 1931, RG 17 vol. 3223, file 160–163, LAC.

34. City of Brandon Commercial Bureau to Minister of Agriculture, Nov. 16, 1910, RG 17, vol. 1128, docket 209948, LAC.

35. Flax Decorticating Co. Ltd. To Premier Walter Scott, October 22, 1915, Motherwell Papers, file II.117; and Board of Trade, Saskatoon to Minister of Agriculture, January 6, 1911, Motherwell Papers, file II.9, Saskatchewan Archives Board-Saskatoon. See the thick file on this (including a preserved envelope of flax fiber sent

to the government in 1919!) in RG 17, vol. 1266, docket 250305B, LAC. On hemp, see Saskatchewan Department of Records, Statistics Branch, R-266, file IV-39 "Hemp," Saskatchewan Archives Board-Regina.

36. Evans, *Bound in Twine*, 166, 197–202.

37. *Hardware and Metal* (Toronto), February 23, 1894, 1.

38. R. R. Hall to Laurier, MG 26-G, microfilm reel 818, vol. 350, Wilfrid Laurier Papers, LAC.

39. n/a, "Binder Twine Situation in Canada," n.d., 2,3, 6, in MG 26, vol. 302, Borden Papers, LAC.

40. F. G. O'Hara, Deputy Minister of Trade and Commerce, to J. H. Grisdale, Deputy Minister of Agriculture, August 7, 1924, RG 17, vol. 3088, file 47–2, part 1, LAC.

41. Inspection and Sale Act, misc. letters from Brantford Cordage Co. to G. H. Clarke, Canadian Department of Agriculture, January 1925; R. L. Brown to W. R. Motherwell, Minister of Agriculture, November 28, 1928, both in RG 17, vol. 3088, file 47–2, LAC.

42. Cotton to Massey-Harris Company, August 5 1899, in *The Wheat King: The Selected Letters and Papers of A. J. Cotton, 1888–1913*, ed. Wendy Owen (Winnipeg: Manitoba Record Society, 1985), 28–29.

43. See Evans, *Bound in Twine*, 149–51, for examples.

44. Ibid., 155.

45. For the history of these prison twine plants, see ibid., 127–31.

46. David Mills, "The Action of the Government in Respect to the Manufacture and Sale of Twine Produced by Convict Labour," Sessional Paper no. 13, Ottawa, 1, 2, 4–7, in MG 26, vol. 302, Borden Papers, LAC. The "on credit" information is from Warden J. W. Platt to Inspector of Penitentiary (Department of Justice), November 29, 1911, RG 13-A-2, vol. 169, file 1911-1347, LAC.

47. "Lots of Binding Twine," *Saturday Evening Review* (Portage la Prairie, Manitoba), August 18, 1894, 1.

48. W. H. Knowlton to W. B. Paremee, Deputy Minister of Trade and Commerce, October 17, 1896, in RG 20-A-1, vol. 1146, file 4371, LAC.

49. *Edmonton Bulletin*, April 8, 1903, 3.

50. "Government Binder Twine Factory," circular, March 6, 1906, in MG 26-J1, vol. 302, file 10, MacKenzie King Papers, LAC.

51. E. L. Newcombe, Deputy Minister of Justice to P. Nutting, Acting Deputy Minister of Trade and Commerce, September 4, 1901, RG 13-A-2, vol. 1901, file 710, LAC.

52. Alex Frank, Member of Parliament to Laurier, June 5, 1900, MG 26-G, vol. 157, microfilm reel C-776, Wilfrid Laurier Papers, LAC.

53. F. G. O'Hara to Prime Minister Wilfrid Laurier, July 5, 1904, reel G813, vol. 326, 87602–87604, Papers of Sir Wilfrid Laurier, LAC.

54. Statutes of 1904, in Memoranda, Clippings, and Reports, 1900–1913, file 7-15, Borden Papers, LAC.

55. George Stairs to Robert Borden, Apr. 5, 1906; and George Wood (London) to Consumers Cordage Co. (Halifax), Mar. 22, 1906, MG 26H2-f, vol. 302, file 7-15, microfilm reel C-4451, Borden Papers, LAC.

56. *Inspection and Sale Act (with Amendments and Revisions)* (Ottawa: Thomas Mulvey, Printer to the King's Most Excellent Majesty, 1920), 36.

57. George Clark, Department of Agriculture to Grisdale, January 26, 1925, and H. K. Small, Plymouth Cordage Co., Canadian Branch to Honourable Minister of Agriculture, Jan. 30, 1925, RG 17, vol. 3088, file 47-2, part 1, LAC.

58. The correspondences, all from early 1925, are in ibid. In an ironic twist to the story, the Ministry of Agriculture informed Brantford Cordage that Customs agents had discovered faulty (deficient in length) Brantford twine in March of that year! Outraged, Brantford officials claimed the inspectors were "incompetent," that it was the first complaint in twenty-one years (the time in which they had gone from a small manufacturer to the "largest producer in the British Empire") that they had received on their twine, and that they would not accept the inspector's report.

59. P. H. Massecar, President of Brantford Cordage Co. to Department of Trade and Commerce, March 19, 1925, RG 20, vol. 287, file T-231, LAC.

60. *Hardware and Metal* (Toronto), October 30, 1926, 1.

61. Canadian Council of Agriculture to Minister of Agriculture, November 9, 1928; and United Grain Growers of Canada to Minister of Agriculture, November 28, 1928, and RG 17, vol. 3088, file 47-2, part 1, LAC.

62. An Act Respecting the Inspection of Binder Twine, 2nd Session, 16th Parliament, 18 George V, 1928, LAC.

63. Department of Munitions and Supplies Memorandum, January 4, 1943, RG 28-A, vol. 263, file 196-15-2-1, LAC.

64. Memorandum Brief Relative to Baler Twine Tariff Classification in the United States, December 19, 1949; A. M. James (Brantford Cordage Co.) to Minister of Trade and Commerce, December 22, 1950; Department of Trade and Commerce Interoffice Correspondence, December 18, 1950; and J. A. McKay (Brantford Cordage) to Department of Trade and Commerce, February 10, 1948, in RG 20-A-3, vol. 710, file 4-UI-48, LAC.

65. Potter, "The Positions of Canada and the United States," 132–33.

66. Ibid., 133.

67. In the Introduction to Itty Abraham and Willem van Schendel, eds., *Illicit Flows and Criminal Things: States, Borders, and the Other Globalization* (Bloomington: Indiana University Press, 2005), 9.

68. Ibid., 8, 23, 25.

69. Jeremy Adelman and Stephen Aron, "From Borderlands to Borders: Empires, Nation-States, and the Peoples in Between in North American History," *American Historical Review* 104, no. 3 (June 1999): 816.

70. Josiah McC. Heyman and Howard Campbell, Afterword, in this book.

Chapter 4. Twilight of the Tequileros

1. With the exception of Daniel Okrent's recent book, *Last Call: The Rise and Fall of Prohibition*, most of the historiography on Prohibition is older or popular in nature. Charles Merz's *The Dry Decade* is probably the best comprehensive history of Prohibition. Unfortunately Merz first published his book in 1930, while Prohibition was still ongoing. Edward Behr's *Prohibition* is possibly the best written, if somewhat popular history of the era. Daniel Okrent, *Last Call: The Rise and Fall of Prohibition* (New York: Scribner, 2010); Charles Merz, *The Dry Decade* (Seattle: University of

Washington Press, 1970); and Edward Behr, *Prohibition: Thirteen Years that Changed America* (New York: Arcade, 1996).

2. Norman Brown's *Hood, Bonnet, and Little Brown Jug,* and Lewis Gould's *Progressives and Prohibitionists* both focus on the politics of Prohibition, particularly Anglo teetotalers' lobbying in Austin. Although both are well researched, neither considers liquor smuggling along the US-Mexico border in any depth. Norman Brown, *Hood, Bonnet, and Little Brown Jug: Texas Politics, 1921–1928* (College Station: Texas A&M University Press, 1984); and Lewis Gould, *Progressives and Prohibitionists: Texas Democrats in the Wilson Era* (Austin: Texas State Historical Association, 1992).

3. C. L. Sonnichsen and M. G. McKinney, "El Paso — From War to Depression," *Southwestern Historical Quarterly* 74, no.3 (1971).

4. James A. Sandos, "Northern Separatism during the Mexican Revolution: An Inquiry into the Role of Drug Trafficking, 1919–1920," *Americas* 41 (1984): 208.

5. Robert Buffington, "Prohibition in the Borderlands: National Government-Border Community Relations," *Pacific Historical Review* 63, no. 1 (1994): 19–38.

6. Gabriela Recio, "Drugs and Alcohol: U.S. Prohibition and the Origins of the Drug Trade in Mexico, 1910–1930," *Journal of Latin American Studies* 34, no. 1 (2002): 21–42.

7. Moisés Naím, *Illicit: How Smugglers, Traffickers, and Copycats are Hijacking the Global Economy* (New York: Anchor Books, 2005); and William van Schendel and Itty Abraham, ed., *Illicit Flows and Criminal Things: States, Borders, and the Other Side of Globalization* (Indianapolis: Indiana University Press, 2005).

8. In this chapter, the term *ethnic Mexican* refers to persons of Mexican descent who could be either US or Mexican citizens.

9. Juan Mora-Torres, *The Making of the Mexican Border: The State, Capitalism, and Society in Nuevo León, 1848–1910* (Austin: University of Texas Press, 2001), 60–63.

10. "Laredo Voters against Prohibition Amendment," *Laredo Weekly Times,* June 1, 1919.

11. David E. Kyvig, *Prohibition: The 18th Amendment, the Volstead Act, the 21st Amendment* (Washington, DC: National Archives, 1986), 1.

12. "Local News," *Laredo Weekly Times,* January 5, 1919.

13. "In Battle with Smugglers Charles Hopkins Killed," *Laredo Weekly Times,* May 11, 1919; "Grim Reaper Wins Battle Fought by Brave Officer," *Laredo Weekly Times,* June 8, 1919; and "Fourth Smuggler Is Dead Having Died Yesterday," *Laredo Weekly Times,* May 11, 1919.

14. James Garza, "On the Edge of a Storm: Laredo and the Mexican Revolution, 1910–1917" (MA thesis, Texas A&M International University, 1996), 62–65.

15. Oscar J. Martínez, ed., *U.S.-Mexico Borderlands: Historical and Contemporary Perspectives* (Wilmington, DE: Jaguar Books, 1996), 139–41.

16. Benjamin Heber Johnson, *Revolution in Texas: How a Forgotten Rebellion and Its Bloody Suppression Turned Mexicans into Americans* (New Haven: Yale University Press, 2003), 3.

17. Ethno-racial relations in Laredo have been a contentious issue. Local ethnic-Mexicans claim the community did not suffer the virulent racism that other communities in the Lower Rio Grande Valley experienced. Historians Elliot Young and Gilberto Miguel Hinojosa have provided evidence to support Laredoan's popular memory. Still, other scholars such as Beatriz de la Garza and Roberto Calderón dispute this claim.

Although Calderón and De la Garza are correct in insisting that incidents of ethno-racial discrimination did occur, their scholarship focuses more on the exception rather than the norm. See Elliot Young, "Deconstructing La Raza: Identifying the Gente Decente of Laredo, 1904–1911," *Southwestern Historical Quarterly* 98, no. 2 (October 1994): 226; and Young, "Red Men, Princess Pocahontas, and George Washington: Harmonizing Race Relations in Laredo at the Turn of the Century," *Western Historical Quarterly* 29 (spring 1998): 48–85; Gilberto Miguel Hinojosa, *A Borderlands Town in Transition: Laredo, 1755–1870* (College Station: Texas A&M Press, 1983), 71; Beatriz de la Garza, *A Law for the Lion: A Tale of Crime and Injustice in the Borderlands* (Austin: University of Texas Press, 2003); Roberto Calderón, *Mexican Politics in Texas: Laredo, 1845–1911* (forthcoming); John Adams, *Conflict and Commerce on the Rio Grande: Laredo, 1755–1955* (College Station: Texas A&M Press, 2008), 78; and Jerry Thompson, *Warm Weather and Bad Whiskey: The Laredo 1886 Election Riot* (El Paso: Texas Western Press, 1991).

18. *Biennial Report of the Adjutant General of Texas from January 1, 1917, to December 31, 1918* (Austin: Von Boeckmann-Jones, 1919), 44; "Smugglers Get Surprise and Eight Are Prisoners," *Laredo Weekly Times*, September 26, 1920; and James Randolph Ward, "The Texas Rangers, 1919–1935: A Study in Law Enforcement" (Ph.D. diss., Texas Christian University, 1972), 35.

19. Maude T. Gilliland, *Horsebackers of the Brush Country: A Story of the Texas Rangers and Mexican Liquor Smugglers* (Alpine, TX: Library of Sul Ross State University, 1968), 16; and William Warren Sterling, *The Trails and Trials of a Texas Ranger* (Norman: University of Oklahoma Press, 1959), 86.

20. "Kill the Chief and Bag the Others," *Laredo Weekly Times*, September 18, 1921.

21. Alonzo H. Alvarez, "Los Tequileros," Courtesy of Manuel Guerra; and Gilliland, *Horsebackers*, 33.

22. Gilliland, *Horsebackers*, 33–39; and Walter Prescott Webb, *The Texas Rangers: A Century of Frontier Defense* (Austin: University of Texas Press, 1965), 556.

23. Much of the information on mules and their many talents come from scattered sources. Maude T. Gilliland goes into some depth about the adeptness of mules in her book. Although she also mentions American law enforcement's use of adept mules, we can assume that tequileros, most of whom came from ranching backgrounds, had equally if not better-trained mules. For more information on the ability of pack animals see, Emmett M. Essin, "Mules, Packs, and Packtrains," *Southwestern Historical Quarterly* 74, no. 1 (1970): 52–80; Gilliland, *Horsebackers*, 51–55.

24. Enrique Martínez Limón, *Tequila: The Spirit of Mexico* (New York: Abbeville Press, 2000), 30–31.

25. Gilliland, *Horsebackers*, 16–17.

26. "Kill the Chief and Bag Others."

27. Results based on calculations done through "Measuring Worth." http://www.measuringworth.com/uscompare/?redirurl=calculators/uscompare/

28. William Warren Sterling, *The Trails and Trials of a Texas Ranger* (Norman: University of Oklahoma Press, 1959), 84.

29. Gilliland, *Horsebackers*, 16.

30. Ibid., 16; Sterling, *Trails and Trials*, 84.

31. Américo Paredes, *A Texas-Mexican Cancionero: Folksongs of the Lower Border* (Austin: University of Texas Press, 1995), 81.

32. José A. Ramírez, *To the Line of Fire: Mexican Texans and World War I* (College Station: Texas A&M Press, 2009); Paredes, *A Texas-Mexican Cancionero*, 81.

33. Alejandra Villarreal Zapata, interview by author, September 24, 2003.

34. *Rinche* is an extremely negative term for an American law enforcement agent. For more on rinches see Américo Paredes, *With His Pistol in His Hand: A Border Ballad and its Hero* (Austin: University of Texas Press, 1958), 24.

35. Alejandra Villarreal Zapata, interview by author, September 24, 2003; and Paredes, *A Texas-Mexican Cancionero*, 81.

36. Johnson, *Revolution in Texas*, 103–5.

37. Américo Paredes, *Folklore and Culture on the Texas-Mexican Border*, ed. Richard Bauman (Austin: CMAS Books, 1993), 27.

38. Whereas US law enforcement saw their transgression of American sovereignty as illegal and their liquor as contraband, the culture that tequileros were a part of accepted liquor. Moreover, ethnic Mexicans of the region had few qualms about evading tariffs on consumer goods and tequileros' smuggling of these items fit easily within a moral economy of illicit trade on the border. For more information on the moral economy of smuggling see, George T. Díaz, "Contrabandista Communities: States and Smugglers in the Lower Rio Grande Borderlands, 1848–1945" (Ph.D. diss., Southern Methodist University, 2010).

39. "In Pitched Battle with Smugglers Three of the Smugglers Are Killed," *Laredo Weekly Times*, April 4, 1920.

40. Mariano Reséndez was a famous smuggler of the late 19th century who trafficked American consumer goods into Mexico. Reséndez's *corrido* reveals locals' attitudes about the widespread contraband trade that occurred in northern Mexico at the time. For more information on Mariano Reséndez, see Paredes, *A Texas Mexican Cancionero*, 96–100, and Díaz, "Contrabandista Communities," 58; for more information on smuggling in northern Mexico in the late 19th century see, Mora-Torres, *The Making of the Mexican Border*, 35.

41. Webb, *Texas Rangers*, 556.

42. Gilliland, *Horsebackers*, 17; and "In Pitched Battle with Smugglers Three Smugglers Are Killed."

43. Period newspapers occasionally mention that US law enforcement recovered quantities of consumer goods from traffickers, but stronger evidence of smugglers bearing holiday gifts is lacking. Still, today untold numbers of gifts are smuggled into Mexico each holiday season, and tequileros' Christmas contraband may fit into this pattern.

44. "Rodríguez, Jorge. Informe el Consulado que este individuo se dedice al contrabando." 1929. file IV 225–254. Secretaría de Relaciones Exteriores. Mexico City.

45. George T. Díaz, "When the River Ran Red: Tequileros, Texas Rangers, and Violence on the Central South Texas Border during Prohibition, 1919–1933" (MA thesis, Texas A&M International University, 2004), 18.

46. "Kill the Chief and Bag Others"; and W. L. Wright to Adj. Gen. Barton, September 13, 1921. Walter Prescott Webb Papers, Center for American History, University of Texas at Austin.

47. E. J. Hobsbawm, *Primitive Rebels: Studies in Archaic Forms of Social Movement in the 19th and 20th Centuries* (New York: W. W. Norton, 1959).

48. Although Anglo–ethnic Mexican conflicts led to a great degree of "social banditry," these occurrences came mostly out of Anglo racism and conflicts over land. For

examples of ethnic Mexicans as "social bandits," see Robert J. Rosenbaum, *Mexicano Resistance in the Southwest: The Sacred Right of Self-Preservation* (Austin: University of Texas Press, 1981); and Jerry Thompson, *Cortina: Defending the Mexican Name in Texas* (College Station: Texas A&M Press, 2007).

49. Gilliland, *Horsebackers*, 17.

50. John R. Peavey, *Echoes from the Rio Grande* (Brownsville: Springman-King, 1963), 228–39.

51. Gilliland, *Horsebackers*, 17; Peavey, *Echoes from the Rio Grande*, 228; and Sterling, *Trails and Trials*, 84–85.

52. Webb, *Texas Rangers*, 556.

53. Gilliland, *Horsebackers*, 38.

54. Webb, *Texas Rangers*, 551.

55. Ibid., 557.

56. "Three Smugglers Killed Just East of Mirando City," *Laredo Weekly Times*, December 24, 1922.

57. Ibid.

58. "3 Rum-Runners Slain: Customs Men Win in Fight with Gang," *San Antonio Express*, December 19, 1922.

59. "Funeral of Bob Rumsey Held Sunday and Largely Attended," *Laredo Weekly Times*, August 27, 1922; "This Horse Riderless because Bootleggers Killed Its Owner," *San Antonio Express*, September 24, 1922; "Fearless Custom Inspector's Murder in 1922 Is Recalled," *Laredo Times*, August 29, 1972; and *The State of Texas v. Santos Salinas*, Webb County Court Records, Texas A&M International, Killam Library Special Collections.

60. "This Horse Riderless because Bootleggers Killed Its Owner."

61. Sterling, *Trails and Trials*, 91.

62. James L. White, letter to Manuel Guerra, May 19, 1994; and "Man Indicted of Killing Rumsey Arrested Saturday," *Laredo Weekly*, August 31, 1928.

63. Díaz, "When the River Ran Red," Appendix.

64. Guillermo E. Hernández, ed., *Corridos Sin Fronteras / Ballads without Borders: Cancionero / Song Book* (Washington, DC: Smithsonian Institution, 2002); and Elijah Wald, *Narcocorrido: A Journey into the Music of Drugs, Guns, and Guerrillas* (New York: Rayo, 2001), 186–87.

65. Hernández, *Corridos Sin Fronteras*.

66. Ibid.

67. "Customs Officers Fled From Gang of Bootleggers," *Laredo Weekly Times*, October 1, 1922.

68. "Need for Action," *Laredo Weekly Times*, October 1, 1922.

69. "Are Now Prepared to Meet the Droves of Bootleggers," *Laredo Weekly Times*, January 12, 1924.

70. "Officers Make Big Seizure," *Laredo Weekly Times*, January 7, 1924.

71. Sterling, *Trails and Trials*, 84.

72. "Patrol Kills Rum Runner in Jim Hogg Co." *Laredo Daily Times*, February 5, 1927.

73. Gilliland, *Horsebackers*, 61–62.

74. Ibid., 16.

75. "Customs Officers Fled From Gang of Bootleggers"; and Gilliland, *Horsebackers*, 16.

76. "Pro Guardian Ambushed By 'Leggers,'" *Laredo Times*, September 25, 1929.

77. Díaz, "When the River Ran Red," 120.

78. Sterling, *Trails and Trials*, 85.

79. Perkins, *Border Patrol*, 110–11.

80. Many corridos describe American law enforcement officers as cowards. See "Gregorio Cortez," "Pistoleros Famosos," "Los Tequileros," and "Dionisio Maldonado," in Américo Paredes's *A Texas-Mexican Cancionero* and *Corridos Sin Fronteras / Ballads without Borders*.

81. "Two Smugglers are Slain and Quantity of Booze Taken," *Laredo Weekly Times*, January 9, 1921; "Kill the Chief and Bag the Others"; Gilliland, *Horsebackers*, 15–17; and Sterling, *Trails and Trials*, 84–86.

82. Paredes, *Texas-Mexican Cancionero*, 101.

83. Dagoberto Gilb, ed., *Hecho en Tejas: An Anthology of Texas Mexican Literature* (Albuquerque: University of New Mexico Press, 2006), 39.

84. Gilb, *Hecho en Tejas*, 39.

85. "Pro Guardian Ambushed By 'Leggers.'"

86. Ibid.

87. Américo Paredes, *A Texas-Mexican Cancionero*, 87.

88. Ibid.

89. "Dapper Youth Once Held Here Charged in Stevens's Death," September 27, 1929. Aldrich (Roy Wilkinson) Papers. Center for the Study of American History, University of Texas at Austin.

90. "Officers Seize $20,000 Smuggled Liquor," *Laredo Daily Times*, February 5, 1927.

91. "Ghost Flier Sought as Border Bootlegger," *Laredo Times*, January 25, 1931.

92. Ibid.

93. "Customs Officers May Patrol Border Beats in Airplanes," *Dallas Morning News*, November 28, 1922.

94. "Alleged Booze Flier Held For Probe," *Laredo Times*, January 18, 1932; and Romayn Wormuth to Secretary of State, Nuevo Laredo, Mexico, February 2, 1932. Records of the Department of State Relating to the Internal Affairs of Mexico, 1930–39. LC 812.00 Tamaulipas.

95. "Rum Runners Chased by Planes," *Laredo Times*, July 20, 1932; "War Air Ace Taken with Booze," *Laredo Times*, May 26, 1932; "Air Booze Chasers Praised for Work," *Laredo Weekly Times*, June 13, 1932; and "Anti-Booze Planes Guard Rio Grande about Laredo," *Laredo Times*, November 29, 1932.

96. Díaz, "When the River Ran Red," 116.

Chapter 5. Detroit's Border Brothel

1. An earlier version of this chapter appeared in the *American Review of Canadian Studies* 40, no. 3 (September 2010): 362–78.

2. "Probe Heat Hasn't Cooled Off Joints: Many Brothels, Blindpigs, Still Running Wide Open," *Windsor Daily Star*, March 14, 1950, 6.

3. Ibid., 6.

4. Karen Dubinsky, *The Second Greatest Disappointment: Honeymooning and Tourism at Niagara Falls* (Toronto: Between the Lines, 1999), 13

5. Chris Ryan and C. Michael Hall, *Sex Tourism: Marginal People and Liminalities* (London: Routledge, 2000), 22.

6. Dubinsky, *Second Greatest Disappointment*; Dan Malleck, "An Innovation from Across the Line: The American Drinker and Liquor Regulation in Two Ontario Border Towns, 1927–1944," *Journal of Canadian Studies* 41, no. 1 (winter 2007): 151–71.

7. Itty Abraham and Willem van Schendel, eds., *Illicit Flows and Criminal Things: States, Borders, and the Other Side of Globalization* (Bloomington: Indiana University Press, 2005), 24.

8. Gerald Anglin, "He Blew the Whistle on Windsor Vice," *Maclean's*, May 1, 1950, 62.

9. Donna J. Dunkley, *All Through the Years: A History of the Salvation Army in Windsor, Ontario 1886–1986* (Windsor: Preney, 1986), 1.

10. Joan Poole, "The Evolution of Social Services in the Border Cities during the Great Depression" (Ph.D. diss., University of Windsor, 1990), 20.

11. Mary Hill, "A City Looks at Itself," *Canadian Business* 25 (April 1952): 28.

12. Poole, "Evolution of Social Services," 13.

13. Joseph Louis Veres, "History of the United Automobile Workers in Windsor, 1936–1956" (MA thesis, University of Western Ontario, 1956), 8.

14. Nancy E. Zettlemoyer, *An Assessment of Immigrant Needs and Their Fulfillment in Metropolitan Windsor* (Windsor: Windsor Citizenship Committee, 1961), 1.

15. Veres, "History of the United Automobile Workers," 6.

16. Canada, Dominion Bureau of Statistics, *Report on the 8th Census of Canada, 1941, VII Gainfully Occupied by Occupations, Industries, etc.* (Ottawa: Edmond Cloutier, 1946), 210.

17. Rudolf A. Helling, *The Position of Negroes, Chinese, and Italians in the Social Structure of Windsor, Ontario* (Ottawa: Ontario Human Rights Commission, 1965), 25.

18. Ibid., 47.

19. Bruno Ramirez, *Crossing the 49th Parallel: Migration from Canada to the United States, 1900–1930* (Ithaca: Cornell University Press, 2001), 110.

20. For further analysis on the gendering of "leisure," see Craig Heron, "The Boys and Their Booze: Masculinities and Public Drinking in Working-Class Hamilton, 1890–1946," *Canadian Historical Review* 86, no. 3 (September 2005): 411–52; and Robert A. Campbell, *Sit Down and Drink Your Beer: Regulating Vancouver's Beer Parlours, 1925–1954* (Toronto: University of Toronto Press, 2001).

21. Steven Meyer, "Rugged Manhood: The Aggressive and Confrontational Culture of Male Auto Workers during World War II," *Journal of Social History* 36 (2002): 126.

22. Liquor Control Board of Ontario, Establishment Files, RG-3, Archives of Ontario.

23. Thomas Sugrue, *The Origins of the Urban Crisis: Race and Inequality in Postwar Detroit* (Princeton: Princeton University Press, 2005), 19.

24. Canada, Dominion Bureau of Statistics, *Ninth Census of Canada*, vol. 1 (Ottawa: Edmond Cloutier, 1953), 65–72.

25. The Greater Windsor Industrial Commission, *Industrial Prospects Are Bright in Windsor* (Windsor: Dominion Bureau of Statistics, 1957), 5.

26. Ewing Laverty and Melwyn Breen, "Windsor: Border — Not Barrier," *Saturday Night* 36 (April 25, 1950): 10.

27. Canada, *Dominion Bureau of Statistics*, 1941 and 1951.

28. "M.O.H. Will Lead Drive: Urges Police Morality Squad Enlarged to Meet Situation," *Windsor Daily Star*, January 18, 1944, 3.

29. "Attracted to Windsor," *Windsor Daily Star*, May 24, 1943, 3.

30. Ibid., 3.

31. Windsor Police Department, *Annual Registers*, 1940–1960.

32. Ibid.

33. "Say Montreal Vice Ring Nets $10,000,000 Yearly; Citizens Accuse Police," *Globe and Mail*, December 15, 1945, 1; "A New Petition to Give Names in Vice Charges," *Globe and Mail*, January 4, 1946, 3; "Citizens Reject Sawed-Off Probe of Montreal Vice," *Globe and Mail*, October 23, 1946, 3; "Rooming Houses Next in Montreal Anti-Vice Drive," *Globe and Mail*, February 18, 1947, 9; "Won't Allow Vice Chief to Resign: Must Face Action by Police Officials," *Windsor Daily Star*, July 31, 1946, 1.

34. Windsor Police Department, *Annual Reports*, 1946.

35. R. M. Harrison, "Now," *Windsor Daily Star*, July 5, 1943, 7.

36. Ibid., 7.

37. Jeff Keshen, "Revisiting Canada's Civilian Women during World War II," in *Rethinking Canada: The Promise of Women's History*, ed. Veronica Strong-Boag, Mona Gleason, and Adele Perry (New York: Oxford University Press, 2002), 258.

38. Canadian Census, 1951, 6–72.

39. Windsor Police Department, *Annual Registers*, 1940–1960; Anglin, "He Blew the Whistle on Windsor Vice," 62.

40. Windsor Police Department, *Annual Registers*, 1940–1960.

41. According to the Annual Reports of the Windsor Police Department, the number of vehicles entering Windsor each year were as follows: 2,543,924 in 1954; 2,789,369 in 1955; 2,637,790 in 1956. Unfortunately these are the only years in which the annual reports recorded the number of border crossings during the postwar period.

42. Windsor Police Department, *Annual Registers*, 1940–1960.

43. "Code Section," *Windsor Daily Star*, July 26, 1946, 3.

44. Windsor Police Department, *Annual Registers*, 1940–1960.

45. Sugrue, *Origins of the Urban Crisis*, 23.

46. Carol Smith and Stephen Sarasohn, "Hate Propaganda in Detroit," *Public Opinion Quarterly* 10, no. 1 (spring 1946): 27–28.

47. Janet Langlois, "The Belle Isle Bride Incident: Legend Dialectic and Semiotic System in the 1943 Detroit Race Riots," *Journal of American Folklore* 96, no. 380 (April–June 1983): 185.

48. Betty De Ramus quoted in ibid., 185.

49. Sugrue, *Origins of the Urban Crisis*, 29.

50. The racialized nature of the Detroit-Windsor border also reinforces Alejandro Lugo's argument that borders are as much about inspection as they are about crossing, and that the difference between these two processes is about power and privilege. Lugo emphasizes the need to recognize not just border crossings but also the process of *border exclusions*, which more often than not result in *failed border crossings* for members of marginalized communities. See Alejandro Lugo, *Fragmented Lives, As-*

sembled Parts: Culture, Capitalism, and Conquest at the U.S.-Mexico Border (Austin: University of Texas Press, 2008), chap. 6.

51. Denise Brennan, "Selling Sex for Visas: Sex Tourism as a Stepping-Stone to International Migration," in *Global Woman: Nannies, Maids, and Sex Workers in the New Economy*, ed. Barbara Ehrenreich and Arlie Russell Hochschild (New York: Metropolitian Books, 2002), 156.

52. Harrison, "Now," 9.

53. Though debates about vice span Windsor's history, the most recent discussions were brought up when Super Bowl XL was held in the city of Detroit. See Louis Aguilar, "Is Windsor the Super Sin City? Canadian Town's Sex Trade May Lure Game Revellers to Cross Border," *Detroit News* (online), January 1, 2006; "Windsor Hopes Super Bowl Can Show it More Than Just Sin," *USA Today* (online), January 11, 2006; Wayne Drehs, "For the Bare Super Bowl Necessities, See Windsor," *ESPN.COM* (online), February 4, 2006; Tom Krisher, "For American, Windsor Is Sin City," *Globe and Mail* (online), January 11, 2006.

54. F. H. Leacy, ed., *Historical Statistics of Canada* (Ottawa: Statistics Canada, 1983), J560–567.

55. Windsor Police Department, *Police Registers*, 1943–1950.

56. "Probe Heat Hasn't Cooled Off Joints," 6.

57. Patrick Brode, Interview with Jim Ure, January 20, 2006.

58. "Police Keep Pressure on 'Hot Spot,'" *Windsor Daily Star*, August 14, 1950, 5.

59. "Five Charged After Raid," *Windsor Daily Star*, October 4, 1948, 3.

60. Liquor License Board of Ontario, Blue Water Public House Case Files, RG-3 B335026, Archives of Ontario. Names have been changed for privacy purposes.

61. LLBO, Blue Water Public House Case Files, RG-3 B335026, Archives of Ontario.

62. Gerald Anglin, "He Blew the Whistle on Windsor Vice," 62.

63. "Probe Heat Hasn't Cooled off Joints," 3.

64. Ibid., 3.

65. For a discussion of automation in Canada, see Steven High, *Industrial Sunset: The Making of North America's Rust Belt, 1969–1984* (Toronto: University of Toronto Press, 2003).

66. Robert A. Heuton, "Urban Sprawl: A Comparative Study of the Detroit-Windsor Region" (Ph.D. diss., Wayne State University, 2005), 142.

67. For studies on Cold War moral politics, see Mary Louise Adams, *The Trouble With Normal* (Toronto: University of Toronto Press, 1997); Lizabeth Cohen, *A Consumer's Republic: The Politics of Mass Consumption in Postwar America* (New York: Vintage Books, 2003); Franca Iacovetta, "The Sexual Politics of Moral Citizenship and Containing 'Dangerous' Foreign Men in Cold War Canada, 1950s–1960s," *Social History/Histoire Sociale* 33, no. 66 (2000): 361–89; Marianna Valverde, "Building Anti-Delinquent Communities: Morality, Gender, and Generation in the City," *A Diversity of Women: Ontario, 1945–1980*, ed. Joy Parr (Toronto: University of Toronto Press, 1995), 19–45.

68. W. L. Clark, "As We See It," *Windsor Daily Star*, October 2, 1946, 2.

69. Harrison, "Now," 7.

70. "Venereal Disease: A Challenge to Leadership," *Windsor Daily Star*, November 30, 1944, 2.

71. Ibid., 2.
72. "Attracted to Windsor," 3.
73. Ibid., 3.
74. See Dan Malleck's article in chapter 7 of this volume.
75. "Local Child Said Victim," *Windsor Daily Star*, September 22, 1941, 3.
76. Ibid., 3.
77. Clark, "As We See It," 2.
78. For studies on adolescents and sexuality, see Adams, *The Trouble With Normal*; Mary Odem, *Delinquent Daughters: Protecting and Policing Adolescent Sexuality in the United States, 1885–1920* (Chapel Hill: University of North Carolina Press, 1995); Joan Sangster, *Girl Trouble: Female Delinquency in English Canada* (Toronto: Between the Lines, 2002); Carolyn Strange, *Toronto's Girl Problem: The Perils and Pleasures of the City, 1880–1930* (Toronto: University of Toronto Press, 1995).
79. "M.O.H. Will Lead Drive," 3.
80. "Parks Here Are Safe, Committee Told: Educational Campaign Decided on in Sex Crime War," *Windsor Daily Star*, July 31, 1946, 1.
81. "Praised For Their Efforts," *Windsor Daily Star*, July 29, 1946, 3.
82. See Gordon McCaffrey, "They're Putting the Squeeze on Gambling," *Saturday Night*, April 18, 1950, 9–10; Ewing Laverty and Melwyn Breen, "Windsor: Border — Not Barrier," *Saturday Night*, April 25, 1950, 8–10, 56; Anglin, "He Blew the Whistle," 61–64.
83. Anglin, "He Blew the Whistle," 7.
84. Robert Earl Stewart, "Portrait of a Scandal," *The Times Magazine* (online) (fall 2005).
85. Windsor Police Department, *Annual Report*, 1959, 52.
86. Anglin, "He Blew the Whistle on Windsor Vice," 62.

Chapter 6. Official Government Discourses about Vice and Deviance

1. Jewell D. Martin to Commissioner of Indian Affairs, July 23, 1917; Commissioner of Indian Affairs, June–September 1917; Jewell D. Martin to Commissioner of Indian Affairs; Sells Indian Agency — Record Group 75 — *National Archives and Records Administration / Pacific Region / Laguna Niguel* (hereafter SIA-RG75-NARA/PR/LN).
2. Janette Woodruff, Report on the Working Girls for the Quarter Ending December 31, 1919; Field Matron Correspondence, Janette Woodruff, 1919–1920; SIA-RG75-NARA/PR/LN.
3. Gustavo A. Serrano to Ezequiel Padilla, Sonora, 18 July 1929, *Archivo Historico de la Secretaria de Eduación Pública-Educación Rural* (hereafter AHSEP-ER), box 8420, exp. 6.
4. Cited in Mary Kay Vaughan, *Cultural Politics in Revolution: Teachers, Peasants, and Schools in Mexico, 1930–1940* (Tucson: University of Arizona Press, 1997), 28. Also, see Regina G. Kunzel's *Fallen Women, Problem Girls: Unmarried Mothers and the Professionalism of Social Work, 1890–1945* (New Haven: Yale University Press, 1993), 36–64; Pablo Piccato's "'El Paso de Venus por el disco del sol': Criminality and Alcoholism in the Late Porfiriato," *Mexican Studies / Estudios Mexicanos* 11, no. 2

(summer, 1995): 203–41; and Piccato, *City of Suspects: Crime in Mexico City, 1900–1931* (Durham, NC: Duke University Press, 2001); and Jürgen Buchenau, *Plutarco Elías Calles and the Mexican Revolution* (Lanham: Rowman and Littlefield, 2007), 59.

5. See Paul Gootenberg, "Between Coca and Cocaine: A Century or More of U.S.-Peruvian Drug Paradoxes," *Hispanic American Historical Review* 83, no. 1 (February 2003): 137–50; and Paul Gootenberg, "The 'Pre-Colombian' Era of Drug Trafficking in the Americas: Cocaine, 1945–1965," *Americas* 64, no. 2 (October 2007): 133–76.

6. Janette Woodruff and Cecil Dryden, *Indian Oasis* (Caldwell, ID: Caxton Printers, 1939), 290.

7. Annual Report — Narrative Section 1917, Jewell D. Martin to Commissioner of Indian Affairs, SIA-RG75-NARA/PR/LN.

8. Eric V. Meeks, *Border Citizens: The Making of Indians, Mexicans, and Anglos in Arizona* (Austin: University of Texas Press, 2007), 17, 37.

9. "'What's to Be Done with 'em?' Images of Mexican Cultural Backwardness, Racial Limitations, and Moral Decrepitude in the United States Press, 1913–1915," *Mexican Studies / Estudios Mexicanos* 14, no. 1 (winter 1998): 23–70.

10. Alan Dawley, *Changing the World: American Progressives in War and Revolution* (Princeton: Princeton University Press, 2003), 81.

11. Susan Yohn, *A Contest of Faiths: Missionary Women and Pluralism in the American Southwest* (Ithaca: Cornell University Press, 1995), 146.

12. Evelyn Nakano Glen, *Unequal Freedom: How Race and Gender Shaped American Citizenship and Labor* (Cambridge: Harvard University Press, 2002).

13. For details, see Will Fowler, *Santa Anna of Mexico* (Lincoln: University of Nebraska Press, 2007), 304–8; and Ramón Eduardo Ruiz, *On the Rim of Mexico: Encounters of the Rich and Poor* (Boulder, CO: Westview Press, 1998), 22.

14. See Oscar J. Martínez, *Troublesome Border* (Tucson: University of Arizona Press, 1988), 38–47.

15. Jewell D. Martin to Commissioner of Indian Affairs, 1 August 1916; Advance Estimate for 1918; Files of the Superintendent, Jewell D. Martin; SIA-RG75-NARA/PR/LN.

16. Jewell D. Martin to Commissioner of Indian Affairs, March 13, 1917; Commissioner of Indian Affairs, January–June 1917; Subject Files of the Superintendent, Jewell D. Martin; SIA-RG75-NARA/PR/LN; Jewell D. Martin to Commissioner of Indian Affairs, July 23, 1917; and Cato Sells, Commissioner of Indian Affairs, to Mr. Jewell D. Martin, July 28, 1917; Commissioner of Indian Affairs, June-September 1917; Subject Files of the Superintendent, Jewell D. Martin; SIA-RG75-NARA/PR/LN; Jewell D. Martin to Commissioner of Indian Affairs, Annual Report, Narrative Section, 1917; Subject Files of the Superintendent, Jewell D. Martin; Commissioner of Indian Affairs, June-September 1917; Subject Files of the Superintendent, Jewell D. Martin; SIA-RG75-NARA/PR/LN.

17. Superintendent to Mr. Dwight B. Heard, May 7, 1917; Dwight B. Heard, Chairman, The Arizona Council of Defense, to Mr. Jewell D. Martin, May 14, 1917; Dwight B. Heard to Superintendent Martin, April 23, 1917; Mexican Conflicts with Papagos, 1916–17; Subject Files of the Superintendent, Jewell D. Martin; SIA-RG75-NARA/PR/LN. See also E. B. Meritt, Assistant Commissioner of Indian Affairs, to Mr. Jewell D. Martin, March 20, 1917 and Commanding Officer, Colonel, 35th Infantry to the Indian Agent, Papago Indian Reservation, May 22, 1917; Mexican Conflict with

Papagos, 1916–17; Subject Files of the Superintendent, Jewell D. Martin; SIA-RG75-NARA/PR/LN; and Friedrich Katz, *The Life and Times of Pancho Villa* (Stanford: Stanford University Press, 1998), 545–614.

18. Tinker Salas, *In the Shadow of the Eagles: Sonora and the Transformation of the Border during the Porfiriato* (Berkeley: University of California Press, 1997), 173.

19. Alan Knight, "The United States and the Mexican Peasantry, circa 1880–1940," *Rural Revolt in Mexico: U.S. Intervention and the Domain of Subaltern Politics,* ed. Daniel Nugent (Durham, NC: Duke University Press, 1998), 40.

20. John Mason Hart, *Revolutionary Mexico: The Coming and Process of the Mexican Revolution* (Berkeley: University of California Press, 1987), 9.

21. See Andrae M. Marak, "Forging Identity: Mexican Federal Frontier Schools, 1924–1935," *New Mexico Historical Review* 80, no. 2 (spring 2005): 163–88.

22. See Josiah McC. Heyman, "The Mexico-United States Border in Anthropology: A Critique and Reformulation," *Journal of Political Ecology* 1 (1994): 43–65.

23. William T. Hagan, "Kiowas, Comanches, and Cattlemen, 1867–1906: A Case Study of the Failure of U.S. Reservation Policy," *Pacific Historical Review* 40, no. 3 (August 1971): 333.

24. Minutes of Council with Papago Indians at Indian Oasis, September 21, 1916; Minutes of Council with Papago, 1916; Subject Files of the Superintendent, Jewell D. Martin; SIA-RG75-NARA/PR/LN.

25. Kunzel, *Fallen Women, Problem Girls,* 57–58; Alan Dawley, *Struggles for Justice: Social Responsibility and the Liberal State* (Cambridge: Harvard University Press, 1991), 93; and John D'Emilio and Estelle Friedman, *Intimate Matters: A History of Sexuality in America* (New York: Harper and Row, 1988).

26. Woodruff and Dryden, *Indian Oasis,* 290.

27. See Stephen E. Lewis, *Ambivalent Revolution: Forging State and Nation in Chiapas, 1910–1945* (Albuquerque: University of New Mexico Press, 2005), 45; and Alexander S. Dawson, *Indian and Nation in Revolutionary Mexico* (Tucson: University of Arizona Press, 2004), xiv–xv.

28. Plutarco Elías Calles, *Plutarco Elías Calles, Pensamiento político y social, Antología (1913–1936),* ed. Carlos Macías (Mexico: Fondo de Cultura Económica, 1988); and *Boletin de la Secretaria de Eduación Pública* 5:6 (1926): 7–8.

29. Proyecto del Plan Sexenal, en lo que Corresponde a la Secretaría de Agricultura y Fomento, *Fideicomiso Archivos Plutarco Elias Calles y Fernando Torreblanco* (hereafter FAPECFT), exp. 1: Plan Sexenal, leg. 1/2, foja 26, inv. 4526. For a description of the situation in Sonora, see Héctor Aguilar Camín, *Saldos de la revolucíon: cultura y política de México, 1910–1980* (México: Editorial Nuevo Imagen, 1982), 22–23.

30. Boletín de la Secretaría de Educación Pública (BSEP) 5, no. 6 (1926): 5–7. See also Manuel Gamio, *Forjando Patria* (México: Porrúa Hermanos, 1916); David A. Brading, "Manuel Gamio and Official Indigenismo in Mexico," *Bulletin of Latin American Research* 7, no. 1 (1988): 75–89; and Dawson, *Indian and Nation,* 14.

31. Luz Elena Galván de Terrazas, *Los maestros y la educación pública en México: un estudio histórico* (Tlalpan: Centro de Investigaciones y Estudios Superiores en Antropología Social, 1985), 91; Calles, *pensamiento político,* 116; and BESP, 5, no. 6 (1926), 8.

32. Gonzalo Aguirre Beltrán, *Teoría y práctica del la educación indígena* (México: Fondo de Cultura Económica, 1992), 68–69.

33. Thomas E. Sheridan, *Landscapes of Fraud: Mission Tumacácori, the Baca Float, and the Betrayal of the O'odham* (Tucson: University of Arizona Press, 2006), 34–38.

34. Eric V. Meeks, "The Tohono O'odham, Wage Labor, and Resistant Adaptation, 1900–1930," *Western Historical Quarterly* 34 (winter 2003): 473–77; See also Reports of the Field Matrons, 1910–1932; SIA-RG75-NARA/PR/LN.

35. Meeks, *Border Citizens*, 20; David Rich Lewis, *Neither Wolf Nor Dog: American Indians, Environment, and Agrarian Change* (New York: University of Oxford Press, 1994), 128–29; A. M. Philipson, Individual Weekly Report for Extension Workers, February 1934; Farmer, A. M. Philipson, 1933–1934; Reports of the Agency Farmers and Stockmen, 1910–1934; SIA-RG75-NARA/PR/LN.

36. Executive Order, February 1917; Land, 1916–1917; Subject Files of the Superintendent, Jewell D. Martin; SIA-RG75-NARA/PR/LN.

37. Robert Wiebe, *The Search for Order, 1877–1920. The Making of America* (New York: Hill and Wang, 1967), 119; and Devon Mihesuah, *Cultivating the Rosebuds: The Education of Women at the Cherokee Female Seminary, 1851–1909* (Urbana: University of Illinois Press, 1993), 21.

38. Dawley, *Struggles for Justice*, 266.

39. Elizabeth Jameson, "Women as Workers, Women as Civilizers: True Womanhood in the American West," *Frontiers: A Journal of Women Studies* 7, no. 3 (1984): 1.

40. Nancy Cott, *The Grounding of Modern Feminism* (New Haven: Yale University Press, 1987).

41. Gary Paul Nabhan, *Enduring Seeds: Native American Agriculture and Wild Plant Conservation* (New York: North Point Press, 1989), 61–62.

42. David Rich Lewis, "Native Americans and the Environment: A Survey of Twentieth-Century Issues," *American Indian Quarterly* 19, no. 3 (summer, 1995): 424–25; and Nabhan, *Enduring Seeds*, 46–65. See also E. B. Merritt, Assistant Commissioner, to Mr. Jewell D. Martin, August 8, 1916; Commissioner of Indian Affairs, 1916; Subject Files of the Superintendent, Jewell D. Martin; SIA-RG75-NARA/PR/LN.

43. A. M. Philipson to Mr. T. F. McCormick, Superintendent, February 6, 1918 and A. M. Philipson to J. B. Brown, Superintendent of Phoenix Indian School, February 14, 1918; Reports of the Agency Farmers and Stockmen, 1910–1934; Farmer A. M. Philipson, 1919; SIA-RG75-NARA/PR/LN. See also Tohono O'odham (27 signatures) to Mr. Cato Sells, Commissioner of Indian Affairs, February 6, 1916; Superintendent to Mr. W. O. Hodgson, February 7, 1916; Efficiency Report on Wilbert O. Hodgson, December 11, 1916; and Superintendent to Commissioner of Indian Affairs, May 17, 1917; Subject Files of the Superintendent, Jewell D. Martin; Employee Record — Farmer Wilbert O. Hodgson; SIA-RG75-NARA/PR/LN. Hodgson's replacement, Philipson, was Catholic if his election as a delegate to the Knights of Columbus for the State Convention at Globe, AZ is any indication. See, A. M. Philipson to Mr. T. F. McCormick, May 5, 1919; Reports of the Agency Farmers and Stockmen, 1910–1934; Farmer A. M. Philipson, 1919; SIA-RG75-NARA/PR/LN.

44. Pablo, José X., Stockman; Reports of the Agency Farmers and Stockmen, 1910–1934; BIA-RG75-NARA/PR/LN. See also Lewis, "Native Americans and the Environment," 425–26.

45. A. M. Philipson to Mr. Jewell D. Martin, August 2, 1916; Subject Files of the

Superintendent, Jewell D. Martin; Education: Tucson Day School, Teacher, A. M. Philipson; SIA-RG75-NARA/PR/LN.

46. Superintendent to Philipson, July 20, 1921; A. M. Philipson to Mr. T. F. McCormick, November 17, 1921; Superintendent to Mr. Philipson, August 4, 1921; A. M. Philipson to Mr. McCormick, July 25, 1921; Reports of the Agency Farmers and Stockmen, 1910–1934; Farmer, A. M. Philipson, 1921–1922; SIA-RG75-NARA/PR/LN.

47. Superintendent to Mr. Philipson, July 7, 1920; Reports of the Agency Farmers and Stockmen, 1910–1934; Farmer A. M. Philipson, 1920 and A. M. Philipson to Mr. McCormick, October, 18, 1921; Reports of the Agency Farmers and Stockmen, 1910–1934; Farmer A. M. Philipson, 1921; SIA-RG75-NARA/PR/LN.

48. A. M. Philipson to Mr. McCormick, May 8, 1923; Reports of the Agency Farmers and Stockmen, 1910–1934; Farmer A. M. Philipson, 1923; SIA-RG75-NARA/PR/LN.

49. A. M. Philipson, Report, n.d.; A. M. Philipson to Mr. McCormick, August 23, 1923; Reports of the Agency Farmers and Stockmen, 1910–1934; Farmer, A. M. Philipson, 1923; SIA-RG75-NARA/PR/LN.

50. Wiebe, *Search for Order*, 149–50; Kunzel, *Fallen Women, Problem Girls*.

51. Yohn, *Contest of Faiths*.

52. Jewell D. Martin to Commissioner of Indian Affairs, July 23, 1917; Commissioner of Indian Affairs, June-Sept. 1917, Jewell D. Martin To Commissioner of Indian Affairs; Subject Files of the Superintendent, Jewell D. Martin; SIA-RG75-NARA/PR/LN.

53. Doyle to J. D. Martin, May 16, 1917. Field Matron's Weekly Reports, Mary Doyle, 1916–1919, Reports of the Field Matrons, 1910–1932, SIA-RG75-NARA/PR/LN.

54. See, for example, Light to J. W. Elliot, Oct 9, 1930, Field Matron, Libbie C. Light, Correspondence, 1929–1930; Frances D. Hall, Senior Placement Matron to Mrs. Libbie C. Light, May 16, 1931; and Field Matron to J. W. Elliott, Nov. 11, 1931, Field Matron, Libbie C. Light, Correspondence, 1931–1932, Reports of Field Matrons, 1910–1932, SIA-RG75-NARA/PR/LN.

55. Cato Sells to Janette Woodruff, Feb. 23, 1917, Field Matron, Janette Woodruff, 1915–1918, Reports of the Field Matrons, 1910–1932, SIA-RG75-NARA/PR/LN.

56. Trennert, "Educating Indian Girls," 283; Woodruff to T. F. McCormick, July 1, 1918, Field Matron, Janette Woodruff, 1915–1918, Reports of the Field Matrons, 1910–1932, SIA-RG75-NARA/PR/LN.

57. Ruth M. Underhill, *The Papago (Tohono O'odham) and Pima Indians of Arizona* (Palmer Lake, CO: Filter Press, 2000), 47–48; Ruth Underhill, *The People of the Crimson Evening* (Palmer Lake, CO: Filter Press, 1982), 97–100.

58. Matron to E. S. Stewart, March 10, 1930, Field Matron, Libbie C. Light, Correspondence, Superintendent E. S. Stewart, Reports of the Field Matrons, 1910–1932, SIA-RG75-NARA/PR/LN.

59. Woodruff to Mr. Martin, July 27, 1917, Field Matron, Janette Woodruff, 1915–1918, Reports of the Field Matrons, 1910–1932, SIA-RG75-NARA/PR/LN. See also E. B. Meritt to T. F. McCormick, May 11, 1918, Commissioner of Indian Affairs, Office of, January–July, 1918, Subject Files of the Superintendent, Thomas F. McCormick, SIA-RG75-NARA/PR/LN.

60. Superintendent to Commissioner of Indian Affairs, July 24, 1917, Commissioner

of Indian Affairs, January–June 1917, Subject Files of the Superintendent, Jewell D. Martin, SIA-RG75-NARA/PR/LN.

61. Woodruff to T. F. McCormick, July 1, 1920, Field Matron, Correspondence, Janette Woodruff, 1919–1920, Reports of the Field Matrons, 1910–1932, SIA-RG75-NARA/PR/LN.

62. Janette Woodruff to T. F. McCormick, April 23, 1920 and May 5, 1920, Field Matron Correspondence, 1919–1920, Reports of the Field Matrons, 1910–1932, SIA-RG75-NARA/PR/LN

63. Matron to Antonio Moreno, San Xavier Village, Nov. 5 1931, Field Matron, Libbie C. Light, Correspondence, 1931–1932, Reports of the Field Matrons, 1910–1932, SIA-RG75-NARA/PR/LN.

64. Field Matron to J. W. Elliot, November 11, 1931, Field Matron, Libbie C. Light, Correspondence, 1931–1932, Reports of the Field Matrons, 1910–1932, SIA-RG75-NARA/PR/LN

65. Janette Woodruff, Annual Report on the Working Girls ending June 30, 1927, Field Matron's Weekly Reports, Janette Woodruff, 1927–1929, Reports of the Field Matrons, 1910–1932, SIA-RG75-NARA/PR/LN.

66. A. M. Philipson to E. S. Stewart, January 27, 1927, Farmer, A. M. Philipson, 1927–1929, Reports of the Agency Farmers and Stockmen, 1910–1934; Field Matron to Miss Mary Stewart, Field Officer, Indian Service, April 14, 1932, Field Matron, Libbie C. Light, Correspondence, 1931–1932, Reports of the Field Matrons, 1910–1932; SIA-RG75-NARA/PR/LN.

67. See, for example, José León to State Government, 27 August 1920; Governor to José León,28 August 1920; José León to Governor, 21 March 1921; Reyes O. Carrasco to Secretary of State, Sonora, 18 April 1921; Antonio L. Bustamante to Governor of Sonora, 25 June, 1921; and Governor to Consulate of Mexico, San Fernando, Arizona, July 4, 1921, *Archivo Historico General del Estado de Sonora* (hereafter AHGES), Aguas / Papagos, Tomo 3411; Jesus M Zepeda to Governor of Sonora, 3 October, 1921; Mose Drachman to Governor of Sonora, 3 October 1921; Governor to Jesus M. Zepeda, 7 October 1921; Mose Drachman to Governor of Sonora, 17 October 1921; Governor to Municipal President of Altar, 24 October 1921; Municipal President of Altar to Governor, 1 November 1921; Antonio L. Bustamante, 12 December 1921; Governor to Antonio L. Bustamante, 31 December 1921; and Governor of Sonora to Comisión Nacional Agraria, 31 December 1921; Secretary General of Sonora to Governor of Sonora, 23 January 1922; José Angel Baviche, Luis Lopéz, and Antonio L. Bustamante to Governor of Sonora, 13 February 1923; Governor to José Angel Baviche, 7 April 1923; El Oficial Primero E. del D. to Lucas Segundo, Lucas Campillo, and José Ventura, 20 July 1923; Local Agrarian Commission to Governor of Sonora, 25 July 1923; José Angel Baviche and Rafael Ortiz to Governor of Sonora, 20 June 1923; AHGES, Tribus / Papagos, Tomo 3472; Municipal President of Sari to Secretary of Government, 14 July 1922; and Secretary of Government to Antonio L. Bustamante, 2 March 1922; AHGES, Tribus / Papagos, Tomo 3546; Raúl Hernández León, Police Commander, to don Alejo Bay, Governor, April 22, 1925; and Jesus Siqueros to Governor, 8 May 1925; AHGES, Tribus / Papagos, Tomo 3814.

68. Fernando F. Dworak to SEP, 25 May 1928, Sonora, AHSEP-ER, box 8420, exp. 6.

69. Pierre Morpeau cited in Dawson, *Indian and Nation*, 19.

70. Ibid., 21.

71. Meeks, "The Tohono O'odham, Wage Labor, and Resistant Adaptation," 473; Lewis, *Neither Wolf Nor Dog*, 126. BIA officials lauded Tohono O'odham dry-farming capabilities. See T. F. McCormick to Commissioner of Indian Affairs, October 24, 1918; Commissioner of Indian Affairs, Office of, July–December 1918; Subject Files of the Superintendent Thomas F. McCormick; SIA-RG75-NARA/PR/LN.

72. Fernando F. Dworak to SEP, 5 June 1928, Sonora, AHSEP-ER, box 8420, exp. 6.

73. Elpidio López, Monthly Report, 25 March 1933, Sonora, AHSEP-ER, box 8446, exp. 21.

74. David Torres Orozco to Fernando F. Dworak, 15 June 1928, Sonora, AHSEP--ER, box 8433, exp. 2.

75. Annual Report, Statistical, 1917; Subject Files of the Superintendent, Jewell D. Martin; SIA-RG75-NARA/PR/LN.

76. Gustavo A. Serrano to Ezequiel Padilla, 18 July 1929, Sonora, AHSEP-ER, box 8420, exp. 6.

77. Minutes of Council with Papago, 1916; Subject Files of the Superintendent, Jewell D. Martin; SIA-RG75-NARA/PR/LN.

78. Mary Kay Vaughan, "Modernizing Patriarchy: State Policies, Rural Households, and Women in Mexico, 1930–1940," in *Hidden Histories of Gender and the State in Latin America*, ed. Elizabeth Dore and Maxine Molyneux (Durham, NC: Duke University Press, 2000), 194.

79. Lewis, *Ambivalent Revolution*.

80. Adrian A. Bantjes, *As If Jesus Walked on Earth: Cardenismo, Sonora, and the Mexican Revolution* (Wilmington, DE: Scholarly Resources, 1998), 6–10; Patience A. Schell, *Church and State Education in Revolutionary Mexico City* (Tucson: University of Arizona Press, 2003), 20.

81. David Torres Orozco to Fernando F. Dworak, 2 June 1928, Sonora, AHSEP-ER, box 8433, exp. 2.

82. Bantjes, *As If Jesus Walked on Earth*, 13.

Chapter 7. Crossing the Line

This chapter draws its primary material from two sets of LCBO records, both in the archives of Ontario. The Standard Hotel Files (RG 36-1) include individual numbers for all files. The Establishment Files (RG 36-8) do not identify the files numerically. For those latter files, I include the name of the establishment as it exists on the file, and the location. Many hotels changed their names when a new owner took over, so while the name on the file may not correspond to the name of the hotel indicated in the text of this chapter, they do refer to the same set of documents.

1. This chapter is a revised and reframed version of "An Innovation from across the Line: The American Drinker and Liquor Regulation in two Ontario Border Communities, 1927–1944," *Journal of Canadian Studies* 40 (winter 2007): 151–71.

2. Carey, Elaine, "'Selling Is More of a Habit than Using': Narcotraficante Lola la Chata and Her Threat to Civilization, 1930–1960," chapter 8 of this book.

3. Authority Holder's Conduct Report (AHCR), September 14, 1935. Archives of Ontario (hereafter AO) RG 36-8, Embassy Hotel (St. Catharines).

4. Robert Campbell, *Demon Rum or Easy Money: Government Control of Liquor in British Columbia from Prohibition to Privatization* (Ottawa: Carleton University Press, 1991); Campbell, *Sit Down and Drink Your Beer: Regulating Vancouver's Beer Parlours, 1925–1954* (Toronto: University of Toronto Press, 2001); Craig Heron, *Booze: A Distilled History* (Toronto: Between the Lines, 2004); Sharon Jaeger, "From Control to Customer Service: Government Control of Liquor in Ontario, 1927–1972" (Ph.D. diss., University of Waterloo, 2000); Mariana Valverde, *Diseases of the Will: Alcohol and the Dilemmas of Freedom* (Cambridge: Cambridge University Press, 1998); Greg Marquis, "'Brewers and Distillers Paradise': American Views of Canadian Alcohol Policies, 1919 to 1935," *American Review of Canadian Studies* 34: 135–66.

5. Stephen T. Moore, "Defining the 'Undefended': Canadians, Americans, and the Multiple Meanings of Border during Prohibition," *American Review of Canadian Studies* 34 (2004): 3–36. He builds and expands considerably on the suggestive work of Richard Kottman's "Volsted Violated: Prohibition as a Factor in Canadian-American Relations," *Canadian Historical Review* 43 (June 1962): 63–81. Prohibition-era border studies are more frequent, usually involving studies of rum running. See, for example, Ryan Potter, "Enforcing National Prohibition along the Detroit River 1920–1933" (MA thesis, Eastern Michigan University, 2000); Ernest R. Forbes, "The East Coast Rum-running Economy," in *Drink in Canada: Historical Essays*, ed. Cheryl Krasnick Warsh (Montreal: McGill-Queen's University Press, 1993), 166–71. Greg Marquis has looked at the way Americans perceived and reacted to Canadian liquor control efforts in "'Brewers and Distillers Paradise': American Views of Canadian Alcohol Policies, 1919–1935," *Canadian Review of American Studies* 34 (2004): 135–66.

6. Dan Malleck, *Try to Control Yourself: Regulating Public Drinking in Post-Prohibition Ontario, 1927–1944* (Vancouver: UBC Press, forthcoming).

7. See Paul Gootenberg, "Talking like a State: Drugs, Borders, and the Language of Control," in *Illicit Flows and Criminal Things: States, Borders, and the Other Side of Globalization*, ed. Willem van Schendel and Itty Abraham (Bloomington: Indiana University Press, 2005), 101–27.

8. The beer was 4.4 percent proof spirit, also called "4.4 beer."

9. "Declares Latest Beer Bill Is to Becloud Real Issue," *Toronto Star*, March 22, 1934; Jaeger, "From Control to Customer Service," 66–114.

10. Robin Room, "Alcohol and Harm Reduction, Then and Now," *Critical Public Health* 14 (2004): 329–44.

11. David W. Gutzke, "Gothenburg Schemes / Disinterested Management," in *Alcohol and Temperance in Modern History: An International Encyclopedia*, ed. Jack S. Blocker Jr., David M. Fahey, and Ian R. Tyrrell (Santa Barbara, CA: ABC-Clio Press, 2003), I: 274–75.

12. Robert A. Campbell, "Profit Was Just a Circumstance: The Evolution of Government Liquor Control in British Columbia, 1920–1988," in *Drink in Canada*, ed. Warsh, 172–92.

13. Campbell, *Sit Down and Drink Your Beer*; Valverde, *Diseases of the Will*; Heron, *Booze*.

14. John Burnham, *Bad Habits: Drinking, Smoking, Taking Drugs, Gambling, Sexual Misbehavior, and Swearing in American History* (New York: New York University Press, 1994).

15. In 1969 John Burnham argued that Prohibition did not fail, because it fundamentally restructured the way individuals drank. This may be the case, but at the

time, Prohibition was seen as a resounding failure because it was unenforceable. It had been the prime motivator for dry forces for well over a half century, and the repeal of the Eighteenth Amendment with the Twenty-first (the only time an amendment was repealed) was considered an unqualified failure.

16. Michel Foucault's ideas about biopolitics and biopower have been explored in some great depth, and often found to be confusing. He first explored the ideas in his lectures to the College de France, published posthumously in *The Birth of Biopolitics* (New York: Palgrave-Macmillan, 2008), but the idea was published a decade earlier in his *The History of Sexuality* vol. 1, *The Will to Knowledge* (London: Penguin 1998). I have found Mitchell Dean's discussion in *Governmentality: Power and Rule in Modern Society* (London: Sage, 1999) to be especially useful, most notably chapter 5, "Biopolitics and Sovereignty," 98–112.

17. Philip Corrigan and Derek Sayer, *The Great Arch: English State Formation as Cultural Revolution* (Oxford: Blackwell, 1985).

18. Government of Ontario, "Liquor Control Act," *Statutes of Ontario* 17 Geo V, Cap 70 Sec 71 (1).

19. William Katerberg, "The Irony of Identity: An Essay on Nativism, Liberal Democracy, and Parochial Identities in Canada and the United States," *American Quarterly* 47 (1995): 493–524.

20. Linda Colley, "Britishness and Otherness: An Argument," *Journal of British Studies* 31 (1992): 309–29; 327–28.

21. Ibid., 311.

22. "Regulations for Liquor Are Approved," *Niagara Falls Review* (Ontario), May 27, 1927.

23. Unsigned photo, *Niagara Falls Gazette* (New York), June 22, 1927.

24. "Peace Bridge Opens but without Any Frills," *Toronto Star*, June 1, 1927.

25. "Report of the Liquor Control Board of Ontario," *Sessional Papers of Ontario* (1927), 7; Jaeger, "From Control to Customer Service."

26. Dingman to Collins, 27 June 1928, AO/RG 36-1-0-1576.

27. Elliott to Coultard 7 August 1932, AO/RG 36-8 Ambassador Hotel (Windsor).

28. Brisson to Smith, 7 October 1937, AO/RG 36-8 Embassy Hotel (Windsor).

29. Brown to LCBO, 3 December 1938, AO/RG 36-8 Hebert's Hotel (Crystal Beach).

30. Jaeger, "From Control to Customer Service," 66–72.

31. Dingman to Fort Erie Hotel Co., 23 March 1929, AO/RG 36-8 Fort Erie Hotel (Fort Erie).

32. OPP Report, 5 July 1929, AO/RG 36-1-0-1576.

33. Pitt to Mair, 25 July 1931, AO/RG 36-1-0-245.

34. Gulliver to LCBO, 15 May 1930, AO/RG 36-1-0-304.

35. Elliott to Dingman, 22 May 1931, AO/RG 36-1-0-1792.

36. Various files AO/RG 36-1-0-1792.

37. "Report of the Liquor Control Board of Ontario," *Sessional Papers of Ontario* (1934).

38. AHCR, 9 January 1938 AO/RG 36-8, Mather Arms Hotel (Fort Erie).

39. Ibid., 2 June 1935, AO/RG 36-8 Palmwood Hotel (Crystal Beach).

40. Cheeseman to Smith, 30 April 1939 AO/RG 36-8, Anglo-American Hotel (Fort Erie).

41. OPP Report, 1 July 1940, AO/RG 36-1-0-262.

42. Ibid., 2 September 1935, AO/RG 36-8 Emery's Corners Hotel (Essex Co).

43. James Briand to LCBO, 11 December 1936, AO/RG 36-8 Venetian Hotel (Niagara Falls).

44. Reaume to Smith, 19 May 1936, AO/RG 36-8 Arcade Public House (Windsor).

45. Boyd to LCBO, 7 June 1940, AO/RG 36-8 Maple Leaf Hotel (Niagara Falls).

46. Smith to Polsky, 11 May 1937, AO-LCBO Highway Hotel (Windsor).

47. For example, LCBO to Williams, 11 July 1935, AO/RG 36-8 St. Clair Hotel (Windsor).

48. AHCR, 16 January 1935, AO/RG 36-8 New Drake Hotel (Fort Erie).

49. Sinclair to Gordon, 24 March 1941, AO/RG-36-8 Edgewater Hotel (Riverside).

50. Ibid.

51. OPP Report, 12 July 1935, AO/RG-36-1-0-314.

52. Mrs. J S to LCBO, 25 March 1937, AO/RG-36-8 Arcade Hotel (Windsor).

53. AHCR, 10 Nov 1937, AO/RG 36-8 GTR Hotel (Fort Erie)

54. Pitt to Coulthard, 1 September 1934, AO/RG 36-1-0-1575.

55. Authority Holder's Monthly Conduct Report (AHMCR), 4 November 1943, AO/RG 36-8 Prince Edward Hotel (Windsor).

56. AHCR, 7 June 1938, AO/RG 36- 8 Bellvue Hotel (Windsor).

57. Inspector's Report, 18 January 1939, AO/RG 36-1-0-262.

58. Buchanan to Smith, 3 February 1941, AO/RG 36-8 Dwarf Village Inn (Jordan).

59. Reaume to Mair, 14 April 1941, AO/RG 36-1-0-305.

60. Bolus to LCBO, 10 October 1940, AO/RG 36-8 Dwarf Village Inn (Jordan).

61. Lond to LCBO, 14 September 1939, AO/RG 36-8 Bridge Ave Inn (Windsor).

62. Ibid., 5 October 1939.

63. Black to LCBO, 8 June 1940, AO/RG 36-8 Royal Hotel (Niagara Falls).

64. Poole to LCBO, 10 June 1940, AO/RG 36-8 Clifton Hotel (Niagara Falls); Briand to LCBO, 8 June 1940, AO/RG 36-8 Venetian Hotel (Niagara Falls).

65. Adelman and Aron, 840.

66. On licit and illicit, see van Schendel and Abrahams, eds., "Introduction," in *Illicit Flows and Criminal Things*, 1–37

Chapter 8. Selling Is More of a Habit than Using

1. An earlier version of this article originally appeared in the *Journal of Women's History* 21, no. 2 (summer 2009): 62–89.

2. S. C. Peña, Special Employee, to Commissioner of Customs, July 7, 1945, Drug Enforcement Administration, Subject Files of the Bureau of Narcotics and Dangerous Drugs, 1916–1970, RG 170, box 161, National Archive College Park (hereafter DEA-BNDD).

3. The history of crime and women has developed in the last fifteen years. In many of these pioneering works, when female offenders — whether prostitute, street vendor, or violent criminal — were perceived as not absorbing the cost of their deviancy, their actions held a disproportionate threat to themselves, other people, and the nation. For examples, see Katherine Elaine Bliss, *Compromised Positions: Prostitution, Public Health, and Gender Politics in Revolutionary Mexico City* (University Park: Pennsylvania State University, 2001); Robert Buffington, *Criminal and Citizen*

in Modern Mexico (Lincoln: University of Nebraska Press, 2000); Nancy Campbell, *Using Women: Gender, Policy, and Social Justice* (New York: Routledge, 2000); and Donna Guy, *White Slavery and Mothers Alive and Dead: The Troubled Meeting of Sex, Gender, Public Health, and Progress in Latin America* (Lincoln: University of Nebraska Press, 2000).

4. The production and distribution of alcohol and narcotics has long been an economic activity that is shared by both men and women. See, for instance, Luis Astorga, *Drogas sin frontera: Los expedients de una guerra permanente* (México, DF: Grijalbo, 2003); Paul Gootenberg, ed., *Cocaine: Global Histories* (New York: Routledge, 1999); and George Peter Murdock, *Social Structure* (New York: Macmillian, 1949).

5. For a discussion of the reasons for feminine addiction in the United States in the 1930s, see E. Mebane Hunt, Executive Secretary, Women's Prison Association of New York, "The Experience of the Women's Prison Association with Women Drug Addicts," paper presented at the American Prison Congress, October 5, 1938, box 42, File Female Addicts, DEA-BNDD. For a discussion of feminine addiction and behavior in Mexican prisons, see H. J. Anslinger, Commissioner of Narcotics, to James Bennett attachment "Letter to the President from the prisoners of the penitentiary, Mexico City," May 18, 1948, Drug Enforcement, box 23, DEA-BNDD. For a contemporary discussion of women falling prey to the vices of narcotrafficking, see Gabriela Vazquez, "La población feminina, escudo de narcotraficante," *La Jornada*, March 25, 2002; and Margath A. Walker, "Guad-narco-lupe, Maquilarañas, and the Discursive Construction of Gender and Difference on the U.S-Mexico Border in Mexican Media Representations," *Gender, Place, and Culture* 12 (March 2005): 95–110.

6. Judith Butler, *Gender Trouble* (New York: Routledge Press, 1999). In regards to the movement across borders, see Sam Truett and Elliot Young, "Introduction: Making Transnational History: Nations, Regions, and Borderlands," in *Continental Crossroads: Remapping U.S.-Mexico Borderlands History*, ed. Truett and Young (Durham, NC: Duke University Press, 2004), 6

7. See Nancy Folbre, *Why Pay for Kids? Gender and the Structure of Constraint* (New York: Routledge, 1994); for a discussion on women's addiction as a threat to US civilization and "structure of constraint," see Campbell, *Using Women*. The concept of constraint and restraint within the bourgeois class in Mexico and its support of the creation of working-class "family values" may be found in Mary Kay Vaughn, *The State, Education, and Social Class in Mexico, 1880–1928* (DeKalb: Northern Illinois University Press, 1982); and William French, "Prostitutes and Guardian Angels: Women, Work, and the Family in Porfirian Mexico," *Hispanic American Historical Review* 72, no. 4 (1992): 529–53. In 1933, the Academia Mexicana de Ciencias Penales published *Criminalia* that reflected a growing concern over crime and policy.

8. For a discussion of the FBN's agents in Mexico, see William O. Walker, "Control across the Border: The United States, Mexico, and Narcotics, 1936–1940," *Pacific Historical Review* 47, no. 1 (February 1978): 92–93. See also Josephus Daniels's autobiography *Shirt Sleeve Diplomat* (Chapel Hill: University of North Carolina Press, 1947). Daniels was the US ambassador to Mexico in the 1930s. For a contemporary analysis, see Peter Andreas, *Border Games: Policing the U.S.-Mexico Divide* (Ithaca: Cornell University Press, 2000).

9. Biographical material on La Chata is available in Jorge Robles García, *La bala perdida: William S. Burroughs en México, 1949–1952* (México, DF: 1995); and

Michael Span, "Unforgettable Characters," in *William S. Burroughs, Unforgettable Character: Lola la Chata and Bernabé Jurado* (Providence: Bisbane Books, 2001); and James B. Stewart, American Consul General to Secretary of State, Head of Narcotics writes an open letter to Lola La Chata, attachment Leopoldo Salazar Viniegra, "Open Letter to Lola la Chata," box 22, DEA-BNDD.

10. Pablo Piccato, *City of Suspects: Crime in Mexico City, 1900–1930* (Durham, NC: Duke University Press, 2001), 30.

11. For a study of La Merced, see Enrique Valenica, *La Merced: Estudio ecológico y social de una zona de la ciudad de México* (México, Instituto Nacional de Antropología e Historia, 1965). Valencia noted that as the commercial activity grew, so too did the criminal element. The increasing markets also brought *pulqerías, piqueras* (illegal alcohol vendors), cantinas, billiard halls, cabarets, and "hoteles de paso" that served prostitutes (92).

12. US Consulate, Nuevo Laredo to Treasury Department, translation of "Inducia su hijo a vender drogas," *La Prensa*, December 22, 1939, box 22, DEA-BNDD. Margarito Oliva was arrested for selling marijuana. His son was also turned in by one of his schoolmates for selling marijuana cigarettes at school.

13. For a discussion of familial connections, see Eloise Dunlap, Gabriele Stürzenhofecker, and Bruce D. Johnson, "The Elusive Romance of Motherhood: Drugs, Gender, and Reproduction in Inner-City Distressed Households," *Journal of Ethnicity and Substance Abuse* 5 (2006): 1–27; Barbara Denton, *Dealing: Women in the Drug Economy* (Sydney: University of New South Wales, 2001); Eloise Dunlap and Bruce D. Johnson, "Family and Human Resources in the Development of a Female Crack Seller: Case Study of a Hidden Population," *Journal of Drug Issues* 26, no. 1 (winter 1996): 175–98; and Patricia Adler, *Wheeling and Dealing: An Ethnography of an Upper-Level Drug Dealing and Smuggling Community* (New York: Columbia University Press, 1993).

14. Luis Astorga, *Drogas sin fronteras*; and Nicole Mottier, "Organized Crime, Political Corruption, and Powerful Governments: Drug Gangs in Ciudad Juárez, 1928–1933" (MA thesis: Oxford University, 2004). There is little information on who Lola la Chata had contact with in Ciudad Juárez.

15. Attorney General of the Republic to Commissioner of Narcotic Treasury Department, January 22, 1962, box 161, DEA-BNDD. This document disclosed the arrests of one of her daughters as well as nieces.

16. In 1898, the pharmaceutical company Bayer introduced heroin in Mexico as a treatment for respiratory illnesses. In 1925, Mexican president Calles announced a decree controlling the importation of opium, morphine, and cocaine. By the decree in 1931, opium for smoking, all marijuana, and heroin became illegal. For a general history of drugs, see Jordan Goodman, Paul Lovejoy, and Andrew Sherratt, *Consuming Habits: Drugs in History and Anthropology* (New York: Routledge, 1995); and David Courtwright, *Forces of Habit: Drugs and the Making of the Modern World* (Cambridge: Harvard University Press, 2001).

17. *Excélsior*, July 8, 1919. Because of the connection of poppy production to the Chinese, Chinese immigrants were targeted for attack. See Jorge Gómez Izquierdo, *El movimiento anti-chino en México (1871–1934): Problemas del racismo y el nacionalismo durante la Revolución Mexicana* (México, DF: INAH, 1991).

18. "Mexico to Join U.S. in Fight on Drugs," *New York Times*, May 10, 1925.

19. Gabriela Recio, "Drugs and Alcohol: U.S. Prohibition and the Origins of the Drug Trade in Mexico, 1900–1930," *Journal of Latin American Studies* 34 (2002): 21–42.

20. Hearings before the Committee on Ways and Means, House of Representatives, Seventy-first Congress, HR 10561, March 7 and 8, 1930 (Washington, DC: GPO, 1930). The urgency of the problem is illustrated by an attached map of the United States representing the "Estimated Average Drug Addiction among Violations of the Harrison Narcotic Law," (1922–1928). See also William O. Walker, *Drug Control in the Americas* (Albuquerque: University of New Mexico Press, 1989).

21. Douglas Clark Kinder and William O. Walker III, "Stable Force in a Storm: Harry J. Anslinger and United States Narcotic Foreign Policy, 1930–1962," *The Journal of American History* 72, no. 4 (March 1986): 919.

22. Consul Henry C. A. Damm, Opium Poppy Planted in Northern Sonora, August 16, 1927, DEA-BNDD. In 1927, Damm wrote about receiving information from US informants living in Mexico about the Chinese in Sonora. He stated, "The large Chinese population on the Mexican West Coast would undoubtedly offer a market for a large quantity of opium produced, but this consulate has not heard of any attempts to smuggle the drug of Sonora origin into the United States directly across the border." See also H. S. Creighton to the Commissioner of Customs, Treasury Dept. United States Custom Service, Houston, December 11, 1940; Translation from an *El Centinela*, a weekly tabloid in Cd. Juárez, editorial "El Escandalo del Robo a los Chinos," December 1, 1940, box 22, DEA-BNDD.

23. Benedict Anderson, *Imagined Communities: Reflections of the Origins and Spread of Nationalism* (New York: Verso Press, 1991). For a discussion of the Chinese in Mexico, see Gómez Izquierdo, *El movimiento anti-chino en México*; and Humberto Monteón González and José Luis Trueba Lara, *Chinos y antichinos: Documentos para su estudio* (Guadalajara: Gobierno de Jalisco, 1988).

24. Leopoldo Salazar Viniegra, "El mito de la marijuana," *Criminalia* (December 1938): 206–37.

25. Ibid. In 1931, the Mexican government amended the Federal Penal Code to make the using, buying, and selling of drugs a criminal offense (currently Article 195). For an extensive discussion of the 1930s, see Luis Astorga, *El siglo de las drogas: El narcotráfico, del Porfiriato nuevo milenio* (México, DF: Plaza Janés, 2005), 43–60.

26. League of Nations. Advisory Committee on Traffic in Opium and Other Dangerous Drugs, Twenty-fourth session, June 2, 1939, box 22, DEA-BNDD; Daniel Bailey, Customs Agent in Charge, Intelligence Bulletins, No. 8, September 19, 1936 and Bulletin No. 9, September 26, 1936, Henry Morgenthau Correspondence, box 206, Franklin D. Roosevelt Library, New Hyde Park, NY (hereafter FDR).

27. Denton, *Dealing*. In Denton's research, La Chata fits the profile of women who grow up in the trade and then forge alliances with men in the business.

28. *La Prensa*, May 1937. *La Prensa* published a series of exposés about the Federal Judicial Police, the attorney general, and the narcotics police involvement in the distribution of heroin for Lola La Chata. The stories in *La Prensa* connected her to high levels within the Health Department and to judges and Customs agents. Other arrests of traffickers in the 1940s supported the tie of police and government officials to traffickers. James B. Stewart, American Consul General, to Secretary of State, February 28, 1940, clippings of newspaper articles, "Funcionarios en fabuloso trafico de drogas,"

Excélsior December 7, 1940; and "Es Tremendo el trafico de drogas," *Excélsior*, December 8, 1940, box 22, DEA-BNDD.

29. Despite her difference in class, La Chata's alliances with men as furthering her own career are echoed in the testimony of Cristal in Howard Campbell's *Drug War Zone: Frontline Dispatches from the Streets of El Paso and Juárez* (Austin: University of Texas Press, 2009), 60–75. Also see his, "Female Drug Smugglers on the U.S.-Mexico Border: Gender, Crime, and Empowerment," *Anthropological Quarterly* 81, no. 1 (2008): 233–68. Campbell demonstrates that women in the trade make strategic sexual alliances rather than sleeping their way to the top as portrayed by other writers.

30. George White to H. J. Anslinger, newspaper clipping "Blow to Narcotic Traffic," DEA-BNDD.

31. Ibid.

32. S. J. Kennedy, Treasury Representative in Charge, to Supervising Customs Agent, Treasury Department, July 27, 1944, DEA-BNDD.

33. The Narcotics Division was housed in the Department of Pensions and National Health. Sharman, an ex-member of the Canadian Royal Mounted Police, remained a staunch ally of Anslinger. He represented Canada on many international narcotics commissions.

34. H. J. Anslinger to Colonel G. H. L. Sharman, Chief Narcotics Division, Dept. of National Health and Welfare, Ottawa, Canada, "Maria Dolores Estevez Zuleta," DEA-BNDD.

35. S. J. Kennedy to the Supervising Agent, Treasury Department, United States Customs Service.

36. Harry S. Anslinger and Will Oursler, *The Murderers: The Story of the Narcotics Gangs* (New York: Farrar, Straus, and Cudahy, 1961), 4. This scene was repeated in Steven Soderbergh's *Traffic* when Caroline, the daughter of the US's drug czar, becomes a heroin addict.

37. Nancy Campbell, *Using Women*, 144–68. Also see Harry S. Anslinger and Will Oursler, *The Murderers: The Story of the Narcotics Gangs*. His nativist views were widely circulated in his talks as well as the press. See H. J. Anslinger and Courtney Ryley Copper, "Marijuana: Assassin of Youth," *American Magazine* 124 (July 1937): 18–19, 150–53.

38. Lic. Arnulfo Martinez Lavalle, Visitador General, Procuraduría General de la Republica to H. J. Anslinger, Feb. 21, 1950, box 29, DEA-BNDD.

39. Campbell, *Using Women*, 64.

40. H. J. Anslinger to Colonel G. H. L. Sherman, Chief Narcotics Division, Dept. of National Health and Welfare, Ottawa, Canada, "Maria Dolores Estevez Zuleta." Astorga, *Drogas sin Fronteras*, 166. The description of La Chata also builds on Anslinger and the Bureau of Narcotics view of the typical dealer. In his book, *The Murderers*, he focused on the "Negro" drug gangs.

41. Adler, *Wheeling and Dealing*. In her research, Adler noted that women involved with traffickers were very beautiful. She argued that they were drawn to the wealth and the lifestyle. The image of the beautiful lover of the drug dealer is celebrated in popular culture. For example, in Brian de Palma's *Scarface* (1983), Michelle Pfeiffer's character becomes the archetype of the traffickers' companion.

42. Leopoldo Salazar Viniegra, "Open Letter to Lola la Chata."

43. Elaine Scarry, *The Body in Pain: The Making and Unmaking of the World*

(New York: Oxford University Press, 1985), 39; and Claudia Schaefer, *Textured Lives: Women, Art, and Representation in Modern Mexico* (Tucson: University of Arizona Press), 18.

44. Julia Sudbury, "Celling Black Bodies: Black Women in the Global Prison Industrial Complex," *Feminist Review* 80 (2005): 162–79.

45. H. J. Anslinger, Memorandum for the Secretary, Treasury Department, Bureau of Narcotics, September, 3, 1936, Henry Morgenthau Papers, FDR Archive.

46. Walker, "Control across the Border," 94.

47. R. W. Artis to H. J. Anslinger, Dec. 12, 1947, and Terry A. Talent to H. J. Anslinger, Treasury Dept, Bureau of Narcotics, El Paso, TX December 1, 1947, box 23, DEA-BNDD. This document contains a list of names of Mexican citizens who have been reported for narcotics violations since 1940, 125 names were listed, seven were women and six were active. Lola la Chata was listed as imprisoned.

48. See William French, "Prostitutes and Guardians Angels: Women, Work, and the Family in Porfirian Mexico," *Hispanic American Historical Review* 72, no. 4 (1992): 530–53.

49. Although focused on the Victorian era explorers of Africa, for a discussion of transgressive sexual fantasies of interracial sex, see Robert J. C. Young, *Colonial Desire: Hybridity in Theory, Culture, and Race* (New York: Routledge, 1995). Jack Kerouac's, *Tristessa* (New York: McGraw Hill, 1960) exemplifies Young's theories, for it is about an affair between a gringo and a Mexico City heroin addicted prostitute. Burroughs work also shows an interest in interracial sexuality.

50. Burroughs's interest in criminals was evident in his circle of friends and his interest in criminal networks in the United States and Mexico. See Oliver Harris, ed., *Letters of William S. Burroughs, 1945–1959* (New York: Viking Press, 1993).

51. Burroughs, *Naked Lunch* (New York: Grove Press, 1992). Lola la Chata appears in a number of Burroughs's works: *Cities of the Night: A Novel* (New York: Picador, 2001), and *The Wild Boys: A Book of the Dead* (New York: Grove Press, 1992).

52. Jorge Robles García, *La bala perdida: William S. Burroughs en México (1949–1952)* (México, DF: Ediciones del Milenio, 1995). Even shortly before his death, Burroughs was still fascinated by La Chata. Robles García gave Burroughs an image of La Chata where one could make out her gold cap jewel studded teeth. Burroughs made a mixed media piece using the photo with the words, "Folk Hero," inscribed on the bottom. See photo in *William S. Burroughs, Unforgettable Characters*, 26.

53. Burroughs, *Cities of the Night*, 145.

54. Ibid.

55. William Burroughs, *The Burroughs File* (San Francisco: City Light Books, 1984), 137–39. In this short story, Lola la Chata hosts an annual party on her birthday where everything is free and where police receive their payoffs in drugs. Burroughs wrote: "Yes, it's once a year on her birthday that Lola la Chata gives this party and on that day everything is free. On that day she gives. On other days she takes."

56. Leopoldo Salazar Viniegra, "Open Letter to Lola la Chata."

57. For a contemporary discussion of street vending, see John C. Cross, *Informal Politics: Street Vendors and the State in Mexico City* (Stanford: Stanford University Press, 1998).

58. For a discussion of the intersection between the private and the public in marginal women's lives, see Sandra Lauderdale-Graham, *House and Street: The Domestic*

World of Servants and Masters in Nineteenth-Century Rio de Janeiro (Austin: University of Texas Press, 1992).

59. Catherine Gilbert Murdock, *Domesticating Drink: Women, Men, and Alcohol in America, 1870–1910* (Baltimore: Johns Hopkins University Press, 1998), 47–49. Gilbert Murdock argues that by 1900, middle-age women made up the majority of opium addicts. Women comprised 40 to 50 percent of addicts in treatment facilities.

60. Silvia Mariana Arrom, *The Women of Mexico City, 1790–1857* (Stanford: Stanford University Press, 1985), 180.

61. Katherine Elaine Bliss, *Compromising Positions: Prostitution, Public Health, and Gender Politics in Revolutionary Mexico* (University Park: Penn State Press, 2001), 69.

62. Burroughs, "Tío Mate Smiles," in *The Wild Boys*, 11.

63. League of Nations, Advisory Committee on Traffic in Opium and Other Dangerous Drugs, Twenty-fourth session, June 2, 1939.

64. Leopoldo Salazar Viniegra, "Open Letter to Lola la Chata."

65. H. J. Anslinger to John Edgar Hoover, July 28, 1945," DEA-BNDD.

66. "Opium Smugglers Are Using Planes," *New York Times*, July 6, 1947.

67. "No Antiwoman Job Bias in the Narcotics Trade," *New York Times*, April 22, 1975; and "Los dos mayores carteles de México son dirigidos por mujeres: UEDO," *La Jornada*, September 3, 2002. Campbell's ethnographic studies taken over years demonstrates the complexities surrounding women in the contemporary drug trade. See *Drug War Zone*, 1–117, and "Female Drug Smugglers."

68. Burroughs, *Naked Lunch*, 193.

Chapter 9. Preventing the Invasion

1. *Toronto Daily Star*, February 10, 1967, 24.

2. Catherine Carstairs, *Jailed for Possession: Illegal Drug Use, Regulation, and Power in Canada, 1920–1961* (Toronto: University of Toronto Press, 2006); Erika Dyck, *Psychedelic Psychiatry: LSD from Clinic to Campus* (Baltimore: Johns Hopkins University Press, 2008); Kyle Grayson, *Chasing Dragons: Security, Identity, and Illicit Drugs in Canada* (Toronto: University of Toronto Press, 2008); Marcel Martel, *Not This Time: Canadians, Public Policy, and the Marijuana Issue, 1961–1975* (Toronto: University of Toronto Press, 2006).

3. See the stimulating study by John J. Bukowczyk, ed., *Permeable Border: The Great Lakes Basin as Transnational Region, 1650–1990* (Calgary: University of Calgary Press, 2005).

4. On the issue of state sovereignty and international drug regulations, see Kettil Bruun, Lynn Pan, and Ingemar Rexed, *The Gentlemen's Club: International Control of Drugs and Alcohol* (Chicago: University of Chicago Press, 1975), but in particular William B. McAllister, *Drug Diplomacy in the Twentieth Century: An International History* (London: Routledge, 2000).

5. Library and Archives Canada [LAC], R-923, vol. 12, file 12-5H.B, Dr. Beatty Cotnam, Supervising Coroner, Continuing Education Course for Coroners, 6 May 1966.

6. "Potency of Morning Glory Seeds Probed," *Globe and Mail*, July 12, 1963, 3.

7. On the American debate about drug use and how to regulate it, see John C. Burnham, *Bad Habits: Drinking, Smoking, Taking Drugs, Gambling, Sexual Misbehavior, and Swearing in American History* (New York: New York University Press, 1993); David Courtwright, *Forces of Habit: Drugs and the Making of the Modern World* (Cambridge: Harvard University Press, 2001); Richard Davenport-Hines, *The Pursuit of Oblivion: A Global History of Narcotics* (New York: W. W. Norton, 2001); Philip Jenkins, *Synthetic Panics: The Symbolic Politics of Designer Drugs* (New York: New York University Press, 1999); Jill Jonnes, *Hep-Cats, Narcs, and Pipe Dreams: A History of America's Romance with Illegal Drugs* (Baltimore: Johns Hopkins University Press, 1996); Kenneth J. Meier, *The Politics of Sin: Drugs, Alcohol, and Public Policy* (Armonk, NY: M. E. Sharpe, 1994); David F. Musto, *The American Disease: The Origins of Narcotic Control* (New Haven: Yale University Press, 1973).

8. Carstairs, *Jailed for Possession*, 19–32; Robert R. Solomon and Melvyn Green, "The First Century: The History of Non-medical Opiate Use and Control Policies in Canada, 1870–1970," in *Illicit Drugs in Canada: A Risky Business*, ed. Judith C. Blackwell and Patricia G. Erickson (Scarborough, Ontario: Nelson Canada, 1988), 88–116.

9. Carstairs, *Jailed for Possession*, 19–32.

10. LAC, R 923, vol. 20, file 20-9, Survey of newspapers and magazines for the Le Dain Commission, by Claude Hénault, May 21, 1971, 167a, Commission Research Paper, Commission of Inquiry into the Non-Medical Use of Drugs, Project No 81, 197.

11. Martin Goldfarb Consultants, *The Media and the People: A Report*, Report of the Special Senate Committee on Mass Media, Ottawa, 1970, 19, 23.

12. LAC, R 923, vol. 20, file 20-9, Survey of newspapers and magazines for the Le Dain Commission. . . .

13. Dyck, *Psychedelic Psychiatry*, 107.

14. *Globe and Mail*, October 20, 1962, 1, 3; "Drug Found to Aid Alcoholic," June 15, 1963, 5; David Farber, "The Intoxicated State/Illegal Nation: Drugs in the Sixties Counterculture," in *Imagine Nation: The American Counterculture of the 1960s and '70s*, ed. Peter Braunstein and Michael William Doyle (New York: Routledge, 2002), 21.

15. *Toronto Star*, February 10, 1967, 24; February 13, 1967, 1.

16. Ibid., February 6, 1967, 6.

17. Ibid., February 9, 1967, 35.

18. *Globe and Mail*, March 20, 1967, 1.

19. *Toronto Telegram*, March 20, 1967, 1–2.

20. *Globe and Mail*, March 21, 1967, 4.

21. "Nude Couple Killed after Wild LSD Revel," *Globe and Mail*, October 10, 1967, 11.

22. "Use of LSD among Average Teens Likely to Grow, Parents Warned," *Globe and Mail*, January 4, 1968, W2.

23. *Globe and Mail*, February 26, 1968, 5; 3 May 1968, 5.

24. Ibid., October 11, 1968, 3.

25. Dyck, *Psychedelic Psychiatry*, 129.

26. LAC, RG 25, vol. 10488, file 45-9-1-1 part 2.2, Resolution adopted by the United Nations Economic and Social Council, 16 May 1967; LAC, RG 25, vol. 10487, file 45.9.1 part 1, Resolution adopted by the United Nations Economic and Social Council, Plenary Meeting, 23 May 1968.

27. Dyck, *Psychedelic Psychiatry*, 108.

28. Reginald Whitaker, *Drugs and the Law: The Canadian Scene* (Toronto: Methuen, 1969), 147.

29. Province of British Columbia, *Statutes*, chap. 37, 1967.

30. Ibid., chap. 21, 1967.

31. *Globe and Mail*, January 29, 1970, 9.

32. See Martel, *Not This Time*.

33. Archives of Ontario [AO], RG 3-26, box 123, file Alcoholism and Drug Addiction Health, Apr. 63–Dec. 65, Letter from H. David Archibald, Executive Director, ARF, to D. Richmond, Prime Minister's Office, 26 November 1964.

34. See Meier, *The Politics of Sin*; Martin A. Lee and Bruce Shlain, *Acid Dreams: The CIA, LSD, and the Sixties Rebellion* (New York: Grove Press, 1985), 89.

35. Reginald G. Smart and David Jackson, *A Preliminary Report on Attitudes and Behaviour of Toronto Students in Relation to Drugs* (Toronto: Alcoholism and Drug Addiction Research Foundation of Ontario, 1969), 4, table 5.2.

36. Reginald G. Smart, Dianne Fejer, and Jim White, *The Extent of Drug Use in Metropolitan Toronto Schools: A Study of Changes from 1968 to 1970* (Toronto: The Addiction Research Foundation, 1970), 8, table 2.

37. Reginald G. Smart, Dianne Fejer and Jim White, *Drug Use Trends among Metropolitan Toronto Students: A Study of Changes from 1968 to 1972* (Toronto: The Addiction Research Foundation, 1972), 16, table 4; Reginald G. Smart and Dianne Fejer, *Changes in Drug Use in Toronto High School Students between 1972 and 1974* (Toronto: The Addiction Research Foundation, 1974), 6.

38. AO, RG 4-2, file 445.3, Addiction Research Foundation of Ontario, Facts about LSD (revised October 1969).

39. Dyck, *Psychedelic Psychiatry*, 128–29.

40. *Senate Standing Committee on Banking and Commerce*, November 22, 1967, 64–70.

41. *Toronto Daily Star*, August 21, 1969, 1; August 22, 1969, 1.

Afterword

1. Josiah McC. Heyman, ed., *States and Illegal Practices* (Oxford: Berg, 1999). For a general review of the anthropology of legality and illegality, see Jane Schneider and Peter Schneider, "The Anthropology of Crime and Criminalization," *Annual Review of Anthropology* 37: 351–73.

2. Willem van Schendel and Itty Abraham, eds., *Illicit Flows and Criminal Things: States, Borders, and the Other Side of Globalization* (Bloomington: Indiana University Press, 2005).

3. Jeremy Adelman and Stephen Aron, "From Borderlands to Borders: Empires, Nation-States, and the Peoples in Between in North American History," *American Historical Review* 104 (1999): 814–41; John A. Agnew and Stuart Corbridge, *Mastering Space: Hegemony, Territory, and International Political Economy* (London: Routledge, 1995); Michiel Baud and Willem van Schendel, "Toward a Comparative History of Borderlands," *Journal of World History* 8 (1997): 211–42; Hastings Donnan and Thomas M. Wilson, *Borders: Frontiers of Identity, Nation, and State* (Oxford:

Berg, 1999); Josiah McC. Heyman, *Life and Labor on the Border: Working People of Northeastern Sonora, Mexico, 1886–1986* (Tucson: University of Arizona Press, 1991); Josiah McC. Heyman, "The Mexico–United States Border in Anthropology: A Critique and Reformulation," *Journal of Political Ecology* 1:43–65, http://www.library .arizona.edu/ej/jpe/volume_1/HEYMAN.PDF, accessed Nov. 19, 2009; Adam Mc-Keown, *Melancholy Order: Asian Migration and the Globalization of Borders* (New York: Columbia University Press, 2008); Joseph Nevins, *Operation Gatekeeper: The Rise of the "Illegal Alien" and the Making of the U.S.-Mexico Boundary* (London: Routledge, 2002); Peter Sahlins, *Boundaries: The Making of France and Spain in the Pyrenees* (Berkeley: University of California Press, 1989); John C. Torpey, *The Invention of the Passport: Surveillance, Citizenship, and the State* (Cambridge: Cambridge University Press, 2000); Samuel Truett and Elliott Young, eds., *Continental Crossroads: Remapping U.S.-Mexico Borderlands History* (Durham, NC: Duke University Press, 2004).

4. Marshall D. Sahlins, *Stone Age Economics* (Chicago: Aldine-Atherton, 1972), 195–96.

5. Thomas W. Gallant, "Brigandage, Piracy, Capitalism and State-Formation: Transnational Crime in an Historical World-systems Perspective," *States and Illegal Practices*, ed. Heyman, 23–61.

6. In addition to chapters by Rensink, Díaz, and Marak and Tuennerman in this book, see Sally Engle Merry, *Colonizing Hawai'i: The Cultural Power of Law* (Princeton: Princeton University Press, 2000).

7. We draw heavily on Howard Campbell's work on the US-Mexican illegal drug system. See Campbell, "Drug Trafficking Stories: Everyday Forms of Narco-Folklore on the U.S.-Mexico Border," *International Journal of Drug Policy* 16 (2005): 326–33; "Female Drug Smugglers on the U.S.-Mexico Border: Gender, Crime, and Empowerment," *Anthropological Quarterly* 81 (2008): 233–68; and *Drug War Zone: Frontline Dispatches from the Streets of El Paso and Juárez* (Austin: University of Texas Press, 2009).

8. We employ the term *cartel* advisedly despite its vague and imprecise use in news media reports about Mexican drug trafficking organizations and crime issues. Given the widespread usage of the term in Mexico and the United States, however, we prefer to maintain it rather than replace it with a cumbersome neologism. By "cartels" we mean large networks of criminal syndicates that traffic prohibited substances. In this chap. we refer only to the most powerful of such organizations. Nonetheless, we recognize that "cartels" are much more loosely structured, temporary, and fragmented than assumed in popular discussions (Campbell, *Drug War Zone*, 19–20). The qualifications surrounding the term are instructive of the need to approach carefully the discursive frames about illegalities provided by states, mass media, and so forth.

9. Josiah McC. Heyman, "State Escalation of Force: A Vietnam / US-Mexico Border Analogy," in *States and Illegal Practices*, ed. Heyman, 285–314; Peter Andreas, *Border Games: Policing the U.S.-Mexico Divide* (Ithaca: Cornell University Press, 2000).

10. Peter Kwong, *Forbidden Workers: Illegal Chinese Immigrants and American Labor* (New York: New Press, 1997).

11. Joel Best, ed., *Images of Issues: Typifying Contemporary Social Problems* (New York: Aldine de Gruyter, 1989); Best, ed., *How Claims Spread: Cross-National Diffusion of Social Problems* (New York: Aldine de Gruyter, 2001).

12. Stuart Hall, Charles Critcher, Tony Jefferson, John Clarke, and Brian Robert, *Policing the Crisis: Mugging, the State, and Law and Order* (London: Macmillan, 1978); also see Stanley Cohen, *Folk Devils and Moral Panics: Creation of Mods and Rockers* (London: MacGibbon and Kee, 1972).

13. See Peter Andreas and Ethan Nadelmann, *Policing the Globe: Criminalization and Crime Control in International Relations* (New York: Oxford University Press, 2006); and Peter Adey, "Secured and Sorted Mobilities: Examples from the Airport," *Surveillance and Society* 1: 500–519, http://www.surveillance-and-society.org/articles1(4)/sorted.pdf, accessed November 19, 2009.

14. See Heyman, ed., *States and Illegal Practices.*

15. In addition to those members of drug cartels that are overtly recognized as such, many other bribed members of mainstream society, such as policemen, politicians, border guards, taxi drivers, lawyers, accountants, auto body workers, truckers, and even journalists, cooperate with cartel operations and in a sense form part of the cartels.

16. See, however, Campbell "Drug Trafficking Stories," and "Female Drug Smugglers."

17. By no means do all these kinds of borders neatly coincide, though the territorialized nation-state strives to make them align. Maintaining awareness of multiple meanings of "border" is important in doing the sort of analysis we offer here, but we do mainly focus on political borders.

18. In this we include borders of novel legal / administrative entities, such as the European Union and in a much weaker way, NAFTA, as well as mid-twentieth-century nation-states.

19. See Nevins, *Operation Gatekeeper.*

20. Mary Douglas, *Purity and Danger: An Analysis of Concepts of Pollution and Taboo* (London: Routledge and Kegan Paul, 1966).

21. Josiah McC. Heyman, "Constructing a Virtual Wall: Race and Citizenship in U.S.-Mexico Border Policing," *Journal of the Southwest* 50 (2008): 305–34.

22. On the multivocal character of the word *border,* see Heyman, "The Mexico-United States Border in Anthropology."

23. On social constructionism in criminology, see Stephen Hester and Peter Eglin, *A Sociology of Crime* (London: Routledge 1992). Certainly, social construction does not mean that there are no cross-historical and cross-cultural moral patterns in what is regarded as criminal or deviant. An example might be murder. However, even murder is highly socially constructed. Organized warfare often is not considered murder. Systematic social killing, such as promotion of tobacco use or workplace deaths, might be handled as a public health matter and at most a matter of liability, and not the criminal charge of murder. Even when murder is regarded as a morally offensive crime, its sanctions vary considerably. It sometimes is discharged by revenge, and in other cases by payment of material goods. Its treatment is also inflected by race (murder of whites may be taken more seriously than of African Americans) and by gender (murder of women and murder by women varies enormously, according to various forms of gendered social relationships). This is to say that the fact of social construction of crime is uncontestable, whatever other theories we might want to add to constructionism.

24. Jonathan Xavier Inda, *Targeting Immigrants: Government, Technology, and Ethics* (Oxford: Blackwell, 2006).

25. Josiah McC. Heyman, "Trust, Privilege, and Discretion in the Governance of the U.S. Borderlands with Mexico," *Canadian Journal of Law and Society / Revue Canadienne Droit et Société* 24 (2009): 367–90.

26. There is a long-standing radical tradition in criminology that situates crime in wider power processes. See William J. Chambliss, *Exploring Criminology* (New York: Macmillan, 1988); William J. Chambliss and Milton Mankoff, *Whose Law? What Order? A Conflict Approach to Criminology* (New York: Wiley, 1976); Richard Quinney, *Critique of Legal Order: Crime Control in Capitalist Society* (Boston: Little, Brown, 1974); and Richard Quinney, *Class, State, and Crime* (New York: Longman, 1980). An alternative but also critical approach to law and power is Foucauldian; see Alan Hunt, *Governing Morals: A Social History of Moral Regulation* (Cambridge: Cambridge University Press, 1999).

27. Greg Gordon, "Goldman Left Foreign Investors Holding the Subprime Bag," McClatchy Newspapers, November 3, 2009, http://www.mcclatchydc.com/100/story/77844.html, accessed November 19, 2009.

28. Raymond Baker and Eva Joly, "Illicit Money: Can It Be Stopped?" *New York Review of Books* 56, no. 19 (December 3, 2009): 61–64.

29. The literature on elite individual–group deviance and crime, and dominant system crime and immorality, and why these phenomena are so often erased or excused, is quite large. For a start, see Raymond J. Michalowski and Ronald C. Kramer, eds., *State-Corporate Crime: Wrongdoing at the Intersection of Business and Government* (New Brunswick, NJ: Rutgers University Press, 2006); and Maurice Punch, "Suite Violence: Why Managers Murder and Corporations Kill," *Crime, Law, and Social Control* 33 (2000): 243–80. Also see works by Quinney and Chambliss cited above.

About the Contributors

Howard Campbell is a professor of cultural anthropology at the University of Texas at El Paso. He is the author or editor of six volumes about Mexico, including a new book from University of Texas Press called *Drug War Zone: Frontline Dispatches from the Streets of El Paso and Juárez*. Dr. Campbell received his Ph.D. and two master's degrees from the University of Wisconsin. He also received a BA from the University of Idaho. Dr. Campbell is a specialist in Latin American Studies with a primary focus on Mexico. He has conducted ethnographic fieldwork among the Zapotec people of Oaxaca, Mexico, at various times since 1982. Dr. Campbell has also conducted extensive research with the Piro-Manso-Tiwa Indian tribe of Las Cruces, New Mexico. His academic expertise is concerned primarily with ethnicity, political anthropology, social and intellectual movements, US-Mexico border culture, and drug trafficking. Dr. Campbell has been a professor at UTEP since 1991.

Elaine Carey is an associate professor at St. John's University in Queens, New York, and she is the Lloyd Sealy Research fellow at John Jay College of Criminal Justice. Her research and teaching interests include Latin American social movements, international human rights, globalization, history of narcotics, and gender studies. She has received numerous grants, including Fulbright-García Robles fellowships 1996–97 and 2007–8, and funding from the National Endowment for the Humanities. While completing her Ph.D. at the University of New Mexico, she worked as an editor and ultimately the managing editor of the *New Mexico Historical Review*. She is the author of *Plaza of Sacrifices: Gender, Power, and Terror in 1968 Mexico* (University of New Mexico Press, 2005). Currently, she is working on a book-length project entitled "Selling Is More of a Habit than Using: Women and Drug Trafficking in North America, 1900–1970."

George T. Díaz majored in history at Texas A&M International University and graduated summa cum laude in May 2002. He earned his Masters of Arts in history at Texas A&M International University in May 2004. He has one publication, "Tracking Tequileros: The Bloody Origins of a Border Ballad," which appeared in the fall 2004 issue of *Journal of South Texas* and was presented at the Texas State Historical Association's annual conference in 2005. He presented his latest research paper, "Contrabandista Community: The Moral Economy of Smuggling in the Two Laredos, 1890–1900," at the 2007 Western Historical Association meeting in Oklahoma City. He is currently a fourth year doctoral candidate at Southern Methodist University working on his dissertation titled "Contrabandista Communities: States and Smuggling in Los dos Laredos, 1848–1988."

Sterling Evans holds the Louise Welsh Chair in Southern Plains and Borderlands History at the University of Oklahoma. He previously taught at Brandon University in Manitoba, Humboldt State University, and the University of Alberta, and received both his master's and doctoral degrees from the University of Kansas. He is the author of *Bound in Twine: The History and Ecology of the Henequen-Wheat Complex for Mexico and the American and Canadian Plains, 1890–1950* (College Station, 2007) and edited *The Borderlands of the American and Canadian Wests: Essays on Regional History of the 49th Parallel* (Lincoln: 2006). He is currently writing a transnational history of water, agriculture, and environmental change for the state of Sonora, Mexico.

Josiah McC. Heyman is professor of anthropology and chair of sociology and anthropology at the University of Texas, El Paso. He has researched the US-Mexico border since 1982, including the historical making of border society and culture and the operations of the US state in the border region, including immigration law enforcement. He is the author of *Life and Labor on the Border* (University of Arizona Press, 1990) and *Finding a Moral Heart for US Immigration Policy* (American Anthropological Association, 1998) and the editor of *States and Illegal Practices* (Berg, 1999). He is also the author of more than fifty articles, essays, chapters, and other scholarly works on borders, state power, bureaucracies, migration, work and working classes, and consumption. His ethnographic studies of US Immigration and Naturalization Service officers are widely cited, and one article, "Respect for Outsiders? Respect for the Law? The Moral Evaluation of High-Scale Issues by US Immigration Officers," *Journal of the Royal Anthropological Institute* (2000), won the Curl Essay Prize of the Royal Anthropological Institute of Great Britain and Ireland. He is currently working on state governance of movement and on critically examining how concepts of "border security" and "national security" have been applied to migration processes.

Holly Karibo is a doctoral candidate in the collaborative program in history and women's studies at the University of Toronto. Her doctoral dissertation, "Ambassadors of Pleasure: Sexual Geographies of the Detroit-Windsor Borderland, 1920–1960," explores the sexual implications of the US-Canada border, paying particular attention to notions of "vice" as they developed in the mid-twentieth century. Holly has previously published in *The Social History of Alcohol and Drugs* and *Neoamericanist*, and is this year's recipient of the Barbara Frum Memorial Award in Canadian History.

Dan Malleck teaches medical history in the Department of Community Health Sciences at Brock University. He researches pharmacy and medical professionalization and drug and alcohol regulation and Prohibition in Canada. He is currently completing a manuscript on the development of post-Prohibition liquor regulation in Ontario, Canada. He is also editor-in-chief of *Social History of Alcohol and Drugs: An Interdisciplinary Journal* and is the secretary-treasurer of the Alcohol and Drugs History Society. He thinks about drinking a lot, though the field research is not nearly as interesting as most people want to believe.

Andrae Marak is an associate professor of history and political science and the division head of liberal arts at Indiana University–Purdue University Columbus and an associate of the Center for Latin American and Caribbean Studies at Indiana University. His book, *From Many, One: Indians, Peasants, Borders, and Education in Callista Mexico, 1924–1935*, was published by the University of Calgary Press in 2009. He is currently working on a manuscript with Laura Tuennerman on the social construction of gender on the Tohono O'odham Indian Reservation in southern Arizona entitled "Gendering the Periphery of Empire: The Tohono O'odham, Gender, and Assimilation, 1880–1934." He has published articles in the *Journal of the West*, *Paedagogica Historica*, the *New Mexico Historical Review*, the *Journal of the Southwest*, and the *Review of International Political Economy*. He earned a Ph.D. in Latin American Studies at the University of New Mexico.

Marcel Martel is an associate professor of Canadian History at York University in Toronto, Canada. His research interests are on the state, identity, nation, and moral regulation. His most recent publications include *Not This Time: Canadians, Public Policy and the Marijuana Question, 1961–1975* (University of Toronto Press, 2006); *Envoyer et recevoir: Lettres et correspondances dans les diasporas francophones* (with Yves Frenette and John Willis) (Presses de l'Université Laval, 2006); "'The Age of Aquarius': Medical Expertise and the Prevention and Control of Drug Use Undertaken by the Quebec and Ontario Governments," in *The Sixties: Passion, Politics, and Style*, ed. Dimitry Anastakis (McGill-Queen's, 2008); "Law versus Medicine: the Debate over Drug Use in the 1960s," in *Creating Postwar Canada, 1945–75*, ed. Magda Fahrni and Robert Rutherdale (University of British Columbia Press, 2008).

Brenden Rensink holds a Ph.D. in history from the University of Nebraska–Lincoln. Originally from Bellingham, Washington, Brenden completed a BA in history at Brigham Young University in 2003 and a MA in history from the University of Nebraska–Lincoln in 2006. His scholarship centers on the North American West with emphases on comparative borderlands studies and the Native American experience. His dissertation explored transnational comparisons between the experience of indigenous immigrants and refugees along the Mexican-American and Canadian-American borderlands. The primary purpose of this research is to examine how the narratives of Sonora-Arizona Yaquis and Alberta-Montana Chippewa-Crees in the late nineteenth and early to mid-twentieth centuries were affected by the strong influence of local borderlands economic, political, and social interests on the formation of federal policy.

Robert Chao Romero is an assistant professor in the UCLA César E. Chávez Department of Chicana/o Studies. He received his Juris Doctor from U.C. Berkeley in 1998 and Ph.D. in Latin American history from UCLA in 2003. He was a Ford Foundation Predoctoral Fellow as well as a U.C. President's Postdoctoral Fellow from 2003–5. Romero's research examines Asian immigration to Latin America and historical and contemporary relations between Asians and Latinos in the Americas. His first book project, *The Chinese in Mexico, 1882–1940* (University of Arizona Press, 2010), provides a comprehensive historical examination of Chinese immigration and settlement in Mexico between the years 1882 and 1940. The dissertation on which this manuscript is based received the Hubert Herring Award for best dissertation from the Pacific Coast Council on Latin American Studies. In addition to this current book project, he has also published several articles on the Chinese of Mexico, including "El Destierro de los Chinos: Popular Perspectives of Chinese-Mexican Interracial Marriage in the Early Twentieth Century," *Aztlan: A Journal of Chicano Studies* 32, no. 1 (spring 2007); "Transnational Chinese Immigrant Smuggling to the United States via Mexico and Cuba, 1882–1916," *Amerasia Journal* 30, no. 3 (2004–5); and "California and the Chinese Transnational Commercial Orbit of the Late 19th Century," an essay chapter to appear in *Blackwell Companion to California History* (Project of Huntington-USC Institute on California and the West, 2008).

Laura Tuennerman is a professor of history at California University of Pennsylvania. Her monograph *Helping Others, Helping Ourselves* was published by Kent State University Press in 2001. Tuennerman's more recent research focuses on the interaction between women reformers, both in the public and private sphere, and women in the communities they served. She earned a Ph.D. in history at the University of Minnesota.

Index

241

women: alcoholics, (*continued*)
Lola); drug use, 149–150, 154–155,
156, *155*, 225n5, n7, 230n59; Tohono
O'odham, 101, *102*, 107–108, 112,
113–117, 119, 120; victims of drug traffickers, 141–142, 150
Woodruff, Janette, 104, 107–108, 115,
116
working-class: liquor consumption, 126,

127; prostitution in, 7, 87, 88, 91, 92,
93; women, 106–107
Wright, William, 70–71, 72–73
Wylie, Wilson, 122, 133, 135, 136

Yucatán Peninsula, 47, 51

Zapata County, Texas, 60, 70
Zetas, 182, 183–184